KT-524-524

Caryl Phillips, David Dabydeen and Fred D'Aguiar

Representations of slavery

ABIGAIL WARD

Manchester University Press
Manchester and New York

distributed exclusively in the USA by Palgrave Macmillan

Copyright © Abigail Ward 2011

The right of Abigail Ward to be identified as the author of this work has been asserted by her in accordance with the Copyright, Designs and Patents Act 1988.

Published by Manchester University Press
Oxford Road, Manchester M13 9NR, UK
and Room 400, 175 Fifth Avenue, New York, NY 10010, USA
www.manchesteruniversitypress.co.uk

Distributed exclusively in the USA by
Palgrave Macmillan, 175 Fifth Avenue, New York, NY 10010, USA

Distributed exclusively in Canada by
UBC Press, University of British Columbia, 2029 West Mall,
Vancouver, BC, Canada V6T 1Z2

British Library Cataloguing-in-Publication Data
A catalogue record for this book is available from the British Library

Library of Congress Cataloging-in-Publication Data applied for

ISBN 978 0 7190 8275 7 *hardback*

First published 2011

The publisher has no responsibility for the persistence or accuracy of URLs for any external or third-party internet websites referred to in this book, and does not guarantee that any content on such websites is, or will remain, accurate or appropriate.

BATH SPA UNIVERSITY
NEWTON PARK LIBRARY
Class No.
820.9358 WAR
10/05/11

Typeset in Aldus
by Koinonia, Manchester
Printed in Great Britain
by MPG Books Group, UK

For Adrian and Joy Ward

Contents

Acknowledgements

This book began life as a PhD thesis at the University of Leeds, where I had the good fortune to be supervised by John McLeod, who has proven to be a source of endless support and advice, and above all else, a very dear friend.

I am especially grateful to Gail Low, for first introducing me to the works of Caryl Phillips and Fred D'Aguiar, and to Niké Imoru, for her early enthusiasm about this project. Thanks are also due to Mick Gidley and Graham Huggan, and especial thanks to Shirley Chew, Sam Durrant, Dave Gunning, Caroline Herbert and David Richards, who all helpfully commented on earlier versions of this work.

I am grateful to the editors and publishers for permission to reprint work from the following essays: '"Words are All I Have Left of My Eyes": Blinded by the Past in J. M. W. Turner's *Slavers Throwing Overboard the Dead and Dying* and David Dabydeen's "Turner"', *Journal of Commonwealth Literature*, 42(1) (2007): 47–58; 'David Dabydeen's *A Harlot's Progress*: Re-presenting the Slave Narrative Genre', *Journal of Postcolonial Writing*, 43(1) (2007): 32–44; and 'An Outstretched Hand: Connection and Affiliation in *Crossing the River*', *Moving Worlds: A Journal of Transcultural Writings*, 7(1) (2007): 20–32.

I would also like to thank John Thieme, whose editorial guidance and support have proved invaluable; the team at Manchester University Press, and David Dabydeen, Fred D'Aguiar and Caryl Phillips for their kind assistance with this project.

Finally, thanks to family and friends for their love and good humour, particularly Kate Clark, whom I cannot thank enough.

Series editor's foreword

Contemporary World Writers is an innovative series of authoritative introductions to a range of culturally diverse contemporary writers from outside Britain and the United States or from 'minority' backgrounds within Britain or the United States. In addition to providing comprehensive general introductions, books in the series also argue stimulating original theses, often but not always related to contemporary debates in post-colonial studies.

The series locates individual writers within their specific cultural contexts, while recognising that such contexts are themselves invariably a complex mixture of hybridised influences. It aims to counter tendencies to appropriate the writers discussed into the canon of English or American literature or to regard them as 'other'.

Each volume includes a chronology of the writer's life, an introductory section on formative contexts and intertexts, discussion of all the writer's major works, a bibliography of primary and secondary works and an index. Issues of racial, national and cultural identity are explored, as are gender and sexuality. Books in the series also examine writers' use of genre, particularly ways in which Western genres are adapted or subverted and 'traditional' local forms are reworked in a contemporary context.

Contemporary World Writers aims to bring together the theoretical impulse which currently dominates post-colonial studies and closely argued readings of particular authors' works, and by so doing to avoid the danger of appropriating the specifics of particular texts into the hegemony of totalising theories.

List of abbreviations

AS	*The Atlantic Sound*
B	*Bloodlines*
C	*Cambridge*
CH	*The Counting House*
CO	*Coolie Odyssey*
CR	*Crossing the River*
ES	*Extravagant Strangers*
FG	*Feeding the Ghosts*
HP	*A Harlot's Progress*
LM	*The Longest Memory*
NWO	*A New World Order*
SS	*Slave Song*
T	*Turner*

Chronology

Caryl Phillips

1958	Caryl Phillips born in St Kitts. Travels to Britain.
1979	BA (Hons) English Literature, Oxford University.
1980	Play *Strange Fruit* produced.
1980–82	Writer-in-residence, Arts Council of Great Britain, The Factory Arts Centre, London.
1982	Play *Where There is Darkness* produced.
1983	Play *The Shelter* produced.
1985	*The Final Passage* published.
1986	*A State of Independence* published. Writes screenplay for the film *Playing Away*.
1987	Travelogue *The European Tribe* published. Writer-in-residence, Literary Criterion Centre, University of Mysore, India.
1989	*Higher Ground* published. Writer-in-residence, University of Stockholm, Sweden.
1990–92	Visiting writer, Amherst College, Massachusetts.
1991	*Cambridge* published.
1992–98	Writer-in-residence (later, Professor of English) and (until 1997) Co-Director of Creative Writing Center, Amherst College, Massachusetts.
1993	*Crossing the River* published. Visiting Professor in English, New York University.
1994	Writer-in-residence, National Institute of Teaching, Singapore.
1997	*Nature of Blood* published. Editor of *Extravagant Strangers*.
1998–2005	Professor of English and Henry R. Luce Professor of

David Dabydeen

1994	*Turner* published.
1996	*The Counting House* published. Co-editor of *Across the Dark Waters*.
1999	*A Harlot's Progress* published.
2004	*Our Lady of Demerara* published.
2007	Co-editor of *The Oxford Companion to Black British History*.
2008	*Molly and the Muslim Stick* published.

Fred D'Aguiar

1960	Fred D'Aguiar born in London.
1962	Travels to Guyana.
1972	Returns to Britain.
1985	BA (Hons) African and Caribbean Studies, University of Kent. *Mama Dot* published.
1986–87	Writer-in-residence, London Borough of Lewisham.
1987	Play *High Life* produced.
1988–89	Writer-in-residence, Birmingham Polytechnic.
1989	*Airy Hall* published.
1989–90	Judith E. Wilson Fellow at Cambridge University.
1990–92	Northern Arts Literary Fellow.
1991	Play *A Jamaican Airman Foresees His Death* produced.
1992–94	Visiting writer, Amherst College, Massachusetts.
1993	*British Subjects* published.
1994	*The Longest Memory* published.
1994–95	Assistant Professor of English, Bates College, Lewiston, Maine.
1995–2003	Professor of English, University of Miami.
1996	*Dear Future* published.
1997	*Feeding the Ghosts* published.
1998	*Bill of Rights* published.
2000	*Bloodlines* published.
2001	*An English Sampler* published.
2003	*Bethany Bettany* published. Professor of English and Co-Director of the Master of Fine Arts in Creative Writing, Virginia Tech.
2009	*Continental Shelf* published.

1

Contexts and intertexts

Slavery is a recurring subject in the works of Caryl Phillips, David Dabydeen and Fred D'Aguiar, yet their return to this past arises from an urgent need to understand the racial anxieties of twentieth- and twenty-first-century Britain. As the narrator of D'Aguiar's long poem *Bloodlines* comes to realise, 'Slavery may be buried, | but it's not dead, its offspring, Racism, still breeds.'[1] This book specifically focuses on these writers' differing representation of Britain's involvement in the transatlantic slave trade. I examine the ways in which their return to this past may shed light on current issues in Britain today, particularly concerning what might be thought of as continuing legacies of the UK's largely forgotten slave past. This study is informed by two primary contexts: the first is the theoretical, and I provide a close textual analysis of literary works, enabled by novel engagements with postcolonial, post-structuralist and Holocaust theory. The second context is the historical. In order to explain some of the problems in accepting a conventionally historical approach to the past of slavery, some detail is required concerning slavery and much later twentieth-century black arrivals to Britain. There are two significant problems with taking an entirely historical approach to the past of slavery; the first is that most received historical accounts have downplayed, or ignored completely, Britain's role as a slaving nation. The second problem is that, if slavery *is* remembered, the focus falls on the abolitionists, so Britain's role in this past is remembered only in terms of ending, rather than perpetuating, the trade.

Nearly one hundred and fifty years after the abolition of the British slave trade, the *S.S. Empire Windrush* docked at Tilbury on 22 June 1948 with 492 Caribbean migrants on board. These people had been granted British citizenship by the Nationality Act of the same year, and arrived in Britain in response to pleas from the British government for workers from the colonies to alleviate the post-war British labour shortage. In the next ten years, some 125,000 migrants from the Caribbean were to enter the country.[2] This concentrated influx of black people to Britain has arguably eclipsed earlier arrivals, to the extent that the *Windrush* immigration is often considered to be the beginning of black arrival in Britain. As James Procter argues in his introduction to *Writing Black Britain: An Interdisciplinary Anthology* (2000), 'it is important to distinguish between 1948 as an *initiatory* rather than an *originary* moment, in terms of black settlement in Britain. This becomes especially urgent given that the narration of that year has tended to erase a black British presence before it.'[3] I propose that the different ways in which the authors Phillips, Dabydeen and D'Aguiar return to the past of slavery offer responses to the apparent eclipsing of a pre-*Windrush* black British past in accounts of received history. This approach might also be thought of as imaginatively returning to the past of slavery in order to creatively revise the way in which this past is understood and remembered.

Britain's involvement in slavery began in 1562, with the first voyage of John Hawkins to Guinea, and the trade was abolished in Britain in 1807. The Slavery Abolition Act to end slavery in the British colonies, however, was not introduced until 1833, and the first slaves were freed around five years later.[4] Britain's entry into the slave trade has been considered a relatively late arrival into an already established and lucrative trade, but its part should not be underestimated. Before long, it was the leading slave-trading nation, and the wealth it amassed was unparalleled. Largely unrecognised benefits of the trade included generating the wealth which enabled the construction of Britain's grand houses and public buildings in primary slave ports like Bristol, Liverpool and London. Today, these buildings may be thought of as visible reminders of Britain's involvement in this trade, yet British slavery continues to be a history that is largely unacknowledged. As James Walvin has claimed in his study of the slave trade, *Making the Black Atlantic: Britain and the African Diaspora* (2000), received historical accounts have tended to downplay the importance of slavery to Britain's economy in the most lucrative period of the trade:

> It is generally true that historians of Britain have persistently overlooked or minimized the degree to which British life in the seventeenth and eighteenth centuries was integrated into the Atlantic slave system ... British historians have tended to regard slavery as a distant (colonial, imperial, American, maritime) issue, of only marginal or passing interest to mainstream Britain.[5]

Walvin not only emphasises the way in which historians have ignored the importance of the slave trade to Britain during the seventeenth and eighteenth centuries, but also raises the crucial issue that slavery is the point of intersection of multiple histories (he names just four). Those dissatisfied with the received narration of Britain's involvement in slavery may offer alternative narratives of Britain in which the slave trade is far from marginal. There have been several attempts by contemporary black writers in Britain to articulate these alternative histories in their works, arguably in response to the racially homogeneous received history of Britain. Returning to Walvin's point, slavery has seemed 'distant' because, unlike the United States, Britain has never had slave societies in the 'motherland'. Aside for a relatively small number of black servants in the UK between the sixteenth and nineteenth centuries, Britain's slavery took place in the Caribbean, at a convenient distance which allowed the majority of sugar-consuming Britons to forget about the source and production of this staple.

The inadequacy of received historical narratives of Britain's slave past ensures that accounts either gloss over the UK's involvement in the trade or focus exclusively on the role of British abolitionists. The former approach can be seen as indicative of the way in which received accounts of British history have tended to concentrate on what has occurred in Britain, rather than developments in the colonies, recalling the oft-cited comment of Salman Rushdie's character Whiskey Sisodia from *The Satanic Verses* (1988): the 'trouble with the Engenglish is that their hiss hiss history happened overseas, so they dodo don't know what it means'.[6] The latter approach ensures that when slavery *is* written about, Britain remembers its role as ending, rather than instigating, the trade. It would seem that even sympathetic representations of this past may add to the obfuscation of the nature of Britain's true involvement in the slave trade. Historians Alex Tyrrell and James Walvin have acknowledged that, while there has been a debate in Britain over how to remember the past of slavery, it has concerned the relative importance of different British abolitionists, rather than how best to remember this past overall.[7] Writing specifically about the memorial to Thomas Clarkson erected at Westminster abbey in 1996, they argue: 'In addition to his birthplace and dates of birth and death, the inscription ... proclaimed only that he was "A friend to slaves"; those who read it were to recall the virtues of a man who had campaigned against slavery – not slavery itself.'[8] This inadequate inscription is arguably typical of a Britain which, if remembering slavery at all, chooses to focus on those figures instrumental in ceasing the slave trade, rather than the perpetuation of slavery by Britain over many years.

Although the mid-twentieth-century Caribbean migration that has come to be symbolised by the arrival of the *Windrush* is often understood to be the 'beginning' of black arrival in Britain, therefore, there was a black presence in Britain long before the late 1940s. In order to find the origin of black habitation in the UK we would, in fact, need to go back to Roman Britain, though black people have lived continuously in Britain since about 1505.[9] Numbers grew steadily over the following century until the number of black citizens in London in the early seventeenth century prompted Elizabeth I to issue a declaration calling for their deportation. The slave trade was responsible for bringing more Africans to England and Scotland, to be used as servants and status symbols from the seventeenth century onwards in the houses of the wealthier classes, a practice which continued into the twentieth century. Also, following the American War of Independence, many enlisted black men came to Britain and were unable to secure work, leading to large numbers of black beggars on the streets of prominent towns and cities, and the establishment of the Committee for the Relief of the Black Poor, which devised the disastrous Sierra Leone resettlement project. Although the black presence in Britain may have declined during the nineteenth century, as Jan Marsh writes in *Black Victorians* (2005), throughout this period, 'in certain cities and localities, such as London, Liverpool, Edinburgh and Kent, black residents were relatively common. So, while the African diaspora was not large, neither was it negligible.'[10]

If we look at the post-war period, however, there is little sense of this wider history of black residence in the UK. The apparent 'forgetting' of this pre-1948 black history in Britain has been crucial in refuting the legitimacy of black habitation in the post-war years. Admitting that black people have lived in Britain since Roman times makes it difficult to cast them as recent intruders to the country. This rhetoric was used by figures like Enoch Powell, who gave voice to a discontent earlier expressed in the series of post-war 'anti-black' riots, such as those of 1958 in Nottingham and Notting Hill, and the associated increase in racist violence and police brutality. The violent rejection of non-white Britons was compounded by media portrayals of black people as violent, unruly and unwanted visitors to a racially homogeneous Britain. Furthermore, it would seem that this racism was legitimised by the introduction of various repressive legislative measures between 1948 and 1981 designed to regulate the entry of black and Asian arrivals into Britain.[11] Race was undeniably a central factor in the desire to stem immigration into Britain; as Bob Carter, Clive Harris and Shirley Joshi have pointed out, the government seemed to take an 'inordinate interest' in the 36,000 black immigrants who arrived in the UK between 1950 and 1955, yet little notice of the 250,000 Southern Irish or the thousands of European workers who came over during this period.[12]

Yet, the moment that has come to symbolise most clearly what Robin Cohen has called the 'racialisation of the "immigration issue"' was the speech made by Powell in Birmingham in April 1968 against a new race-relations bill, commonly termed the 'Rivers of Blood' speech.[13] In this address, Powell read aloud a letter allegedly written by an anonymous white British woman terrified and terrorised by the influx of black immigrants into 'her' neighbourhood, to whom she refused to let rooms. As Paul Gilroy has argued, 'Britannia is portrayed as an old white woman, trapped and alone in the inner city. She is surrounded by blacks whose very blackness expresses not only the immediate threat they pose but the bleak inhumanity of urban decay.'[14] Powell depicted the woman as a helpless victim and used the letter to attack the legal system and the proposed race-relations bill which would criminalise the woman's actions. His vocabulary in this speech is telling, recounting a constituent's warning that 'in fifteen or twenty years' time the black man will have the whip hand over the white man'.[15] Powell provocatively reanimates a slave environment to scare a racist Britain. His metaphor can be seen as achieving two things: first, it reminds his audience of the supposed inferiority of black people, which was the argument used in the previous centuries to justify their enslavement. Secondly, it suggests that there may be a reversal of roles if immigration trends continue – within two decades, Powell prophesises, white people would almost certainly be dominated by black people. Elsewhere in contemporaneous speeches he panders to imperialist sensibilities through his rhetoric concerning loss of Empire:

> In so short a time have a globe with one quarter of the land surface coloured red, our naval and air predominance, and our commercial, industrial and financial primacy become things of the past. History is littered with nations that have been destroyed for ever by the stress of lesser changes than these.[16]

Powell was clearly indicating that, although Britain's Empire may have ended, it was possible to halt Caribbean immigration into Britain, and so prevent the reversal of roles outlined above;

he was extremely careful to indicate that this kind of transformation was a 'preventable evil'.[17]

Powell's mention of slavery as a means of mobilising anti-immigration support in the above example is rare; the portrayal of non-white people in the post-war period as alien to Britain is, on the whole, a consequence of *not* remembering slavery. By denying their habitation and involvement within Britain before 1948, the casting of them as outsiders by figures such as Powell was more easily facilitated. However, at the same time, by talking about a slave environment, he bypasses the black presence in Britain by suggesting that black people do not belong in the UK, but in the plantation fields, so once again Powell casts them as outsiders.

While racism may have had a long history in Britain, it only became the 'official', legitimised narrative through the passing of the 1981 Nationality Act, which enforced Powell's ideas about race and nation and arguably led to a form of legalised racism as national identity. The 'forgetting' of a pre-1948 black involvement and habitation in Britain, and the emphasis on the *Windrush* immigration as the original moment of black arrival in Britain, has supported a larger governmental campaign (which also included the series of repressive legislation mentioned above and propagandist speeches made by Powell and Margaret Thatcher) to portray black people as alien threats to Britain, and so legitimise their exclusion from both Britain (where possible to do so) and British national identity. I contend that, alongside the initial appeals for workers from the colonies, which were made possible only by Britain's role as a slaving and colonising nation, the racism sanctified by the post-war immigration legislation may also be thought of as a continuing legacy of slavery.

Phillips, Dabydeen and D'Aguiar can be seen as exploring what is missing from both standard accounts of British history and historical accounts of slavery: namely, the effects of slavery's legacies in the late twentieth and early twenty-first centuries on racism, identity and the politics of belonging. Through close reading of the works of Phillips, Dabydeen and D'Aguiar, I engage with such issues as the difficulty of representing slavery, and the ethics involved in so doing, the impossibility of accessing or 'returning to' this past, and the problem of remembering and memorialising Britain's involvement in the slave trade. While two of the texts I explore by D'Aguiar are set in the United States, on the whole, the focus of this study is on British slavery, as the subject of American slavery has attracted much scholarly attention both in Britain and the United States throughout the twentieth century. I examine how these authors portray the involvement of British men and women in the past of slavery, a neglected area at the intersection of literature and history. Although historians such as Peter Fryer, Ron Ramdin and James Walvin have made vital contributions to the wealth of available information on British slavery, as yet, literary representations of this past have been comparatively under-explored.[18]

The last two decades of the twentieth century were especially productive years for black writers in Britain examining the past of slavery. Alongside Phillips, Dabydeen and D'Aguiar, we might think of Grace Nichols, who provides a female perspective on plantation slavery in her poetry collection *I is a Long Memoried Woman* (1983), which won the Commonwealth Poetry Prize and was subsequently adapted for film and radio. In the 1990s, the novelists Beryl Gilroy and S. I. Martin also turned to this past; Gilroy's *Stedman and Joanna* (1991) is based on John Gabriel Stedman's narrative and journals of his travels in Surinam in the late eighteenth century, whereas Martin's *Incomparable World* (1996) explores the black presence in London following the American War of Independence. There were, of course, earlier Anglophone Caribbean attempts to write about this past, with Edgar Mittelholzer's trilogy *Children of Kaywana* (1952), *Kaywana Stock* (1954), *Kaywana Blood* (1958) and Orlando Patterson's *Die the Long Day* (1972). Yet, the concentration of works on slavery towards the end of the twentieth century, in particular, may be indicative of a need to understand this past in order to progress more smoothly into the new millennium. Sam Durrant has argued that the 'principal task' of postcolonial narrative, 'structured by a tension between the oppressive memory of the past and the liberatory promise of the future,

...[is] to engender a consciousness of the unjust foundations of the present and to open up the possibility of a just future'.[19] Through their writing, poised between past and present, Phillips, Dabydeen and D'Aguiar also seek to investigate the past not only in order to reveal the reasons for the 'unjust foundations of the present' – the continuing legacies of slavery into the twentieth and twenty-first centuries – but also to begin to envisage the possibility of a 'just future'. There exists a contradiction between the 'unjust' Britain, described by Phillips as 'culturally and ethically homogeneous',[20] and the assertions made by other black Britons, such as Trevor Phillips, that 'Multicultural Britain is already a fact of life.'[21] The relevancy of understanding slavery is therefore perhaps all the more keenly felt at a time when ongoing racial tensions and anxieties continue to undermine claims of Britain's identity in the twenty-first century as a multicultural society.

When these three writers have been brought together previously, it has often been under the guise of 'black British literature'. Procter, for instance, includes writing by each author in his anthology *Writing Black Britain 1948–1998*, and Phillips, Dabydeen and D'Aguiar also all feature in Mark Stein's *Black British Literature* (2004). However, while these authors may be thought of as important figures in black British literature, Procter and Stein both acknowledge that defending the term is fraught terrain.[22] As Stein writes:

> For a variety of reasons, terms such as *post-colonial literature* or *black British literature* are often considered problematic. The heterogeneity of texts so labeled seems to defy the logic of these categories, which also applies to designations such as *English literature* or *British literature*. This raises the question whether a group of texts indeed has to be homogenous in order to be considered 'a group of texts' – whether English, British, or black British.[23]

The term 'black British literature' is problematic, not only in its potential for the homogeneous grouping of ethnically diverse texts, but also because both 'black' and 'British' are deceptively complex terms.

In this book, I use the term 'black' to refer to Caribbean-descended persons, whether of Indian- or African-Caribbean origin, fully aware that any racial category is, to quote Paul Gilroy, 'imagined – socially and politically constructed'.[24] In a similar way, I employ the term 'white' to describe people of European origin; in neither case do I wish to dismiss the diversity and heterogeneity of people that fall within these constructed categories. I therefore apply these labels as political alignments rather than biological categories, conscious of their inadequacy in doing so.[25] It would seem that whiteness has been particularly under-conceptualised in debates about race and identity, which is a serious problem, as Richard Dyer recognises: 'As long as race is something only applied to non-white peoples, as long as white people are not racially seen and named, they/we function as a human norm. Other people are raced, we are just people.'[26] There is a need to critically think about 'whiteness' in order to ensure the 'normalcy' of the term ends. As Dyer acknowledges, 'white' needs to be open for debate and continual definition, rather than taken for granted as the starting point from which to begin defining other ethnic or political identities.

In contrast to the perceived critical invisibility of whiteness, the concept of blackness has a high visibility in contemporary debate. The political deployment of the term 'black' is traced by Alison Donnell in the introduction to her *Companion to Contemporary Black British Culture* (2001). She argues that 'an articulation of specifically black British concerns' began to emerge in the late 1970s, and suggests that there was a gradual shift from projects being thought of as 'the black British presence in Britain to the black dimension of Britain by the 1980s'.[27] Through the gradual integration of black cultures into mainstream Britain, by the 1980s the terms 'black' and 'British' were no longer thought of as completely incompatible, but it was not long before internal 'fractures' appeared.[28] Such fractures might include D'Aguiar's assertion more than twenty years ago in his essay 'Against Black British Literature' (1989) that 'The dual function of black, as adjective and noun seems all-embracing. In fact it serves to enclose and prejudice the real and imaginary scope of that creativity. In addition it syphons off so-called blackness from the general drive of creativity in Britain.'[29] Far from being an empowering identity, he suggests that the term 'black British' instead marginalises black creativity. 'Black', then, is clearly not a straightforward or unproblematic term but, returning to Donnell, it would seem there is value in its continuing role as a political and identificatory alliance:

> As difference becomes both more marketable and more nuanced, the notion of black as an identificatory category will surely both demand and seek constant re-definition; nevertheless, while institutionalised racism persists, it would seem that for many in Britain black remains a politically resonant and historically significant sign of alliance.[30]

The repeated definition and assessment of the term 'black' is crucial; Stuart Hall has stressed the shifting nature of diasporan identities, which are, he writes, 'constantly producing and reproducing themselves anew, through transformation and difference'.[31] Importantly, for Donnell, 'black' provides a historicised political identity which is vital in contemporary challenges to the racism arguably institutionalised within British society.

As I have suggested, the term 'black British literature', as a description of the literary works produced by black men and women in Britain, is inevitably contentious. As Dabydeen is the only one of this study's authors currently residing primarily in Britain, the label 'black British' seems a particularly inappropriate way of describing them. Furthermore, in the following chapters it will become clear that many of the conclusions reached by Phillips, Dabydeen and D'Aguiar surrounding exclusionary national identities and problems with British history have been reached precisely because their habitation outside the UK enables their different critical perceptions on Britain. In his essay 'Some Problems with "British" in a "Black British Canon"' (2002), John McLeod employs the alternative phrase 'black writing in Britain'.[32] This phrase suggests the potential for movement, heterogeneity and migration, recalling Hall's emphasis on diasporan identities 'constantly producing and reproducing themselves anew'. The phrase 'black writing in Britain' indicates a non-static, or non-fixed, identity that is perhaps particularly suited to Phillips, Dabydeen and D'Aguiar, whose transatlantic movements would seem to shake off attempts to fix identities as being rigidly, and solely, black *British*.[33]

Caryl Phillips

Caryl Phillips was born on the small Caribbean island of St Kitts in 1958, brought to Britain as an infant, and raised in Leeds. He attended Oxford University and initially began his literary career as a playwright; his first play, *Strange Fruit*, was produced in 1980 at the Crucible theatre in Sheffield. Phillips's works, which include fiction, non-fiction and plays, range from the sixteenth-century Venice of his novel *The Nature of Blood* (1997) to the twentieth-century Britain of such novels as *The Final Passage* (1985), *A Distant Shore* (2003) or *In the Falling Snow* (2009). The varied settings for his works reflect his interest in tracing connections between seemingly diverse subjects, as Phillips has revealed: 'When I finished [the novel *Higher Ground* (1989)...] I remember thinking, I've written about Africa, about the USA, and a Jewish girl – slavery, civil rights, the Holocaust in one book – and I thought, your canvas is a lot broader than perhaps you realised.'[34]

Prizes awarded to his works include the Malcolm X Prize, Martin Luther King Memorial Prize, Sunday Times Young Writer of the Year Award, the James Tait Black Memorial Prize for Fiction, a Guggenheim Fellowship and a Lannan Fellowship. His novel *Crossing the River* (1993) was short-listed for the Booker Prize and *A Distant Shore* won the 2004 Commonwealth Writers' Prize. Having previously taught at Amherst College and Columbia University, he is now Professor of English at Yale University. To a greater extent than the other authors considered in this book, Phillips engages closely with the historical archive, and close reading of his work reveals a web of intertextual relationships with older sources. His prevailing interest lies in exploring those voices absent from received historical accounts of slavery, whether that of a slave or of a plantation-owner's daughter. One of Phillips's central contentions is that slavery does not just belong to the realm of so-called 'black history', but is central to the past and fortunes of white Britons as well. This contention has an important bearing on this book, and is all too often overlooked by both standard and revisionary accounts of slavery.

Phillips's fascination with the historical archive is evident from his early novels about the slave trade, *Cambridge* (1991) and *Crossing the River*, and the work of Edward Said may be useful in thinking about Phillips's motivation for returning to this past. In *Culture and Imperialism* (1993) Said argues that contemporary 'Appeals to the past' are in part motivated by 'not only disagreement about what happened in the past and what the past was, but uncertainty about whether the past really is past, over and concluded, or whether it continues, albeit in different forms, perhaps'.[35] Here, Said identifies three impulses in returning to the past. While one is a broadly philosophical question about historiography and what exactly the past was, he adds the important contention that the past may continue into the present in altered forms. Phillips suggests in his works that, while slavery may have ended, the legacies of this past – such as racism and the attempted exclusion of non-white people from British national identity – continue into the late twentieth century in related, if different, forms. Said's final point concerning 'appeals to the past' introduces the notion of inter-pretation, and the inevitable disagreements about what actually happened in the past. The proliferation of conflicting viewpoints leads, in turn, to the notion of multiple histories. As we shall see, these disagreements are fundamental in approaching the work of Phillips, who seeks to destabilise the assumption that one version of received history, or homogeneous main narrative, is adequate representation for Britain's diverse citizens. Referring to Western literature, Said has argued:

> As we look back at the cultural archive, we begin to reread it not univocally but contrapuntally, with a simultaneous

awareness both of the metropolitan history that is narrated
and of those other histories against which (and together
with which) the dominating discourse acts.[36]

Said indicates the necessity of reading the separate pasts simultaneously; each history is distinct, but needs to be read contrapuntally, alongside and in dialogue with the others. If we look
carefully at the received history of Britain, therefore, we may be
able to discern traces of other forgotten histories that challenge
the prevailing narrative of this past.

What Said demands in reading, Phillips produces in a contrapuntal writing. The work of Said is helpful in reading the novels
Cambridge and *Crossing the River* and non-fictional works *The
Atlantic Sound* (2000) and *A New World Order* (2001) in a way
that complicates the Manichean polarisation of slavery and its
legacies. Counter-narratives – articulated in Phillips's creation
of contrapuntal texts – may indeed serve to disrupt the notion
of one main narrative, with implications for racialised models
of British national identity. In *Cambridge*, for example, we
find the narrative of a slave placed alongside that of a slave-
owner's daughter and, in *Crossing the River*, an eighteenth-
century slave-ship captain's log is juxtaposed with a narrative
about a nineteenth-century black female pioneer. In *Cambridge*
and *Crossing the River* Phillips aims, via polyphonic voices, to
counter the homogeneity of the narrative of received British
history, from which, he proposes, several of these voices have
been excluded as slavery has been quietly forgotten. Frequently,
Phillips's use of historical sources is undisguised – for example,
he acknowledges his debt to John Newton's *Journal of a Slave
Trader* at the start of *Crossing the River*. His gathering of often
disparate sources which rest alongside each other within his
novels prompts the reader to question the historical archive and
admit the many competing versions of the past.

Phillips has also acknowledged the influence of African
American authors on his work. In his travelogue *The European
Tribe* (1987) he admits that reading Richard Wright's *Native
Son* catalysed his desire to become a writer: 'I felt as if an explo-
sion had taken place inside my head. If I had to point to any

one moment that seemed crucial in my desire to be a writer, it was then'.[37] Despite Phillips's interest in Caribbean literature, therefore, he has explained that the 'first generation' of twentieth-century black writers in Britain largely failed to depict his reality of growing up in an urban British environment: 'Lamming's fiction, like V. S. Naipaul's, tended to be rooted in an exotic geography I didn't recognize. Black Americans wrote about an urban experience I understood, and they were angry.'[38] For Phillips, an important exception was Sam Selvon's novel *The Lonely Londoners*, in which he found

> a sense of being both inside and outside Britain at the same time. The literature was shot through with the uncomfortable anxieties of belonging and not belonging and these same anxieties underscored my life and the lives of many people of my generation in the Britain of the 1970s and early 1980s.[39]

Given the significance of African American writers to Phillips, it is perhaps unsurprising that transatlantic connections between the UK and US permeate his works. For example, he has cited the importance to *Crossing the River* of US author Toni Morrison's novel *Beloved*,[40] and his recent novel *Dancing in the Dark* (2005) explores the life of black Broadway vaudeville performer Bert Williams in early twentieth-century America. It reveals Phillips's ongoing concerns with the complexities of identity, race, sexuality and gender, as well as his interest in the historical: Williams is not a figment of Phillips's imagination, but was a popular entertainer at the start of the last century. Phillips's fascination with the historical archive, and with the intersecting complexities mentioned above, are staged again in his 2007 dramatisation of Simon Schama's historical epic *Rough Crossings*. In this play, he investigates the role performed by black soldiers on the British side in the American War of Independence alongside the drive to abolish slavery in the British Caribbean. While Phillips's play considers the past of slavery, simultaneously it raises questions important to twenty-first-century Britain concerning belonging and the seemingly persistent coalition of race and national identity. These apparent legacies of slavery are also traced in non-fictional works *A New World Order* and *The Atlantic Sound*. In these texts, Phillips's ultimate rejection of an exclusive national identity is captured by his conception of what he calls his 'Atlantic home' – a point in the middle of the Atlantic Ocean between the UK, Africa and the Caribbean. While this may seem a liberating alignment, this notion of what he calls the 'watery crossroads' of identity is not a realistic or plausible solution to the complexities of diasporan identity, and a sense of restlessness, or unbelonging, characterises much of his writing, both fictional and non-fictional.[41]

David Dabydeen

David Dabydeen was born in Guyana in 1955 and, in 1969, joined his father and elder sister in Britain. He was soon taken into care by local authorities, but was determined to go to the university of either Oxford or Cambridge, as he has explained: 'if I was to survive and to progress from the conditions in which I was living at the time, I might as well aim for the very "best". I had nothing to lose.'[42] He succeeded in this ambition, reading English at Cambridge University, and Dabydeen was awarded his doctorate on eighteenth-century literature and art from University College London in 1982. Since 1984, he has been based at the University of Warwick, where his most recent role has been as Professor and Acting Director at the Centre for British Comparative Cultural Studies. His collections of poetry include *Slave Song* (1984), *Coolie Odyssey* (1988) and *Turner* (1994), and novels span from the twentieth-century Britain of *The Intended* (1991), as viewed from a Guyanese immigrant's perspective, back to the eighteenth-century Hogarthian world of *A Harlot's Progress* (1999). Dabydeen has also edited a range of non-fictional works which include, together with Nana Wilson-Tagoe, *A Reader's Guide to West Indian and Black British Literature* (1987) and, with Brinsley Samaroo, the essay collection *Across the Dark Waters: Ethnicity and Indian Identity in the Caribbean* (1996). He has, in addition, completed two studies of

William Hogarth's works, *Hogarth's Blacks* (1985) and *Hogarth, Walpole and Commercial Britain* (1987). Dabydeen's work has been awarded a number of prizes; *Slave Song*, for example, won the Commonwealth Poetry Prize and the Quiller-Couch Prize. On three occasions he has been awarded the Guyana Prize for Literature (for *The Intended*, *A Harlot's Progress* and *Our Lady of Demerara*), and *A Harlot's Progress* was also short-listed for the James Tait Black Memorial Prize for Fiction. In 2004 he was awarded the Raja Rao Award for outstanding contribution to the Literature of the South Asian Diaspora and, in 2007, the Hind Rattan Award by the Non-Resident Indian Society of India for outstanding contributions to the literary and intellectual life of the Indian diaspora. In 2008 he received the Anthony Sabga Prize for Literature.

The chapter on Dabydeen sees a move away from the historical archive in responding to the past of slavery. Instead, he exhibits a deliberate vandalisation of, and irreverence towards, received history; as a result, his is a much more confrontational and deliberately provocative approach to writing about this past. Dabydeen's primary concern is with the ethics of representing slavery. His works reveal his anxieties about audience and received readers for his texts, drawing comparisons between the eighteenth-century slave narrator's reliance on the abolition market and twentieth-century readers' desire to 'consume' books on slavery. In his novel *The Counting House* (1996) Dabydeen also explores the role of Indian indentured labourers; although this is not part of the African slave trade, it remains important to this study. Often referred to as 'the new slavery', Indian indentured labour, like African-Caribbean slavery, is an overlooked part of British history which Dabydeen attempts to imagine using the surviving fragments and objects of this past.[43] Significant for Dabydeen is the neglect of the past of Indian indenture in literature by earlier Caribbean authors. Important Indo-Caribbean texts like Selvon's *A Brighter Sun* (1952) or Naipaul's *A House for Mr Biswas* (1961) are inadequate for Dabydeen because neglectful of this history. Dabydeen addresses this absence by imaginatively returning to the site of

Indian indentured labour in his poetry collections *Slave Song* and *Coolie Odyssey*, as well as his aforementioned novel *The Counting House*.

Indentured labourers on British sugar plantations were brought from India to compensate for the substantial loss of African labour in the period following the emancipation of African slaves in the British Caribbean. Initially, planters looked to Europe and the Portuguese Atlantic islands for workers, before turning their gaze towards India. The first Indian indentured labourers arrived in Guyana in May 1838 and, by the demise of this system, some 238,909 Indian labourers had been brought to Guyana alone.[44] Yet, despite the vast numbers involved in this mass relocation, the past of the Indian indentured labourer is a curiously neglected one. Their history is largely absent from standard accounts of Caribbean, Indian and British histories, as well as from most revisionary accounts of the slave trade which, in tracing the role of the African slave, subsequently tend to eclipse the significant part played by Indian indentured labourers on the British plantations in the Caribbean.

While these indentured labourers were not, strictly speaking, slaves, they endured the same harsh conditions and punishments as plantation slaves and sometimes toiled alongside their African counterparts in the fields. Indian indentured labour was seen by many as a continuation of slavery under a different guise. Mortality rates were high for those indentured labourers who had survived the journey to the Caribbean and, whenever able, immigrants fled the harsh life on the estates. Although slavery had officially ended, Indian indentured labour can be viewed as its immediate legacy, and a continuation of enslavement. It was not until 1917 that Indian indenture stopped – a system of exploitation around which 'The taint of slavery would always linger'.[45]

If Britain's involvement in the slave trade has not been afforded the due amount of historical representation, the role played by Indian indentured labourers is especially overlooked. The insufficient historical information on these labourers and lack of literary precedent mean both historical and literary representations are inadequate for Dabydeen – his unease with representations of Indian- and African-Caribbean people is a major issue in his works. In order to think imaginatively about the past of slavery and Indian indenture, it is not to books that he turns for inspiration. Instead, Dabydeen looks at what he refers to in *The Counting House* as the discarded 'scraps' of this past: the remnants of lives found in the plantation counting houses and in eighteenth-century paintings and etchings.

This juncture brings me to the second important arena of Dabydeen's work, his interest in the interaction between literature, history and art – exploring through his literary works representations of black people in Britain during the eighteenth and nineteenth centuries by artists such as William Hogarth and J. M. W. Turner. His fascination with eighteenth-century art is evident from the subject of his doctorate and two books on Hogarth, and is a particularly important intertext for much of his fictional work: most obviously, his novel *A Harlot's Progress* is inspired by Hogarth's engravings of the same name of 1732. Dabydeen's interest in art from this period stems from, in his words, 'an attempt to show that English art has had a dimension of blackness to it; in other words, and on a personal level, that I belonged to British society.'[46] Yet, also pertinent to his interest in art is his concern with 'the idea of whether or how you could aestheticize suffering', a dilemma most frequently encountered with reference to the Jewish Holocaust.[47] For this reason, Chapter 3 includes an exploration of Dabydeen's narrative poem 'Turner', where the focus shifts to J. M. W. Turner's infamous pictorial depiction of 'aestheticized suffering' in his painting of 1840, *Slavers Throwing Overboard the Dead and Dying* – the jettison of African slaves in the middle passage. Dabydeen's poem accentuates the exploitation inherent in visual depictions of this journey by reinterpreting the artist as both a paedophile and slave-ship captain. However, criticism of literary audience and the appetite for the 'exotic' finds its strongest articulation in *A Harlot's Progress*. In this novel he critiques the genre of the slave narrative, alongside which is suggested the continuing inadequacy of representations of black people within Britain, still largely typified by their reliance on stereotype and myth.

Dabydeen has made clear in interviews his cynicism for both British literary audiences and prizes, as he has stated:

> I really don't mind being a victim of any British appetite for the exotic, if it means that I can get some royalties here and there. As to the British guilt for the Empire which translates into book buying and prize giving, I'll gladly jostle in the queue for handouts and reparations. (I've even contemplated writing a sombre novel on slavery to cash in on White angst.)[48]

However much his comments are meant ironically, Dabydeen nevertheless seems quick to draw distinct racial lines, especially when referring to the apparent desire of white readers to consume 'exotic' literature, leading to his denial of a 'genuine audience' for his works within Britain.[49]

In returning imaginatively to the history of slavery, Dabydeen writes from an especially troubled position: aware of the literary and historical gaps surrounding this past and unusually sensitive to the impossibility of such an act of representation – in particular, of the inappropriateness of attempting to 'speak for' either Indian indentured labourers or African slaves. He finds himself wrestling with this conundrum as much as with earlier, and inadequate, literary or historical precedents. As we shall see, the works of Dabydeen explored in this study point to his compulsion to return to the history of slavery, yet are characterised by his anxieties generated by the act of representing this past, illustrative of the crisis of representation at the heart of his writing.

Fred D'Aguiar

Fred D'Aguiar was born in London in 1960 and raised in Guyana, returning to Britain when he was twelve. Upon leaving school, he worked for three years as a psychiatric nurse before studying African and Caribbean Studies at the University of Kent. D'Aguiar now resides in the United States, where he is

Professor of English and Gloria D. Smith Professor of Africana Studies at Virginia Tech State University. His earliest published works were poems; his first collection *Mama Dot* (1985) was followed by *Airy Hall* (1989), *British Subjects* (1993) and *Continental Shelf* (2009), and the long poems *Bill of Rights* (1998) and *Bloodlines* (2000). D'Aguiar's poetry, which oscillates between the Guyana of his youth and the bleak Britain of the late twentieth century, has received the Malcolm X, T. S. Eliot and Guyana Poetry Prizes. His first novel, *The Longest Memory* (1994), won the Whitbread First Novel Award and David Higham Prize for Fiction, and was followed by *Dear Future* (1996); *Feeding the Ghosts* (1997), which was shortlisted for the James Tait Black Memorial Prize for Fiction, and *Bethany Bettany* (2003). Like Dabydeen, he has also thrice won the Guyana Prize for Literature (for *The Longest Memory, Dear Future* and *Bethany Bettany*). D'Aguiar's primary interest is in the memory of slavery – specifically, how we are to remember this past one hundred and fifty years after slavery's abolition. In imaginatively returning to this past, D'Aguiar, like Phillips and Dabydeen, draws upon a range of historical and literary material. When questioned in interview about his use of sources in writing *Feeding the Ghosts*, for example, D'Aguiar revealed that he learned of the slave ship *Zong* from a trip to the Liverpool Maritime Museum, though he also 'read Linda Brent, Phyllis [*sic*] Wheatley, Sojourner Truth and others to get a feel for the time, tone and place that black women faced.'[50]

D'Aguiar's earliest poetic influences included a grandfather who 'liked Tennyson and Victorian poetry', and calypsos played on the radio: 'alongside heraldic English poetry with its Tennysonian, Victorian metres, we also had some crude creole poetry bursting over the airwaves into our ears.'[51] D'Aguiar intended to complete a doctorate at the University of Warwick on Wilson Harris, and has cited a range of other authors as being influential on his work, including the British and Irish poets John Milton, W. B. Yeats, Philip Larkin and T. S. Eliot; writers of Caribbean origin, like Valerie Bloom, Sandra Agard, Edward Kamau Brathwaite, Derek Walcott, Claude McKay and George

Lamming, and African American authors such as Ralph Ellison and James Baldwin.[52]

D'Aguiar's most recent novel, *Bethany Bettany*, examines the plight of a young girl born of Guyanese parents in London. Following the dissolution of her parents' marriage and suicide of her father, she is taken aged five to live with her father's family in Guyana. Racial incidents remembered in the book include not only racist graffiti in the toilets of her father's workplace, but also marches in 1960s' London denouncing Caribbean immigration. As Bethany's mother recalls: 'Long before they came into view I could hear the order from the megaphone, *Niggers! Niggers! Niggers!* And the crowd's response of, *Out! Out! Out!* I hauled you in the opposite direction. But there was nowhere to go.'[53] Captured in the last sentence of this passage is not only a parent's terror at being unable to escape the pervading racism of England in the 1960s, but also D'Aguiar's ongoing interest, shared by Phillips, in racism as an inescapable legacy of slavery. This issue can be traced in his works concerning the time of slavery, *The Longest Memory* and *Feeding the Ghosts*, through the mid-twentieth-century period of Caribbean immigration in *Bethany Bettany* into the twenty-first century of *Bloodlines*.

Also like Phillips, D'Aguiar explores in his works his uneasiness with a British identity. In his essay 'Further Adventures in the Skin Trade' (2000), he writes of his identity as being divided:

> Born in London but not of London, writing in English but not of the English, British but under the rubric of a racial and cultural difference, my tongue forked, my skin bristled with the scales of my unlikeliness. I became Hydra-headed, speaking from multiple selves to multiple constituencies. Each poem staged my insider-outsider stance.[54]

The notion of being 'unlike' or different is a central concern in many of D'Aguiar's poems – especially those from *British Subjects* which explore the concept of a black British identity. In poems such as 'A Gift of a Rose' the speaker describes an incident of police brutality accompanied by 'epithets | sworn by the police in praise of [his] black skin and mother'.[55] Despite its sustained metaphor of roses for bruises, this poem deals explicitly with racial violence against a black person. In 'Home', D'Aguiar writes of an airport customs official at Heathrow airport informing him

> with Surrey loam caked
> on the tongue, home is always elsewhere.
> I take it like an English middleweight
> with a questionable chin, knowing
>
> my passport photo's too open-faced,
> haircut wrong (an afro) for the decade;
> the stamp, British Citizen, not bold enough
> for my liking and too much for theirs.[56]

We can see in this passage the anxiety that an afro is the 'wrong' haircut for the time and one which functions as a clear racial identifier, marking him specifically as 'black British'. The stamp of 'British Citizen' acts like a protective armour, but is unable to reassure the narrator of the legitimacy of his habitation in the UK. The airport is portrayed as a space where identity is even more keenly felt and questioned than usual – a place of suspicion and interrogation where he can never be too British.

D'Aguiar repeatedly addresses in his works the legacy of belonging, but the concept of fixed 'borders' of identity is rejected in favour of an exploration of overlapping areas of identification. This notion is particularly evident in his depiction of mixed-race characters; Chapel from *The Longest Memory* and the narrator of *Bloodlines* both struggle with identities as 'half a slave, half [a] master'.[57] Simple positions of insider or outsider are complicated in D'Aguiar's texts, as his earlier reference to his own 'insider-outsider' status indicates, positing instead a pivoting identity. As we shall see, his portrayal of mixed-race characters at the time of slavery complicates opposing moral and racial positions of black slave and white master, suggesting a need to think about slavery in a way that is sensitive to the absence of historical representation for those of mixed races.

Phillips, Dabydeen and D'Aguiar are a dynamic trio for study because all three authors choose, in the late twentieth century, to return imaginatively to the past of slavery, and do so in strikingly dissimilar ways. Their varying concerns in returning to this past (which often include the history, ethics, memory and representation of slavery) illuminate very different problems inherent in exploring Britain's involvement in slavery. Despite their sometimes close reliance on historical documents (particularly transparent in the case of Phillips), Dabydeen, D'Aguiar and Phillips deliberately avoid adding to the body of received historical accounts of slavery by choosing to write creatively about this past. Phillips may be seen as seeking to vocalise the past excluded from history by his ventriloquism of neglected voices and histories. In contrast, Dabydeen attempts to question the motivation for, and ethics involved in, exploring the past of slavery. What, he asks, are the consequences of such acts of representation? For D'Aguiar, the question posed concerns what to do with this historical information: how do we manage the legacies of slavery in order to remember this past? Although all three authors are largely preoccupied with the problem of how to commence representing slavery, therefore, their approaches to this problem vary immensely, and this book investigates these differences.

Caryl Phillips and the absent voices of history

Caryl Phillips's most recent play, *Rough Crossings* (2007) juxta-poses late eighteenth-century events occurring in Britain and America in its exploration of the work undertaken by British slavery abolitionists Granville Sharp, Thomas Clarkson and John Clarkson alongside the black troops fighting on the British side in the American War of Independence. Based on Simon Schama's historical epic of the same name, we learn of the black soldiers' subsequent habitation in Nova Scotia and resettlement in Sierra Leone, and the extreme hardships faced by the settlers in each location. Phillips also makes clear that Britain's reluc-tance to accommodate these men and their families is behind the resettlement in these new locations. While the play is set in the eighteenth century, it therefore shares current concerns to do with Britain's apparent reluctance to find a space for non-white citizens within its boundaries. In one of the few critical essays so far written on the play, John McLeod argues that '*Rough Crossings* affords Phillips a way of thinking not so much about the eighteenth century but also the twentieth century, viewed from the vantage of a British-raised writer who has often been worried by the racial inflection of African American politics.'[1] I would concur with McLeod, and suggest that, while much of Phillips's play is set in Africa and North America, Phillips remains concerned with twentieth-century Britain, in particular, and the ways in which belonging has been made difficult for non-white citizens. The black soldiers in *Rough Crossings* soon realise that, although they have been fighting for the British side, there will be no legitimate place for them in the UK after the war. In fact, as Peter Fryer explains, from 1784, Britain's black population was 'swollen by a stream of mostly penniless refugees from north America. The promise of freedom had lured them to the British side ... The promise was kept. But hundreds of these black "loyalists", many of them ex-servicemen, exchanged the life of a slave for that of a starving beggar on the London streets.'[2] As one of the leading characters in Phillips's version of *Rough Crossings* (though a decidedly minor one in Schama's), the freed slave Thomas Peters, reasons: 'In America we fight and we kill for them. What use are we to them on the streets of their cities?'[3] We might detect a link here between Britain's use of black American men to fight as British soldiers in the American War of Independence, and the mobilisation of black men and women from its colonies during the Second World War. In both cases, the subsequent invitation to enter Britain after the wars was undermined by the coldness of the nation's response to these 'foreigners'. It would seem that the UK's apparently unwelcoming attitude towards the black men and women entering the country from 1948 has roots in a much earlier period. In the works explored in this chapter, Phillips traces the origins of this attitude, and the related anxieties surrounding national identity. In his novel *Cambridge* (1991), a white plantation-owner's daughter finds her English identity thrown into confusion in the creolising space of the unnamed Caribbean island, and a male slave reflects on his life as a 'virtual Englishman'. In *Crossing the River* (1993), the black diaspora created by slavery is examined over a two hundred and fifty-year period and in varying locations; for example, the account of a female black pioneer rests against that of a white slave-ship captain, suggesting the need for each story to be heard. Non-fictional works *The Atlantic Sound* (2000) and *A New World Order* (2001) chart Phillips's ongoing interest in what it means to 'belong' in the late twentieth century. In these later works, through visiting, and writing about, the points of the triangular trade (Africa, the Caribbean and US, the UK), and engaging with seemingly disparate notions like football affiliations and Pan-Africanism, Phillips investigates the boundaries of belonging and exactly who is included – or excluded – from national identities.

Cambridge

In writing *Cambridge*, Phillips drew upon a range of eighteenth- and nineteenth-century sources by such authors as the slave narrator Olaudah Equiano; eighteenth-century Scottish travel writer Janet Schaw; the diarist Lady Maria Nugent, whose husband was the governor of Jamaica from 1801–6; the plantation owner and novelist Matthew 'Monk' Lewis and the nineteenth-century British actress Frances Ann Kemble.[4] Often, these sources are not only traceable, but undisguised; in the construction of narratives penned by his protagonists Emily and Cambridge, for example, Phillips quotes entire paragraphs unchanged from the original sources. Such unabashed 'borrowing' led Paul Edwards to criticise a draft of the novel in a letter to Phillips dated 10 August 1990:

> I think rather that the narrative degenerates into easily recognisable pastiche, a kind of impersonal patchwork with little contemporary value, since the original sources have said it all already. I think that the narrative of Cambridge must derive much more from your own imagination, but as it stands, what you do is repeat material from the past. That's not what a modern novelist must do with material like this.[5]

Edwards's criticisms arise from Phillips's heavy reliance on his sources, apparently believing that the latter's use of these disparate accounts was unoriginal. Edwards fails to see that Phillips's act of creating the 'patchwork' of sources is vital. In exposing the mechanics of construction, Phillips reveals the inadequacy of relying upon one source, or standard account (such as that of received history) to narrate the past of slavery. Instead, it is only in comparing accounts, and constructing a contrapuntal montage from these documents, that the complexities and contradictions at the heart of attempts to represent slavery are exposed. The novel's multifaceted form plays a definitive role in Phillips's critique of the historical representation of slavery, and can be seen as engaging with the 'itinerary of silencing' posited by Gayatri Spivak through the juxtaposition of conflicting narratives.[6] In this way, received history may be thought of as the survival of the most dominant of many narratives, thereby dispelling the myth of one authoritative narrative, or truth, of the past. *Cambridge* is more that just a collation of different documents from the slave trade; in blending and constructing his story of plantation life in the nineteenth century, Phillips was, he asserts in his response to Edwards, 'trying to make something "new" out of something "old"'.[7]

Cambridge is a multi-narrated, interwoven tale of plantation life on an unnamed Caribbean island in the period between the abolition of the slave trade in 1807 and emancipation of slaves from 1838. The Caribbean portrayed by Phillips in this novel is a terrifying, unstable and creolised space. While the multiple, and unreliable, narrators make a simple description of the plot no easy task, it would seem that Emily Cartwright has been sent from England to the island in order to report back to her father the state of his plantation. She soon becomes pregnant; the father of her child would appear to be the plantation manager, Mr Brown, who has also been conducting a relationship with the slave Cambridge's wife, Christiania. Not long after, Mr Brown is murdered by Cambridge, and Emily moves from the Great House on the plantation to the deserted Hawthorn Cottage, where she gives birth to a stillborn child. The novel ends as she ponders her now uncertain future in light of her father's decision to sell the plantation, and we learn that Cambridge has been hanged.

The narratives of Emily and Cambridge are placed alongside one another and followed by a sensationalised newspaper report, reproduced almost without change from Mrs Flannigan's *Antigua and the Antiguans* (1844), which details the murder of Mr Brown by Cambridge.[8] This is an important source for Phillips, in providing not only names for Cambridge, Mr Brown and Christiania (Christiana in the original document), but also in sealing the fate of Cambridge. The novel is framed by a prologue and epilogue, narrated by an omniscient narrator, which provide Emily with a more compassionate character than is portrayed by her often condescending and prejudiced first-person account.

Although brief, the title of *Cambridge* is significant for at least four reasons. First, while the novel shares its title with the name of a plantation slave, the longest narrative within *Cambridge* is a travel journal written by Emily. This flawed expectation of the leading narrative voice is typical of Phillips who, throughout the text, creates and positions characters who appear to conform to his readers' expectations, only to confound these expectations with figures that cannot be simply read or understood. As an anglicised African, Cambridge's voice is indicative of such a tactic of flawed expectations, in his refusal to conform to an 'authentic' African voice. Emily, an unmarried middle-class woman at the start of the nineteenth century, also subverts standard expectations by becoming pregnant. In their shared transgressions and refusal to conform to both readers' expectations and the expectations of early nineteenth-century English society, Phillips shows that such characters as Emily and Cambridge are not predictable: they are more complicated than allegorical figures of black slave and white slave owner.

Secondly, Emily's centrality to the novel makes it different to many other twentieth-century novels about slavery. Phillips writes the majority of *Cambridge* from the viewpoint of a person who would not normally be a central figure in accounts of this history, both due to her position as a woman and, as the novel progresses, in relation to the poor whites on the Caribbean island. By the end of *Cambridge*, although Emily is not quite yet a poor white, the forthcoming sale of the plantation indicates her increasing economic insecurity.

Thirdly, Emily's prominent narrative presence within a novel entitled *Cambridge* also suggests the integrated nature of the relationship between the protagonists, despite their minimal contact. Phillips is particularly interested in the connections between black men and white women, a relationship he explores in other works, including, for example, his play *The Shelter* (produced 1983) and novels *Crossing the River, A Distant Shore* (2003) and *In the Falling Snow* (2009). In his introduction to *The Shelter* Phillips writes that the relationship between black men and white women is an area rarely explored: 'An explosive, perhaps the most explosive of all relationships, seldom written about, seldom explained[;] feared, observed, hated'.[9] Phillips does not bring Emily and Cambridge together in a sexual encounter as one can find in, for example, Fred D'Aguiar's poem *Bloodlines* (2000), or in the coarse sexuality of David Dabydeen's collection of poems *Slave Song* (1984). Neither does he revel in the antithesis between the characters, but instead subverts expectations by illustrating their similarities, or what Bénédicte Ledent has called the 'often neglected cross-cultural potentialities of the colonial situation'.[10] Importantly, these similarities include their shared exclusion from narratives of English identity and differing experiences of 'enslavement'. While Emily's enslavement through her gender and, later, economic position, is in no way commensurable with Cambridge's slavery, Phillips posits their accounts in a way which highlights their similarities. Both characters are enslaved by, and excluded from, narratives of English identity, though they are 'enslaved' in very different, and unequal, ways.

In allowing Emily more narrative room in the novel, Phillips also reminds his reader that slavery, though unequally shared, is a shared past nonetheless. As he has explained:

> It wasn't just black people, it was white people too. It was their history [...] British people forget they know very little about history. Why? Because most of their history took place in India and Africa and the Caribbean, where they could pretend it didn't happen.[11]

If British twentieth-century 'amnesia' surrounding the past of slavery has been instrumental in the construction of non-white people as alien to Britain, then Phillips suggests the falsity of such a forgetful position. Slavery is not only 'black history', but the intersection of a number of disparate lives and histories. By calling the novel after a British town as well as a Caribbean slave, Phillips emphasises the novel's dual position as part of both British and Caribbean history.

Finally, by naming the novel *Cambridge*, Phillips also reiterates the point that his male protagonist is no longer African Olumide or English David, but Caribbean Cambridge; like (and yet different from) Emily, Cambridge is of a creole, liminal status. His testimony traces each of his identities, detailing his life in the Africa of his boyhood to his transportation to England and, following his manumission, his subsequent recapture into slavery and remainder of his life on the Caribbean island. As a slave testimony, this narrative draws upon a long history of British writing by slaves, which includes well-known figures such as Olaudah Equiano, Ottobah Cugoano and Ignatius Sancho. Although generally slaves were prohibited from reading or writing, as owners feared the potential for subversion and discontent that might come from their literacy, there were notable exceptions, and the role played in the campaigns of abolitionists by slave narratives should not be underestimated. However, renowned ex-slaves like Sancho, Cugoano and Equiano were unusual figures amid an otherwise illiterate and unprivileged mass of slaves in Britain and its colonies. Furthermore, even when accounts written by slaves were published, there was often significant doubt as to the authenticity of the writing. Such doubt was fuelled in part by assumptions that black people were insufficiently intelligent to produce these narratives, and also by the substantial role played by white editors and ghost writers in the creation of slave testimonies. More recently, historians have questioned the extent to which these accounts were 'fictionalised' to aid the abolitionist cause, something I explore in greater detail in Chapter 3. In addition, many of these accounts will not have survived. In *Cambridge*, Phillips historicises the figure of the slave narrator, arguably in response to the ways in which eighteenth-century writers like Equiano have been held aloft as iconical figureheads for black Britain.

While the accounts of Cambridge and Emily provide different views of largely the same events, we cannot simply think of Cambridge's narrative as being the 'missing piece' of Emily's account, or vice versa. In examining the past of slavery, it is necessary to hear the histories of both slave and slave owner. Yet, only the history of the slave owner has traditionally been recorded, which has proved problematic for those exploring the history of subaltern, or oppressed, groups. In *Cambridge*, Phillips suggests that narratives such as those by Emily or Cambridge are overlapping fragments of an untotalisable past and should be read *alongside* one another, or contrapuntally. His apparent disinterest in paraphrasing perhaps more subtly his sources, or blending the conflicting accounts, can be seen as a refusal to create one homogeneous version of the slave past, instead emphasising its polyphony.

Emily's narrative assumes the form of a travel journal, a popular form in the nineteenth century, though primarily thought to be a male genre. The act of writing her travel narrative indicates Emily's endeavour to 'wear' an identity – that of the male imperial adventurer. She does not, however, assume this new identity with ease. Like her elaborate and confining English clothing, which becomes increasingly ill-fitting and unwearable in her time on the island, the travel-narrative genre does not comfortably accommodate Emily's writing. Its inadequacy is implied by her reluctance to be restricted, or enslaved, by its form: 'I wished to go beyond the commonplace memoirs of previous travellers, [which find] nought worthy of record but the most bizarre features of this tropical life'.[12] We can see in this quotation that Emily desires to transcend, or 'go beyond' the confinements of the travel narrative form with its focus on the 'most bizarre' or exotic aspects of travel, which suggests her reluctance to be bound to the expectations of the form. The apparent masculinity of the genre also leads to a certain tentativeness; Emily is heavily reliant on the information about the slaves imparted to her by the white men on the plantation. In her book *Discourses of Difference: An Analysis of Women's Travel Writing and Colonialism* (1991), Sara Mills has suggested that female travel writers were caught between the twin discourses of imperialism and femininity, 'neither of which they could wholeheartedly adopt'.[13] It is, Mills indicates, in the struggle between these two discourses 'that their writing exposes the unsteady foundations on which it is based'.[14] Although Emily's journal is, of course, a staged nineteenth-century travel journal created by a man in the late twentieth century, if we look at her narrative we can see how Phillips instils these tensions in her writing, most visibly aboard the ship, where shipping terms are crudely spliced into the narrative and left disjointed and unexplained:

> Attached to each *bed* are straps of rope. We have been informed that these are to lash us in of an evening irrespective of the weather appearing clear or inclement.
>
> Sea terms: WINDWARD, whence the wind blows; LEEWARD, to which it blows ... the BOWLINES, those which spread out the sails and make them swell.
>
> Out on deck Isabella and I surveyed the dingy sky. It promised rough sea, sudden squalls and a stormy passage. (C, 8–9)

In this extract, part of the disjunction arises from Phillips's juxtaposition of different sources; the first part would seem to draw on a passage from Janet Schaw's *Journal of a Lady of Quality*, while the sea terms are taken from Matthew Lewis's *Journal of a West India Proprietor*. We perhaps detect here that Emily is enduring a 'stormy passage' with masculine imperial language; the vocabulary of shipping does not quite enable her to successfully articulate her voyage. Like the restraining straps inside the cabin, Emily is to some extent restrained or confined by this language and, at this moment, we can see one example of her several enslavements.

Emily's freedom is also restricted through her position as a wealthy woman in early nineteenth-century Britain. Although there is a continuation of patriarchal values on the Caribbean island, the trip to her father's plantation is clearly an attempt to escape from patriarchal Britain, where she is expected to marry the ageing widower Thomas Lockwood: 'The truth was she was fleeing the lonely regime which fastened her into backboards, corsets and stays to improve her posture. ... Almost thirty. Too old to be secretly stifling her misery into lace handkerchiefs' (*C*, 4). Emily's life in England is one of loneliness, restraint and concealed sadness, where her body is imprisoned in repressive and rigid garments and she 'stifl[es] her misery' into a symbol of English respectability, her lace handkerchief. Indeed, the notion of containment is indicative of her identity as an English woman; once away from England, she is soon able to loosen the vestments of her identity.

If, in some ways, Emily is cast as a Britannia figure – a representative of Britain, or rather England, on the Caribbean island – it is a role she assumes both imperfectly and unwillingly.[15] Here we have another flawed expectation; Emily may appear to be a representative of England in the Caribbean, but her experiences differ widely from this portrayal. In *Gender and Nation* (1997), Nira Yuval-Davis re-examines the familiar notion of the state as divided into two spheres, public and private. While men operate largely in the first of these categories, women have tended to be located in the private sphere, and 'As nationalism and nations have usually been discussed as part of the public political sphere, the exclusion of women from that arena has affected their exclusion from that discourse as well.'[16] Emily's partial exclusion from English national identity is made evident at several points in the novel and is metaphorically linked to notions of clothing, where she feels uncomfortable in items representative of her English identity. Throughout her narrative she writes of feeling confined or smothered; while on board the ship, for instance, she complains: 'I am occasionally seized by a suffocating sensation … I have in consequence thrown off my shop-dress' (*C*, 15). Her increasingly informal standards of dress aboard the ship signify that she is relaxing out of an English identity.

National identity, therefore, is frequently portrayed in the novel in terms of the proper clothing to be worn or removed, according to the situation, and Emily invests much importance in the notion that clothes reflect one's social position. On the island, she objects to what she sees as Christiania's 'insubordination' for sitting at the dining table in the Great House and refusing to serve her. Here we see Emily's belief in the importance of dressing appropriate to one's (social and racial) position: 'I informed this coal-black *ape-woman* that I desired her to put on a serving gown and take up a role among my attendants' (*C*, 73). She therefore seeks out Mr Brown in the field and demands he ban Christiania from the dining table; as Emily describes: 'For some time we stood, toe to toe, two solitary white people under the powerful sun, casting off our garments of white decorum before the black hordes, each vying for supremacy over the other' (*C*, 77). English identity is portrayed as a repressive article of politeness and manners which must be removed in any attempt to demonstrate power. This is an interesting description, as Emily depicts herself and Mr Brown to be united by their race, and very much aware of the audience to their performance, or 'black hordes'. At the same time, they are in clear opposition to one another in their battle for control of the situation. Emily is sufficiently enraged to disregard conventional codes of femininity and challenge Mr Brown's patriarchal authority. Her assertion of power is, however, short-lived, as the encounter quickly ends when she vomits and faints. This reaction is arguably prompted not only by the slave Fox, at Mr Brown's command, placing 'his black hands upon [her] body' (*C*, 78) – an example of what Robert J. C. Young has called 'an ambivalent driving desire at the heart of racialism: a compulsive libidinal attraction disavowed by an equal insistence on repulsion'[17] – but also by the temporary shedding of her respectability. Without the constraints of the 'garments of white decorum' her body cannot be limited; vomiting clearly signals this failure of containment and, therefore, the dramatic effect upon Emily of freedom from English identity.

While Emily imagines casting off her repressive English clothing in her encounter with Mr Brown, she cannot, at this stage, actually disrobe. In her restrictive and burdensome outfit, she envies the slaves' ability to dress according to the climate and 'without concern for conventional morality' (*C*, 21). Quite ironically, then, we see the apparently free Emily expressing envy at the slaves for flouting the rules of polite English society, as she, as we have seen, is frustrated by these very rules. Her anxieties over the seemingly inadequate clothing of the slaves

– the women wearing 'nothing … more substantial than a petti-coat' (*C*, 21) – are partly linked to her fear at the transition she longs to make to a similar creolised state of undress. She is caught between two opposing forces: there is the sense, perhaps, that her identity is coming undone. Emily envies the slaves, yet is aware that their clothing does not conform to the rules of English codes of decency – an indication that her unsteady, 'stormy passage', which began on the ship, continues long beyond the end of her sea voyage.

Emily's twinned responses of fear and desire at trans-gressing the boundaries of both polite English society and her own identity are illustrated in her preoccupation with 'proper' dress and reliance on order. This fixation reveals her concerns about (yet longing for) a collapse of social order and of her own descent into a 'disreputable' creole life; she wonders of her father: 'Does he have no conception of what would claim us all in the tropics were we to slip an inch below the surface of respectability? In these climes all is possible' (*C*, 127). Emily both fears and desires such a conclusion; she craves the freedom that accompanies casting off the rules of polite society, yet fears the consequences of this creolisation.

In contrast to the insubstantial clothing of the slaves, Emily describes the overdressed, and uncomfortable, white inhabitants of Baytown as 'half melting under heavy, richly embroidered coats and waistcoats' (*C*, 102). The English on the island feel it necessary to dress to reflect national identity, yet this is inappro-priate clothing for the climate. Apparel is clearly a badge, a weari-some marker of nationality. Furthermore, it would seem that the maintenance of an English identity is so constrictive that it leads to deformity; the slaves are 'Erect and well-formed, their quality is attributed … directly to their lack of tight clothing, which in infancy and childhood can lead to deformities among white and civilized people' (*C*, 35). Phillips implies, then, the intimate relationship between national identity and racism, and the potentially deforming nature of this alliance.

If English national identity, in its metaphor as clothing, is burdensome, then it is, according to Emily, a burden only white people should endure. Having described the usual flimsy attire of the slaves, she is clear to record her discomfort at their dressing on Sundays and holidays in what she sees as a parody of English clothing:

> The *sable-belles* are no less extravagantly modish in their ornamental silk dresses, gauze flounces and highly coloured petticoats which, though of the best quality, display patterns more commonly employed in England for window-curtains. ... I for one take great comfort in viewing the negroes, male and female, in their filthy native garb, for in these circumstances they do not violate laws of taste which civilized peoples have spent many a century to establish. (*C*, 66)

Just as Emily disapproves of Cambridge's 'highly fanciful English' (*C*, 92), she also objects to black people dressing up in an 'English' fashion. This strategy is employed by Phillips in order to suggest the constructed, and confining, notion of identity, as well as its adaptability. If one overlooks for a moment Emily's condescending tone, the slaves' use of material with 'patterns more commonly employed in England for window-curtains' can be seen as a reflection of their creolisation; their own response to enslavement and a measure of their creativity in bending the rules of 'conventional morality'.[18] Emily's derision comes from her inability to read this creativity; unlike the slaves, she cannot yet break the rules.

While the slaves may adapt English clothing to suit their creolised status, Emily's shedding of her English identity leaves her unsteady and fragmented. In the epilogue, following the loss of her baby, the ensuing exchange takes place with the doctor, Mr McDonald:

> 'And when will you be returning to our country?'
> 'Our country?'
> 'England, of course.'
> England. Emily smiled to herself. The doctor delivered the phrase as though this England was a dependable garment that one simply slipped into or out of according to one's whim. Did he not understand that people grow and

change? Did he not understand that one day a discovery
might be made that this country-garb is no longer of a
correct measure? (C, 177)[19]

The implication here is that Emily no longer 'fits' within England;
far from the familiarity of a 'dependable garment', an English
identity is now ill-fitting and unwearable. She has quite literally
grown on her time on the island, as her pregnancy has altered
her body, yet the notion that her character may have grown, or
developed, may be a positive effect of her visit. Although her
attitudes towards black people on the island remain problematic
throughout *Cambridge*, by the end of the novel Emily is able
to question her satisfaction with English identity, as well as the
necessity of rejoining her father in England. In the time spent
on the island she has changed to such an extent that she does
not know if she can return to what was formerly her 'home'. So,
while she asserts, '"I expect I will soon return to England." Emily
paused. "After all, it is my home"' (C, 178), the pause is significant
in pointing to what is *not* being said, and crucial in signalling her
uncertainty about the statement that follows. Like Cambridge,
Emily now exists in a liminal world between identities; neither
simply English, nor Caribbean, but a diasporan creole misfit. She
ponders her fate, with a new-found acceptance of her creolisation:
'Was I doomed to become an exotic for the rest of my days? This,
it now seemed to me, would be no bad thing' (C, 114).

Emily's ultimate state of nakedness and fragmented identity
is the culmination of a process that began early in the novel. Her
journey into island life has been also an expedition into what she
refers to the 'darkness' of her identity and the disintegration of
self, where she can no longer be certain of anything: 'In these
climes all is possible. Perhaps this is why a certain type of man
(and woman) longs to settle in these parts' (C, 127). Although this
quotation suggests that the island offers her a degree of freedom
not permitted in England, for Emily, it had quickly turned from
a 'tropical paradise' (C, 18) into an altogether more frightening
prospect: 'a dark tropical unknown' (C, 22). Yet, implicit in this
journey is a certain excitement at going beyond the boundaries
and limits of her race and class which she could not transgress

in England; the 'darkness' of the unknown is vital. Earlier in the novel, having rejected the courtship of Mr McDonald, Emily reflects on the white men on the island: 'I retired to my chamber and looked into my mirror. Perhaps the affections of all these men turn in due course to some brown-faced beauty' (C, 122–3). While Christiania may seem to be foremost in her mind at this moment, the mirror signals that Emily is scrutinising her own appearance. By the close of the novel, her stay on the island has transformed Emily into a 'brown-faced beauty'.

The 'dark tropical unknown' can therefore be seen as a creolised space which enables her to achieve a greater degree of freedom, in escaping the enslavement which stems from her position as a wealthy woman in early nineteenth-century England. It is also a less judging society, with different social standards, and where rules are to some extent broken, yet this freedom is dangerous. In the epilogue, with the realisation that she cannot return to England, Emily stands naked in the mirror, disrobed of her cloak of English identity and assessing what she has become. No longer conforming to protocol, her identity is unstable and fragmented. The epilogue moves seamlessly between third- and first-person narrators, articulating a sense of instability and precariousness. We see through the character of Emily that a refusal to conform to the rules of 'conventional morality' leads to feelings of displacement and unbelonging; she fits nowhere. Phillips does not leave the book with a utopian vision of happiness on the Caribbean island. The stillborn child may indicate a resigned pessimism about the future for white individuals upon the island; this is, Phillips reminds us, an uncertain, turbulent time for such people.

If Emily is in some ways enslaved by her gender, she is also towards the close of the novel enslaved through her identification with the poor whites on the island. The end of slavery and her father's decision to sell the plantation leaves her future on the island uncertain. She had earlier recorded her shock at seeing what she refers to as 'pale-fleshed *niggers*' (C, 108); this is our first introduction in the novel to the plight of poor whites in the Caribbean. The position of the poor whites mirrors that of the slaves upon the island, unable to marry without their master's consent, and 'as likely to be subject to a public whipping or imprisonment as the common negro' (*C*, 108). However, while the poor whites are also enslaved, it is on economic rather than racial grounds, and many are now reliant upon the generosity of their ex-slaves:

> the most destitute among them now rely upon the kindly benevolence of negroes. These black Samaritans feel pity for the white unfortunates and take a mess of stewed produce, with a proportion of garden-stuff from their own grounds made savoury by a little salt meat, to their old *misses* and *massa*. (*C*, 108)

This description has later echoes in Emily's residence at Hawthorn Cottage: 'They were kind, they journeyed up the hill and brought her food ... The mistress, she had a position' (*C*, 182–3). Phillips shows through the character of Emily the plight of both women and poor whites in the Caribbean in this period, largely silenced from history and excluded from respectable colonial society. The history of white indentured labourers in the Caribbean is curiously absent from most standard and revisionary histories of British slavery, though Eric Williams has asserted the importance of this labour as the 'historic base upon which Negro slavery was constructed'.[20] Black and white people, Williams reminds us once again, were inextricably intertwined in the course of slavery, and not only as slaves and masters. Paradoxically, while the poor whites are arguably enslaved by their economic status, Emily's growing identification with them seems to offer her a marginally greater freedom, in granting more relaxed social and moral standards than were available to her as an unmarried middle-class woman. Yet, it remains a liminal, difficult location: this is not a celebratory creolisation. In *Cambridge* the poor whites inhabit an interstitial, in-between status; prevented from identification with either wealthier whites in the Caribbean (through their lack of economic power and social standing) or black people (due to race).

   Just as Phillips uses clothing as a metaphor for English identity in Emily's narrative, we also witness Cambridge writing of identity as a garment, and experiencing a similarly unstable, shifting identity. Cambridge's account, as has been established, takes the form of a slave testimony. One can deduce from the poise and stylised writing of slaves such as Sancho or Equiano that they were what we would call anglicised; Cambridge, too, adopts a tone of writing that reflects his anglicised identity, or what Paul Smethurst has referred to as 'the voice of a *translated* slave'.[21] Like Emily, therefore, Cambridge is in some ways enslaved by the formal language of early nineteenth-century England. Ironically, though, while Emily longs to escape from this society, this is exactly the kind of world that Cambridge aspires to be accepted into.

While Cambridge clearly sees himself as English David Henderson, his skin colour is a permanent and visible marker that differentiates him from other Englishmen. This is, for Cambridge, a painful reminder that identity is forged by contact with others. Emily, for example, is quite clear about Cambridge's status as an outsider: 'he seemed determined to adopt a *lunatic* precision in his dealings with our English words, as though the black imagined himself to be a part of our white race' (*C*, 120). This passage highlights that, perhaps as in twentieth-century Britain, in the nineteenth century, English identity was established by identifying those who did not 'belong'. It also indicates that certain linguistic registers were thought to be the preserve of white English people; just as Emily admitted to 'taking great comfort' from the slaves wearing 'filthy native garb' rather than English-styled clothing, she expects Cambridge to speak in an 'exotic' manner. His familiarity with, and employment of, 'correct' English leads her to conclude he is not of sane mind; a black person pertaining to be English was thought incongruous.[22] We might remember Emily's struggles with nautical and imperial language, indicating the ways in which speech, like writing or clothing, is an essential, and performative, component of identity.

Cambridge's belief in his English nationality makes his subsequent recapture into slavery all the harder to accept: 'That I, a virtual Englishman, was to be treated as base African cargo, caused me such hurtful pain as I was barely able to endure' (C, 156). Here, he employs a useful phrase, in describing himself as a 'virtual' Englishman, recalling Smethurst's notion of the 'translated' slave. As an anglicised African, he is not actually English, but virtually so. His race prevents the perfect assimilation of English national identity; in a different way, Cambridge is, like Emily, of a creole, in-between status. Yet, if he may be thought of as a 'virtual Englishman', this is just part of a larger process of shifting identity, and is linked to the tricky concept of 'home'. In a similar way to Emily, who quickly realises that England can no longer be described as her home, Cambridge's conception of home shifts with his changing locations and multiple identities. While Africa is initially his home, it is soon replaced by England, where he 'sheds' his African persona with the acquisition of Christianity. For Cambridge, nationality seemingly is like clothing – easily cast aside: 'My uncivilized African demeanour began to fall from my person, as I resolved to conduct myself along lines that would be agreeable to my God' (C, 144). Stuart Hall's essay 'Cultural Identity and Diaspora' (1990), in which he describes identity as being far from a stable presence, writing instead of 'a "production" which is never complete, always in process', is helpful in thinking about Cambridge's changing identity.[23] The concept of identity as being continually developed and adapted seems particularly relevant when considering how Cambridge and Emily reinvent, or shape, their identities through the use of different dress and language, though it is worth reiterating that Phillips does not portray their unstable identities in an uncomplicatedly positive way.

If Cambridge is able to 'remove' his African identity like a garment, English identity soon becomes burdensome. He is reluctant to assume the new name Thomas, but concedes: 'my condition far out-ranked my betrayed bretheren, whose backs were breaking under perpetual toil while I carried only the featherish burden of a new name' (C, 140–1). While his burden of identity may be light, it is nevertheless still an encumbrance – an identity to be endured rather than enjoyed. Not long after, Cambridge is 'reborn' as David Henderson and enthusiastically casts himself into the role of an Englishman: 'Truly I was now an Englishman, albeit a little smudgy of complexion!' (*C*, 147). It is perhaps not insignificant that, following his conversion to Christianity and assimilation of an English identity, his master buys him new clothing: 'He promptly ordered a new livery for myself, and announced a shilling increase in my allowance' (*C*, 144). This clothing is a reward for Cambridge's 'progress' in learning the rules and language of nineteenth-century England, and is also a recognition of his new status as a 'virtual' Englishman. However, his apparel as 'livery' is a further reminder that he is, at this point, servant to both his master and an imperfect English identity.

Cambridge, in his garb of the 'virtual Englishman', then, impersonates what he believes it means to be an English Christian: 'I earnestly wished to imbibe the spirit and imitate the manners of Christian men, for already Africa spoke to me of a barbarity I had fortunately fled' (*C*, 143). This moment reveals not only his acquired anglicisation, in believing in the 'barbarity' of Africa, but also the performative nature of identity, as an act requiring the correct lines and costume in order to be convincing. Cambridge had earlier referred to himself as 'dressed in the spiritual and physical guise of *Mungo*' (*C*, 136) but, once in England, attempts to learn the language and wear the clothing of the English. We have here an eighteenth-century equivalent to Paul Gilroy's warning of the dangers of assimilation in his analysis of the 1983 Conservative Party election poster proclaiming 'Labour says he's black. Tories say he's British'. As Gilroy argues, 'Blacks are being invited to forsake all that marks them out as culturally distinct before real Britishness can be guaranteed'.[24] The perfect assimilation of Cambridge's identity, however, is impossible due to his 'smudgy complexion', which leads other English people to attempt to cast him into another role: that of the African.[25]

Like Emily, who is in some ways enslaved, or restrained, by her position as an English woman in the early nineteenth century, in his time in England, Cambridge also finds that the bondage of slavery is replaced by a very different enslavement in his adherence to nineteenth-century English identity and codes of conduct. We can see from his descriptions of other black people that he feels himself to be superior; Cambridge, he is clear to emphasise, is no 'common slave' (*C*, 157), and his purpose in returning to Africa is as a missionary. Just as Emily's narrative – often prejudiced and disdainful – may distance her from the reader, so Cambridge, when given his own voice, reveals that he, too, is highly critical of the black people he encounters.

In initially moving Cambridge from Africa to Britain, Phillips not only illustrates the historical bond between the countries, but also dispels the myth that black people came to Britain for the first time in the mid-twentieth century. Cambridge records the substantial black presence in London in the late eighteenth, or early nineteenth, century: 'I went forth into London society and soon discovered myself haunted by black men occupying all ranks of life' (*C*, 142). His use of 'haunted' is pertinent, in revealing his construction of black people as 'other', or ghostly reflections of his racial identity – a reminder that he is a problematic figure. Cambridge describes black people of ranging social positions, from the companions of rich white people, to prostitutes and street performers, yet it is clear from his tone that he does not relate to these 'unfortunate negroes' (*C*, 143).

While in London, Cambridge encounters prejudice surrounding mixed-race relationships. He falls in love with, and marries, a white servant called Anna. Although his master has been conducting a relationship with his black servant, Mahogany Nell, it seems that this is a more socially acceptable pairing. Cambridge reports that, while walking with Anna, he was 'set upon by a swarm of white *gallants* with epithets of *black devil*, while she that was under [his] protection received considerably worse for being in company with a man of colour' (*C*, 145). Once again, we find that the relationships between black men and white women, in particular, would seem to have a history that cannot be cast aside. In *Cambridge* Phillips illustrates the far-reaching nature of such relationships, which did not begin with the arrival of the *Windrush*. He suggests it is therefore necessary to unpick and explore the roots of this antagonism; *Cambridge* allows the reader to see how the relationships between disparate people have been entwined by the process of slavery. While there may have been an effort to separate the histories of black and white people in the twentieth century, Phillips rejoins their narratives within his text, if only to illustrate their separateness in, or absence from, standard versions of history. Slavery he reminds us, though unequally shared, is a shared past nonetheless.

In the perhaps surprising twinning of his protagonists, Phillips demonstrates the scope of enslavement. In revealing the different forms of enslavement experienced by Emily and Cambridge – the former on grounds of gender, the latter on race – Phillips questions what it means to be enslaved. Furthermore, as we have seen, Emily is partially enslaved by her English identity, but at the same time, is denied full participation in this identity because she is female. Cambridge aspires to being English, but is also excluded from the narrative of English nationality because he is black: both are imperfectly assimilated into this identity. The protagonists in some ways write as a protest against these enslavements and exclusions. Their narratives indicate the destabilisation of English identity at the start of the nineteenth century and point to the proliferation of alternative, and difficult, creolised conceptions of identity. Phillips does not write of slavery via an accusatory, dissident, politics of race, but as a way of unravelling the propriety and 'purity' of national identity itself.

However, neither Emily nor Cambridge has a fortuitous outcome from their act of rebellion; Cambridge is killed, and Emily's attempt to write her own script proves hazardous. The slaves' use of language and dress suggests a creolised adaptability and creativity, yet Emily's refusal to conform to English rules of femininity, and subsequent shedding of her English identity, leads to dislocation and instability. Like Cambridge, Emily may seem to no longer belong in England, but neither does she belong in the Caribbean, leading her to ask: 'Are there no ships that might take me away? But take me away to what and to whom?' (C, 183). Phillips therefore questions what there is for those that refuse, or are not allowed to engage with, English rules and society. We can see in the problems experienced by both Emily and Cambridge with English identity Phillips's deep-set dissatisfaction with the related concept of British national identity, as irrevocably flawed in its exclusion and marginalisation of people on grounds of race, gender or class. He reveals how both protagonists labour, in differing ways, with the exclusivity and constraints of English national identity, yet neither is entirely successful in constructing viable alternative identities. Their creolisation does not suggest a celebratory freedom, but precarious and liminal positions which, while indicating the importance of forging new identities, also highlight the dangers of creolisation, revealing the paradox of diasporan identity arguably at the core of this novel.

Crossing the River

Crossing the River is a fragmented novel, split into four distinct parts, with a framing epilogue and prologue set in a transhistorical mode. Letters and diary entries within the sections are often non-chronological and incomplete, and each story tells a tale of broken familial bonds. Slavery, Phillips seems to suggest, is a fractured and untotalisable past. However, despite such fragmentation, *Crossing the River* traces the unexpected connections between people, centuries, countries and histories made possible because of the transatlantic slave trade. Said has argued in *Culture and Imperialism* that

> No one can deny the persisting continuities of long traditions, sustained habitations, national languages, and cultural geographies, but there seems no reason except fear and prejudice to keep insisting on their separation and distinctiveness, as if that was all human life was about. Survival in fact is about the connections between things.[26]

Said indicates that, while differences will always exist between traditions, habitations, languages and cultural terrains, survival is enabled by tracing the affirmative connections between these different elements.

My contention that *Crossing the River* demonstrates that connections are crucial to survival is supported by Phillips's comments that he 'wanted to make an affirmative connection, not a connection based upon exploitation or suffering or misery, but a connection based upon a kind of survival'.[27] Within his novel, the importance of connections is slowly revealed as we follow the fortunes of three children sold into slavery. The survival of these allegorical protagonists depends on their ability to forge bonds with others. Unlike *Cambridge*, which covered a relatively short period of time in the nineteenth century, *Crossing the River* spans two and a half centuries, and its subjects range across the globe; the novel moves from eighteenth- and nineteenth-century Africa, through nineteenth-century America to Britain during, and after, the Second World War.

The prologue reveals the voice of a guilty African father: 'A desperate foolishness. The crops failed. I sold my children. I remember ... And soon after, the chorus of a common memory began to haunt me'.[28] If the plural voices of *Cambridge* suggest a history of slavery comprising separate, but overlapping, stories and lives, then in *Crossing the River*, these histories are simultaneously articulated to create what is described in the epilogue as a polyphonic, intertwined 'many-tongued chorus of the common memory' (*CR*, 235). Phillips's use of 'haunt' stresses the insistence of the past to be resurrected; it would seem that what has happened cannot remain buried, but somehow exists, though 'in different forms', in the present.[29] In *Crossing the River*, the father is haunted by memories of the past and the moment of separation from his children. His voice is interspersed with other apparently irreconcilable voices, such as that of the slave captain of the third section of the novel, James Hamilton. This conjunction recalls Said's advocacy of 'overlapping territories, intertwined histories' in its seamless interchange: 'Three children only. I jettisoned them at this point, where the tributary stumbles and swims out in all directions to meet the sea. *Bought 2 strong man-boys, and a proud girl*' (*CR*, 1). The same intertwining device occurs in the other stories; Phillips implies that we should think not of separate black and white accounts of the past, but of a connected – yet fragmentary – narrative of slavery which interlaces all these histories.

The first section of *Crossing the River* recounts the story of Edward Williams; upon the death of his wife, he journeys from America to Africa to search for his former slave, Nash, with whom it is suggested he has had a sexual relationship. Nash had ventured to Liberia as a missionary, but gradually lost contact with Edward, whose wife had secretly destroyed Nash's letters. After a period of sickness in Sierra Leone, Edward travels into Liberia and learns from another former slave, Madison, that Nash is dead. The second, and shortest, section recounts the life of Martha, an ex-slave, now pioneer, on her way across America to simultaneously join her friend and search for her daughter Eliza Mae in California. Taken in off the streets by an anonymous white woman in the depths of winter, Martha dies that night. The third section comprises the logbook of a slaver captain, James Hamilton, contrasted with love letters written to his wife. This section ends with his purchase of the children of the prologue. The final section, which is by far the longest, is set largely during the Second World War and takes place in the north of England. The narrator, Joyce, is a white working-class woman trapped in an unhappy marriage to the violent and abusive Len. Her diary entries reveal that she falls in love with a black American serviceman, Travis, and becomes pregnant. They marry, but he dies soon after while serving in Italy, and Joyce is persuaded to give up her baby son Greer. Eighteen years later, the remarried Joyce receives a visit from her now grown-up son.

Crossing the River may be a novel about slavery and its continuing legacies, but it is not simply an accusatory novel. Instead of a literature of recrimination and retribution, Phillips's novel envisages a meeting between black and white people; an acknowledgement and understanding of the past of slavery which rejects a rhetoric of blame. It is therefore important to note that Phillips dedicates his book to 'those who crossed the river', which acknowledges all the people – black and white – that journeyed across the Atlantic and other 'rivers', both literal and figurative. In fact, and quite crucially, in the epilogue, the 'children' include Joyce. In *Crossing the River* Phillips may be seen to be transcending racial categories to explore a past, and a future, that comprises black and white.

Although *Crossing the River* is a text rife with broken familial bonds, we subsequently see an emergence of new, non-familial connections. In *The World, the Text, and the Critic*, Said writes that 'Childless couples, orphaned children, aborted childbirths, and unregenerately celibate men and women populate the world of high modernism with remarkable insistence, all of them suggesting the difficulties of filiation.'[30] The apparent 'difficulties of filiation' are not merely traits of 'high modernism'; we can find evidence of almost all the figures listed by Said in *Crossing the River*, where slavery and its aftermath have, it seems, led to problems of filiation. Edward and his wife are childless and Martha is looking for her daughter. Hamilton is searching to retrace the last movements of his late father in Africa, though his desire to trace his family connections contrasts ironically with his role as a slave-trader. Finally, Joyce has an abortion, loses both parents through different wars, and is eventually persuaded to give up the child she has with Travis. Phillips's portrayal of 'families' in this novel as fragmented might suggest his dissatisfaction with the concept of the stable family unit. The families he presents span centuries, yet none fits the standard Western representation of the 'nuclear' family, whether due to war, plantation slavery or (in the case of Edward) perhaps sexuality. The disruption of the stable family unit, one could argue, is one of the legacies of slavery although, as I explain, in this novel it is replaced with affiliative 'families'.

Aside from the guilty father of the prologue, one of the first characters suffering the effects of broken familial bonds is Martha. Her husband Lucas and daughter Eliza Mae were separated from her, and each other, when their owner died and they were resold. Although Martha is journeying across America to join her friend Lucy and find her daughter, there is a simultaneous realisation of the impossibility of this task, as her encounter with the white woman reveals: 'The woman stretched out her gloved hand and Martha stared hard at it. Eliza Mae was gone. This hand could no more lead her back to her daughter than it could lead Martha back to her own youthful self' (*CR*, 75). This movement pre-empts the epilogue's conclusion that 'There is no return' (*CR*, 237). The past cannot be undone, and so Martha's dream of familial reunion will remain only a dream: 'Soon it was time for Martha to leave, but her daughter simply forbade her mother to return east. Martha, feeling old and tired, sat down and wept openly, and in front of her grandchildren. She would not be going any place' (*CR*, 94). At no point in the novel do we find the kind of utopian 'return' or resurrection of filial relationships projected in her dream. The closest Phillips allows us to get to this utopian moment of meeting is in the final section of the text, though this is, in many ways, a far from utopian encounter.

In the section entitled 'Crossing the River', we encounter broken filial bonds in James Hamilton's search to retrace his father's last steps, but it is in the final section of the novel that Phillips explores in greatest depth the figure of the absent father. Joyce's father died during the First World War, and she records searching for his name, lost among the many others, on the town's war memorial: 'his name is scattered among the names of hundreds of others. This is merely a place to find him, but not to discover him' (*CR*, 133). We can see here the impossibility of knowing her father: the war memorial may list the dead, but that is all it does – her father's name is indistinguishable from the numerous names of other men. The anonymity of the soldiers mirrors the anonymity of the slaves in part three of the novel, and here Phillips perhaps raises the problem of memorials to the dead; like monuments to slavery, war memorials are not places 'to discover' the dead. Instead, Phillips's imaginative exploration of slavery in novels like *Cambridge* or *Crossing the River* suggests an alternative means of discovering this past. The war is clearly a time for absent fathers, as Joyce tells her friend Sandra: 'this is a war ... if Tommy [Sandra's child] ends up without a father, he won't be the first and he won't be the last' (*CR*, 157). Travis's death means that he, too, briefly becomes an absent father, before Greer is given up for adoption. Absent fathers are not the extent of familial fragmentation, however; Joyce also suffers the death of her mother, killed by a bomb dropped upon the town. Furthermore, Greer is not the first child she has been unable to keep; before her marriage to Len, she became pregnant by an actor named Herbert and had an abortion.

Yet, if filial relationships are impossible, Said proposes the development of affiliative bonds, borne out of 'the pressure to produce new and different ways of conceiving human relationships'. He asks: 'is there some other way by which men and women can create social bonds between each other that would substitute for those ties that connect members of the same family across generations?'[31] In *Crossing the River*, we can see a similar substitution of familial bonds with affiliative connections; 'social bonds' constructed between biologically unrelated people. However, these bonds may not necessarily prove positive or equal, as in the case of Edward and Nash. The relationship between them is clearly not filial, despite the paternal vocabulary. According to Edward, his yearning for Nash is for the 'unconditional love of a child' (*CR*, 55), though the 'child' in question is an adult, and no kin of Edward. Said has proposed that 'affiliation sometimes reproduces filiation', and this section of Phillips's novel provides an imitation of a paternal relationship (as well as Joyce's transition to 'daughter' in the epilogue).[32] The paternalistic relationship between, in this case, former master and slave, or coloniser and colonised, is complicated by the implication of a sexual relationship between the men. Having received little communication from Edward, Nash's letters to his 'Dear Father' reveal he feels like an abandoned son. Like the father of the prologue, Edward is also a guilty 'father', partly occasioned by sending Nash to Africa (where he dies shortly before Edward's arrival), and also by their implied sexual relationship. Edward's guilt at abandoning his 'son' has, it would seem, an imperfect mirroring in the fourth section, in Joyce's decision to give up Greer for adoption – a point I shall return to in a moment. I would suggest that there is also a simultaneous mirroring between Nash and Greer as both come to terms with, and so acknowledge, the past. For Nash, Liberia is an awakening from the 'garb of ignorance' (*CR*, 61–2) that had been his identity as an American. Here we can see the effect of Nash's crossing of the river, in his growing resentment and anger as he comes to terms with his various exploitations. Nash's anger is directed towards America's continuing involvement in the trade, but it is also personal – at Edward for exploiting, and then abandoning, him: 'Perhaps ... you might explain to me why you used me for your purposes and then expelled me to this Liberian paradise' (*CR*, 62). Nash may suggest ironically that he has found 'paradise' on the other side of the river, but it is at the cost of painful self-discovery. In this part of the book, affiliative relations are not shown to be always positive; it is only by rejecting the relationship with Edward that Nash is able to cross the river, or arrive at an identity that is independent of Edward and awake to his previous manipulation.

Affiliative bonds can also be found in the second section, which examines another connection between black and white people. Though the relationship between Martha and the white woman that offers her shelter is less exploitative than that of Edward and Nash, its uncertainty is manifested in the gesture of an outstretched hand: 'After countless years of journeying, the hand was both insult and salvation, but the woman was not to know this' (*CR*, 75). Despite the ambiguity of the gesture, and their prescribed historical roles ('Perhaps this woman had bought her daughter?' *CR*, 74), a connection is nevertheless forged and, for a while, their lives come together. The woman may not know Martha's name, as we do, but then neither we – nor, it would seem, Martha – know hers. She is just as anonymous; a benevolent, almost allegorical, white figure.

If the bond between Martha and the white woman may seem to be an unlikely one, the third part of *Crossing the River* demonstrates another apparently unusual connection between Hamilton, as a white slave-ship captain, and the children of the prologue. This encounter between black and white characters is arguably the crux of the novel: the transaction upon which the book rests. As if to emphasise the point, this section is positioned at the centre of the text, and is named 'Crossing the River'. Phillips acknowledges in the opening page his reliance on the journal of the slave captain John Newton in order to write this account, and the historical note at the beginning of this section is important, in suggesting its emulation of a historical record. Phillips inserts frequent ellipses into the journal entries, which suggests, first, that the source may have been edited, but also that the history of slavery is fragmented and incomplete. In these gaps we can perhaps sense the unspoken or missing parts of this past, such as the voices, or stories, of the slaves (and of other, poorer, crew members), of whom we hear nothing. For example:

> At 7 p.m. departed this life Edward White, Carpenter's Mate, 7 days ill of a nervous fever. Buried him at once. Put overboard a boy, No. 29, being very bad with a violent body flux. Have now 3 whites not able to help themselves … (CR, 116)

This section, furthermore, serves as a reminder of who exactly crossed the river; we can see from the above quotation that the middle passage was also gruelling for the sailors, who died alongside the slaves, though they at least are named rather than numbered. Phillips also includes at the start of this section a list of crew members and their fates; another stark reminder of the white death toll. The deaths of slaves and crew are all related to the reader in a dispassionate log, as are Hamilton's acquisitions of slaves: 'Was shown 11 slaves, of whom I picked 5, viz., 4 men, 1 woman' (CR, 105). These staccato entries contrast with the passionate, heartfelt letters to his wife:

> I confess that, when alone, the recollection of my past with you overpowers me with a tender concern, and such thoughts give me a pleasure, second only to that of being actually with you. I have written myself into tears, yet I feel a serenity I never imagined till I was able to call you mine. (CR, 110)

Hamilton's letters are written in flowing, eloquent and romantic language, full of hyperbole and sentiment. They demonstrate his loneliness and capacity to love, thereby humanising and complicating his characterisation; in so doing, they pose a testing juxtaposition. Phillips has created a multidimensional and intriguing character, arguably indicative of the complexities of slavery, where ordinary men, often with wives and families, became embroiled in the trade. While Hamilton's letters evince his potential for compassion, he cannot relate this kindness to the slaves – a disjunction that renders this section particularly difficult for the reader. The association with Newton demonstrates the ambiguous position of Hamilton, as Newton evolved from being one of the more notorious slave captains to become a determined speaker against the slave trade.

Like Emily in *Cambridge*, then, Hamilton is an unusual choice of protagonist. In a way typical of Phillips, he returns to a character that has previously been portrayed (especially in abolitionist literature and tracts) as a dehumanised monster, and problematises this image. Eighteenth-century examples of this dehumanisation include pictorial depictions of cruel slave captains, created for the abolitionist cause, such as Isaac Cruikshank's etching *The Abolition of the Slave Trade* (1792), which shows a female slave roped upside down on the deck of the ship, watched by a leering captain and reputedly based on a real event. The case of the *Zong* is another example of a slave-ship captain's behaviour being particularly inhumane. In 1781, Luke Collingwood, captain of the *Zong*, fearing his slaves – many of whom had become ill – may not survive or be healthy enough to provide him with a good return, made the decision to jettison alive one hundred and thirty-two slaves for the insurance money. Cases such as these were further ammunition for the abolitionist cause, and authors contemporary to Phillips have also imaginatively returned to these events. Fred D'Aguiar's novel, *Feeding the Ghosts* (1997), for example, is based on the incidents aboard the *Zong* and the ensuing court case. Unlike Phillips, however, D'Aguiar adheres to more conventional portrayals of the slave-ship captain, and his Captain Cunningham arguably lacks the multidimensionality of Hamilton.[33]

In contrast to D'Aguiar's perhaps more familiar portrayal of the slave-ship captain, then, Phillips's representation of Hamilton is complex. Especially in the early days of slavery, participation in the trade was considered legitimate; there was no conception of its immorality, largely because slaves were not considered to be fully human. We realise the precariousness of the captain's life when, with crew members dying around him, he too contracts an illness. His journal ends not with his safe arrival on land, but somewhere in the ocean; the last entry reads:

> *Friday 21st May* ... During the night a hard wind came on so quick, with heavy rain. Occasioned a lofty sea, of which I was much afraid, for I do not remember ever meeting anything equal to it since using the sea. At dawn brought the ill-humoured slaves upon deck, but the air is so sharp they cannot endure, neither to wash nor to dance. They huddle together, and sing their melancholy lamentations. We have lost sight of Africa ... (*CR*, 124)

Hamilton is suspended in the act of crossing the river and does not, unlike the children he carries, necessarily ever reach the other side; the ellipsis trails off tantalisingly into an uncertain future. This uncertainty concerning his destiny is reinforced by the crew list at the start. The column indicating the crew's fate is left blank for certain men, including the captain; we cannot be sure of what happened to him, only that the ship, and the slaves, reached their destination. The stark list of crew members predicts the anonymous listing of the dead on the war memorial in the last part of the novel. Here, too, in the crew list, we encounter a place to know, but not discover, these men. Slave-ship ledgers, whether real or fictional, lead one to question who actually gained from the slave trade. While it is problematic to compare too closely enslaved Africans with free, if harshly treated, white crew members, Phillips seems to suggest that those who truly profited from the trade cannot be found aboard his ship.

Although this third section of the novel may seem incongruous, in that it is not the 'voice' of one of the children, it is linked to the others, not only in the figure of the absent father, but also in the sale of the three children to Hamilton. Furthermore, we might remember Said's advocacy of reading '*contrapuntally*,' with a simultaneous awareness both of the metropolitan history that is narrated and of those other histories against which (and together with which) the dominating discourse acts'.[34] The dominating discourse in the history of slavery has chiefly been the voice of the wealthy, white male; in this case, arguably represented by the narrative of Hamilton. Yet, even the accounts that have survived, such as the journal of Newton, provide a very one-sided view of these men. It is therefore necessary to read Hamilton's log alongside his letters in order to better understand the complexity of the man, and of the other narratives in the novel.

It would appear that the various histories articulated in *Crossing the River* need to be read together in any attempt to come to terms with the complex history of slavery and imperialism. Hamilton's voice is, as much as the children's, part of the novel's 'chorus of the common memory', though significantly, he is *not* one of the children. James Walvin, in *England, Slaves and Freedom, 1776–1838* (1986), writes of the 'distinctive historical forces which have bound black and white together, over many centuries, in ... a special interdependence'.[35] Like Phillips, Walvin stresses the inextricable nature of the relationship between black and white people. In the case of both *Cambridge* and *Crossing the River*, the most prominent historical 'force' is that of slavery; it makes possible, in its continuing legacies, the positions of all the characters with whom we are confronted. If Hamilton's story is the 'moment', or a microcosm, of slavery, then we see the continuing legacies of this moment in each of the other sections. For example, Nash and Martha were both slaves in America; again, as a direct result of the slave trade. In the last part of the novel, the relationship between Joyce and Travis is made possible precisely because of slavery; like Nash and Martha, Travis is a black American. However, the prejudice and racism Joyce and Travis encounter towards their relationship can also be seen as a legacy of this past. Slavery therefore both enables and hinders their relationship, and their child Greer is also bound to this past.

From the beginning of this final part of the novel, it is immediately clear that Joyce does not 'belong' within the small village community.[36] She is a threat to the villagers because obviously different; her friendly nature contrasts her to the others. Joyce is also, presumably, unique because she is what several critics have called 'colour blind' – it is some time before she reveals that Travis is black.[37] As a newcomer from the town, she is further alienated by her decision to not 'stick' by Len when he is sent to prison for dealing on the black market, and by her subsequent relationship with Travis: 'I knew what they were thinking. That he was just using me for fun. There was no ring on my finger, but I didn't think that they had the right to look at me in that way' (*CR*, 202).[38] In *Imagining Home: Gender, 'Race' and National Identity, 1945–64* (1998), Wendy Webster argues that 'The concept of "miscegenation" – widely used in race discourse in the 1950s – signalled not only the idea that races were biological categories marked by difference, but also that the mixing of these in heterosexual relations was deeply problematic and unnatural.'[39] As Webster affirms, those writing about race at this time were quick to seize upon what they saw as the 'unnaturalness' of mixed-race relationships. Joyce is warned by the army officer that they 'don't want any incidents' (*CR*, 206), or pregnancies, and Len tells her she's a 'traitor to [her] own kind' (*CR*, 217), his vocabulary emphasising the perceived unnaturalness of the attraction between Joyce and Travis, in crossing racial boundaries. His use of 'traitor' also signals that this is, for Len, a kind of war, based on a polarised vision of black and white. Unfortunately, Joyce cannot live with Travis in the United States because of the segregation laws; it seems their relationship is a connection thrown up by slavery that is not approved of.[40]

If the villagers are untrusting of Joyce, they also react with hostility to what they perceive as threats from 'outsiders', demonstrated with the arrival of the American servicemen. In the earlier quotation, Said mentions the 'fear and prejudice' involved in maintaining the 'separation and distinctiveness' of traditions and cultures. The village landlord excepted, the behaviour of the villagers towards the servicemen demonstrates this 'fear and prejudice': 'Some of the villagers couldn't contain themselves. They began to whisper to each other, and they pointed … I wanted to warn them, but in no time at all they were gone. It was too late' (*CR*, 129). The wartime language of invasion that was, in later decades, used by Enoch Powell and Margaret Thatcher to depict post-war Caribbean immigrants is, in this section, employed to describe the Americans: 'It's all over the papers. We're having an invasion all right, but it's not Jerry. We've been invaded by bloody Yanks' (*CR*, 134). It is not only Joyce and the American servicemen that are viewed with suspicion and outright hostility; the children evacuated to the village are also resented: 'They can bloody well go back where they come from' (*CR*, 144), as Len asserts. This statement echoes sentiments expressed towards black men and women in Britain in the latter half of the twentieth century – instructed with some frequency to go back to 'where they [came] from'. Joyce describes: 'Before us stood a dozen frightened children, the farmers eyeing the husky lads, the girls and scrawny boys close to tears' (*CR*, 144). The scene is also reminiscent of a slave auction – the children lined up with 'an identification tag around their necks' (*CR*, 144). Again, Phillips is tracing connections between disparate people and times – in this case, along lines of exploitation. The 'husky lads' are viewed in terms of their physical strength, or economic value, to the farmers; slaves were similarly assessed by potential owners in terms of strength, breeding potential and other criteria. This is, it would seem, another ghost of slavery, or continuation of the past in the present in altered forms.

Although Phillips's three black protagonists die, the ending of *Crossing the River* implies hope for the future in the character of Greer. As the child of Joyce and Travis, and the result of their relationship and love, he is a positive outcome of this meeting between black and white cultures. If Greer's arrival at Joyce's house in 1963 suggests a hope for the future, however, it does not signify the resurrecting of familial bonds, any more than it implies that Greer has returned 'home'. This term is particularly problematic for Phillips, and the delicacy with which it is employed is illustrated by Joyce's reaction to Greer's arrival: 'Come in, come in. He stepped by me, dipping a shoulder as he did so in order that we didn't have to touch ... I almost said make yourself at home, but I didn't. At least I avoided that' (*CR*,

231–2). One might also recall Emily's uncertainty about her 'home' towards the end of *Cambridge*; the problem of 'home' and belonging resurfaces throughout Phillips's works and is something I shall look at in more detail in the context of his non-fictional texts. Greer's arrival, therefore, does not result in a joyous recovering of familial bonds ('There is no return'), but a new relationship. One that is, perhaps, more honest, and replete with an acceptance of the impossibility of changing the past. Phillips does not provide a utopian moment of meeting, but an awkward and difficult moment. This is a key encounter in the novel; it is significant that the chapter ends with a note of painful tentativeness – a hope (but not certainty) for a future of reconciliation and understanding. Joyce cannot be absolved of the guilt of giving up her child for adoption, but is also not blamed by Phillips for her act: 'The silences had become more awkward, but at least they remained free of accusation' (*CR*, 223). I have already mentioned Edward's guilt concerning Nash, and implicit in all these 'silences' is, perhaps, a historical guilt which spans back to earlier rejections by white people; specifically, the refusal of plantation overseers or owners to acknowledge the children that were the product of their sexual union with slaves. In the case of Joyce, however, this acknowledgement *is* made, if somewhat late: 'My God, I wanted to hug him. I wanted him to know that I did have feelings for him. Both then and now. He was my son. Our son' (*CR*, 224). Unlike Edward and Nash, Martha and Eliza Mae or Hamilton and his father, therefore, Joyce and Greer are reunited, though they are unable to recover the past or, in any unproblematic way, be mother and son. It is, as we have seen, impossible to alter what has happened; but it is possible, Phillips seems to suggest, to forge new relationships based on honesty and understanding. *Crossing the River*, there-fore, rejects an accusatory rhetoric; his reluctance to blame men like Edward and Hamilton, or women who have given up their children, like Joyce, ensures Phillips's novel, like the silences between Joyce and Greer, remains 'free of accusation'.

The voices of the protagonists that comprise the main stories are just a few of the numerous diasporic voices of slavery.

These voices feature both in the prologue and, more extensively, in the epilogue:

> I wait. And then listen as the many-tongued chorus of the common memory begins again to swell, and insist that I acknowledge greetings from those who lever pints of ale in the pubs of London. Receive salutations from those who submit to (what the French call) neurotic inter-racial urges in the boulevards of Paris. ('No first-class nation can afford to produce a race of mongrels.') But my Joyce, and my other children, their voices hurt but determined, they will survive the hardships of the far bank. (*CR*, 235)

The global scale of this diasporic living is reflected in references to various countries across the world and to such figures as Toussaint L'Ouverture, Claude McKay, Miles Davis, James Baldwin, Marvin Gaye, Muhammad Ali, The Supremes and Martin Luther King. These diasporic survivors have endured slavery and imperialism, and continue to survive (and not *just* survive) in contemporary society, which is, as we have seen, infused with the ghosts of the slavery. Despite the fractures incurred by diasporic living, there remains an overwhelming sense of connectedness in the novel, though this does not arise only from these recurring hauntings of the past. In *Crossing the River*, we can see the existence of what Said has called the 'massively knotted and complex histories of special but nevertheless overlapping and interconnected experiences',[41] and the way in which, despite the fundamental disruptions incurred by diasporan living, connections can still be made. In the epilogue, Phillips ventriloquises Martin Luther King:

> I have listened to the voice that cried: I have a dream that one day on the red hills of Georgia, the sons of former slaves and the sons of former slave-owners will be able to sit down together at the table of brotherhood. (*CR*, 237)

In *Crossing the River*, this dream is at least partly realised, in the bonds forged between black and white characters. Greer may not be able to call Joyce's house his 'home', but he is invited to sit down with her as they begin to construct their new relationship:

'Sit down. Please, sit down' (*CR*, 232). The act of sitting becomes, for Phillips, a physical manifestation of the affiliative hopefulness projected in this novel. In each of the stories, the children are striving for survival through affiliative bonds – through their determined attempts to connect with their surroundings. As Phillips states:

> I wouldn't say I've always wanted to be an explorer of the fissures and crevices of migration. I have seen connectedness and 'celebrated' the qualities of survival that people in all sorts of predicaments are able to keep hold of with clenched fists. I didn't want to leave this novel as an analysis of fracture, because I felt such an overwhelming, passionate attachment to all the voices, and I kept thinking it seemed almost choral. These people were talking in harmonies I could hear.[42]

Like Said's contrapuntal reading, the emphasis is on consonance – counterpoint that is nevertheless harmonious. While *Crossing the River* comprises different voices, all are part of the 'chorus of a common memory' and linked by affiliative bonds. If the various families are fragmented in this book through the course of slavery and its repercussions, Phillips intimates the necessity of creating new affiliative relationships. These connections fall not just between people and races, but also between centuries.[43]

Yet, in *Crossing the River*, survival is made possible not only, as Phillips suggests, by 'clenched fists' but also, as we have seen, by outreached hands. This gesture first occurs when the white woman reaches out to Martha, but can also be found on a metaphorical level in Joyce's refusal to treat Travis differently on the grounds of his skin colour. We might recall that the gesture is not an attempt to return to the past, just as the epilogue concludes 'There is no return' (*CR*, 237). *Crossing the River*, while acknowledging the past, does not gaze only backwards, nor does it dwell on the politics of blame, concluding with the confirmation that the children 'arrived on the far bank of the river, loved' (*CR*, 237). Instead, it points quite determinedly to a shared future in which all are invited to 'sit down together', irrespective of race. Through Phillips's refusal to be lured into writing a literature of blame or recrimination, his novel becomes a hand outstretched towards people like the African father, Edward or Hamilton. Phillips neither demonises nor blames them and, in not doing so, makes the greatest outreaching gesture of all.

The Atlantic Sound and *A New World Order*

In his essay 'Media, Margins and Modernity' (1986), Edward Said argues that

> culture has to be seen as not only excluding but also *exported*; there is this tradition which you are required to understand and learn and so on, but you cannot really be *of* it. And that to me is a deeply interesting question and needs more study because no exclusionary practice can maintain itself for very long. Then you get the crossings over ... and then of course the whole problematic of *exile and immigration* enters into it, the people who simply don't belong in any culture.[44]

Said's focus on 'crossings over', within the context of migration and diaspora, is particularly relevant to the study of Phillips's works, as the act of crossing is also a central motion in his fictional and non-fictional texts. Said provides a theoretical vocabulary for this idea of crossing as an unfinished or incomplete state, where even when migrants physically cross over to another place, they find that they 'simply don't belong in any culture'. Further, the relevancy of Said's comment about culture's 'exclusionary practice' is evident in its link to what Phillips has called in *Extravagant Strangers* (1997) the British 'mythology of homogeneity' and the fierce policing of British boundaries and identities in attempts to control immigration from non-white citizens.[45] This apparently exclusionary practice is instrumental in engendering feelings of unbelonging for those who are unable to 'participate fully in the main narrative of British life' (*ES*, xiii).

This section focuses on two of Phillips's non-fictional works: the historical travelogue *The Atlantic Sound* and collection of essays *A New World Order*. These partly autobiographical works are vital in exploring what Phillips shows to be the continuing legacies of slavery, including racism and the related problems with national identity facing non-white people in twenty-first-century Britain. I propose that it is precisely this under-explored relationship between the anxieties of contemporary Britain and the past of slavery that motivates Phillips's imaginative return to slavery in his fiction.

Phillips's non-fictional works have received little critical comment in comparison to his novels, which are necessarily more easily categorised by genre. Reviewers have struggled, especially, to position *The Atlantic Sound* within a specific literary category, being part fiction, part travelogue and part historical journey, in which Phillips attempts to unpick the tangled web of diasporan identities. Travel writing was a popular genre for the first generation of twentieth-century Caribbean migrants to Britain. *The Atlantic Sound* is written in a similar travelogue style to V. S. Naipaul's *The Middle Passage* (1962), which splices historical information with Naipaul's current impressions and thoughts on the places he visits. There are further comparisons to be made between Phillips's non-fictional works and Naipaul's *The Enigma of Arrival* (1987) and *A Way in the World: A Sequence* (1994), both of which are written in a style that seamlessly fuses autobiography and fiction – an achievement matched by Phillips in *The Atlantic Sound*. Phillips has suggested, however, that Naipaul's work is tainted by an 'undisguised contempt for the people of the Third World', and he and Naipaul are two very different authors.[46] In comparing their works, I do so with due caution.

The Atlantic Sound and *A New World Order* are both divided into geographical sections; in *A New World Order*, these are the four zones of transatlantic slavery: 'The United States', 'Africa', 'The Caribbean' and 'Britain'. In *The Atlantic Sound*, while there is a similar geographical split, the labelling differs. It begins with the 'Atlantic Crossing', where Phillips travels by 'banana boat' from the Caribbean to Britain, retracing the journey he had undertaken as an infant with his parents as they emigrated from St Kitts. This is followed by a chapter about Liverpool entitled 'Leaving Home'; the first part examines the story of John Ocansey who, in 1881, came to Liverpool from Africa to investigate his father's missing money, owed for goods sent to a Liverpool merchant. In the second part, Phillips returns to Liverpool, where he meets up with a 'Liverpool Born Black' called Stephen. The next chapter, 'Homeward Bound', sees Phillips travel to Ghana, where he attends 'Panafest' and explores the politics and pitfalls of Pan-Africanism. He then travels, in 'Home', to Charleston in the United States, and delves into the life of Judge Waring, who campaigned to ensure the vote for all. Finally, in the Epilogue, entitled 'Exodus', Phillips visits a group of African-Americans who have decided to live in the Negev desert in Israel, returning to the land of their biblical ancestors.

The Atlantic Sound and A New World Order are, like Cambridge and Crossing the River, fragmentary texts, arguably reflecting the fragmentation which, for writers such as Phillips, is an integral part of diasporan identity. As Phillips states in A New World Order, 'I realize that for me – ... born elsewhere – there will never be any closure to this conundrum of "home"' (NWO, 308). This 'conundrum' may be seen as a focal point of both his fictional and non-fictional works, including, as is evident from just the titles of the chapters, The Atlantic Sound. In this book, Phillips explores the multifarious understandings of home, not only from his own perspective, but from the viewpoints of people he encounters, or whose lives he explores, along the way. I have argued in my readings of Cambridge and Crossing the River that Phillips's works transcend a politics of race and that he writes, quite relentlessly, about slavery as a history comprised of black and white people. This trait is not confined to his fiction; indeed, from the beginning of The Atlantic Sound, Phillips is keen to emphasise that black people of the diaspora are not alone in their experience of crossing the Atlantic. He has explained that his trip on the banana boat was an attempt to 'relive not just [his] parents' voyage but Columbus's, the slave ships', and the Irish and Russian flotsam migrating to the New World'.[47] The

Atlantic Ocean has been crossed for many centuries by people of all races – sometimes voluntarily; at others, in chains.

Said has quite simply stated that 'No one today is purely *one* thing',[48] and for Phillips – who was born in St Kitts, raised in Britain, and now resides principally in the United States – identity is necessarily composite. His uneasy position as a black child within post-war Britain is articulated in his introduction to *A New World Order*:

> I am seven years old in the north of England; too late to be coloured, but too soon to be British. I recognise the place, I feel at home here, but I don't belong. I am of, and not of, this place. History dealt me four cards; an ambiguous hand. (*NWO*, 4)

Unlike the first generation of Caribbean migrants to Britain, Phillips reflects a slowly changing country, and an identity that therefore falls between the labels 'coloured' and 'British'. Furthermore, he finds himself caught between the four cards of Africa, Britain, the Caribbean and the United States. Regardless of where Phillips resides, the refrain is the same: 'I recognise the place, I feel at home here, but I don't belong. I am of, and not of, this place'. Phillips's identity is one that is, to use Homi Bhabha's vocabulary, 'interstitial' or 'liminal' – reflected most succinctly in the phrase 'of, and not of, this place'. He also makes the distinction between feeling at home and belonging, implying that, while somewhere may be 'home', it can still be a place one does not belong.[49]

In Chapter 1, I raised the notion that British identity has been predicated on exclusions and argued that, in the post-war period, this was enforced by the passing of legislation designed specifically to exclude non-white people. Phillips has also stated that, 'Across the centuries British identity has been primarily a racially constructed concept. … Race and ethnicity are the bricks and mortar with which the British have traditionally built a wall around the perimeter of their island nation and created fixity.'[50] This defensive wall is, furthermore, fiercely policed, as Rosemary Marangoly George, in her book *The Politics of Home* (1996), writes:

> One distinguishing feature of places called home is that they are built on select inclusions. The inclusions are grounded in a learned (or taught) sense of a kinship that is extended to those who are perceived as sharing the same blood, race, class, gender, or religion. Membership is maintained by bonds of love, fear, power, desire and control.[51]

While George's comments are not directed towards Britain specifically, her idea of an enforced kinship certainly seems relevant to the UK, and links to the notion of 'cultural insiderism' proposed by Gilroy.[52] Gilroy writes that its identifying feature is 'an absolute sense of ethnic difference. This is maximised so that it ... acquires an incontestable priority over all other dimensions of [people's] social and historical experience, cultures, and identities', and is utilised in order to 'construct the nation as an ethnically homogeneous object'.[53] The importance of ethnic difference as signifier of nationality, and twinned conception of the nation as 'an ethnically homogeneous object', in turn anticipates Phillips's comments in *Extravagant Strangers* about the 'mythology of homogeneity'. The persistent attempt to deny black Britons full participation in Britain's 'main narrative', as I have already argued, is one of the continuing legacies of slavery. The 'mythology of homogeneity' relies upon the false, but persistent, notion that the *Windrush* arrival was the primary moment of black arrival in Britain. This, in turn, depends upon the denial of an earlier, and continuous, history of black habitation within Britain – an important part of which is the suppression of Britain's role in the slave trade. When, in fact, as Phillips argues, migration to Britain did not begin with the *Windrush*: 'Britain has been forged in the crucible of fusion – of hybridity. Over the centuries, British life at all levels – its royal family, the nation's musical heritage, Parliament, military, sport, entertainment and the City – has been invigorated and to some extent defined by the heterogenous nature that is the national condition' (*ES*, xiii). Phillips's conclusion to a *New World Order* is correspondingly subtitled 'The "high anxiety" of belonging', and in this he writes:

I grew up in Leeds in the sixties and seventies, in a world in which everybody, from teachers to policemen, felt it appropriate to ask me ... for an explanation of where I was from. The answer 'Leeds,' or 'Yorkshire,' was never going to satisfy them. Of course, as a result, it was never going to satisfy me either. (*NWO*, 303)

We see here Phillips's awareness of the complexity of diasporan identity. His sense of self and identity relies to a certain extent on how he is perceived by others; without an acceptance of his British citizenship from those he meets, it is also rendered unconvincing to him.

Even dictionary definitions of 'home' are confusing; it is both 'the place where one lives' and 'the native land of a person or a person's ancestors', which allows for some considerable contradiction, especially for diasporan people.[54] Phillips wrestles with this ambiguous word throughout his works. We might, for instance, remember Greer's arrival at Joyce's house in *Crossing the River*, which could not, in any terms, be described as a return home. An understanding of what home means, and where it lies, is intimately connected to one's sense of identity, self and belonging and, in *The Atlantic Sound*, Phillips makes various suggestions as to the meaning of this word. One of the most significant, and characteristic of Phillips, is in connection to football: 'Back at the hotel I lie full-length on my bed and watch images of "home". Everton versus Manchester United.'[55] Here, football becomes emblematic of British identity; an idea that is also central to the essay in *A New World Order* entitled 'Leeds United, Life and Me'. In this essay, the racism that is interlaced in the game of football is evinced not only in the behaviour of hostile fans of opponent teams, who showered Phillips with 'torrents of abuse [and] sharpened pennies' (*NWO*, 299), but also in the utter duplicity of white Leeds football fans: 'The same people who would hug you when Leeds scored ... would also shout "nigger" and "coon" should the opposing team have the temerity to field a player of the darker hue' (*NWO*, 299). In some ways, Phillips's uneasy relationship with football would seem to echo his relationship with Britain. While he is, of course, entitled to go to matches, he is made uncomfortable by the number of racist fans that, in his experience, are in attendance; in a related way, his dissatisfaction with a British identity is in part due to the racism he has encountered over many years. Furthermore, football affiliations are, like a British identity, also predicated on exclusions and are reinforced by maintaining a strong sense of the 'other'.

However, football provides Phillips with a temporary, and not uncomplicated, sense of belonging:

> Leeds United reminds me of who I am. All together now, 'We are Leeds, We are Leeds, We are Leeds.' Somewhere, thirty-five years ago, a small black boy in the company of his white teenage babysitter stood on the terraces at Elland Road and muttered those words for the first time. And I say back to that child today, 'And you will always be Leeds, for they are a mirror in which you will see reflected the complexity that is your life.' (*NWO*, 301)

A momentary unity ('All together now') is created as the fans assume a collective identity, repeating their football chant mantra. Belonging, it seems, needs to be continually asserted in order to become believable. Like the difficult representation of slavery in Phillips's novels, his portrayal of the legacies of this past, such as belonging and identity for non-white Britons, is also complicated. Leeds United may remind Phillips of who he is, but this reminder is of his difference; it is not an easy affiliation with the white football fans. This quotation also demonstrates that identities are performative, suggesting Bhabha's notion of the pedagogical and the performative.

In his essay 'DissemiNation: Time, Narrative and the Margins of the Modern Nation' (1990), Bhabha writes of the heterogeneity of the nation; the numerous histories and points of cultural difference that preclude the establishment of a homogeneous national identity. There occurs, he argues, 'a split between the continuist, accumulative temporality of the pedagogical, and the repetitious, recursive strategy of the performative. It is through this process of splitting that the conceptual ambivalence of modern society becomes the site of *writing the nation*.'[56]

For Bhabha, the pedagogical is a continuous history, a linear movement through time, whereas the performative is continually repeating and non-progressive. In *A New World Order*, we can see that, by donning a football shirt, the fans perform an identity as supporters of a certain team and, in so doing, also as British citizens. Against this performative, and repetitive, aspect of British identity runs the pedagogical. The belief in the uninterrupted continuity of British history is expressed in George Orwell's essay 'England Your England', explored by Phillips in *A New World Order*. Ignoring completely centuries of migration to Britain and, of course, the involuntary arrival of slaves from Africa, Orwell is confident in claiming that 'British people had no desire to view themselves as a nation of immigrants, and that a sense of continuity with the past was a crucial determinant of national identity' (*NWO*, 266).[57] This idea of the unbroken continuity of British history has also been used by Enoch Powell, and has a far-reaching historical basis. As Ian Baucom states, the 'strategy of disavowing blackness in order to negatively invoke a racially pure English identity draws on a long history of the reading of Englishness as primarily a racial category'.[58] We also saw Cambridge struggling with the problems of English identity; the persistent belief in the coalition of race and nationality, which prompts the exclusionary tactics deployed against Phillips by fans of opposing teams, is clearly not a late twentieth- or early twenty-first-century phenomenon.

While a temporary solidarity may be introduced by assuming an identity as a Leeds United supporter, therefore, for fans like Phillips, this identity remains volatile and uneasy. The mirror in this case is provided by his football team; in Phillips's works, mirrors can be found in often unexpected things. If, as Phillips argues, he is often perceived by other Britons as not belonging within Britain, his affiliation with Leeds United provides him with a mirror, in which he sees the confirmation that his identity is complex and that he does not, to use his terminology, easily 'belong'.

Phillips suggests, therefore, that moments of belonging are always temporary. When he travelled to France during the

World Cup to watch England play against Colombia, he admits that he rose to sing the national anthem, 'with a vigour that shocked [him]' and

> For a moment the cloud of ambivalence was lifted. I belonged. Why not, I wondered, submit to the moment and cease struggling? After all, what is wrong with a tee-shirt emblazoned with the Union Jack? The sixties and seventies are over ... However, for me, the unequivocal answer to such private urgings is contained in the one word; 'vigilance'. History has taught me that for people such as myself the rules will change. The goalposts will be moved. A new nationality act will be passed. And another. (*NWO*, 308–9)

For Phillips, British identity remains, it seems, locked into a position in which it works by exclusions, and the ever-moving goalposts of British legislation ensure that, for non-white citizens, a Union Jack tee-shirt will continue to be uncomfortably worn. Rather like Cambridge, who clothed himself in the robes of British identity, therefore, Phillips's support for his team provides him with an identity that is more than just an affiliation to Leeds United. It is worth stating here what may easily be overlooked: namely, that as a non-white citizen, belonging is so rare for Phillips that he has to attend a football match in order to experience it momentarily. This is also an instance of belonging based on assimilation; Phillips can briefly belong, but only if he wears the appropriate tee-shirt and chants the correct words. This is a complicated and anxious moment for Phillips, and if his affinity to a football team affords him a sense of belonging, it remains an impermanent condition – it is not long before the 'cloud of ambivalence' once more descends. In *After Empire*, Gilroy also discusses 'Britain's odd culture of sports *spectatorship* and its relationship to xenophobia, racism, and war', focusing on football in particular.[59] As Gilroy writes:

> Those of us who have had to run for our lives from vicious drunken crowds intent on a different, bloodier sport than the one they paid to see on the terraces have always been able to know where nationalist sentiments were wired

in to the raciological circuitry of the British nation and
where Brit racisms and nationalisms were fused together
as something like a single ethnic gestalt.[60]

Gilroy emphasises the integration of race and nationality which,
he suggests, we can see enacted in the drunken, racist behaviour of football supporters, especially. He reveals the dangers of
being lured into a temporary identification with white football
fans. For Gilroy, football affiliations cannot be divorced from
the wider and non-separable issues of nationality and race: 'The
knot of ideas around sport demonstrates that we cannot sanction
the luxury of believing that "race," nation, and ethnicity will be
readily or easily disentangled from each other.'[61] Like Phillips's
urged 'vigilance', Gilroy suggests that the British coalition of race
and nationality continues to exclude non-white people. Perhaps
more emphatically than Phillips, however, Gilroy intimates that
nowhere is this clearer than on the football terraces.

Any ambivalence surrounding a black British identity
arguably stems not only from repressive post-war legislation,
but also from the persistent denial of a history of black habitation in Britain that predates 1948. Instrumental in these attempts
to deny black Britons a pre-*Windrush* history has been Britain's
drive to 'forget' slavery. The city of Liverpool was for some time
at the forefront of Britain's slaving industry – as Ramsay Muir
candidly wrote in *A History of Liverpool* (1907), 'Beyond a
doubt it was the slave trade which raised Liverpool from a struggling port to be one of the richest and most prosperous trading
centres in the world'.[62] It was also in Liverpool in 1779 that the
last sale of a slave on British soil took place. Phillips opens the
postscript to the 'Leaving Home' section of *The Atlantic Sound*
with a quotation about Liverpool from Richard Wright's *Black
Power*: 'Along the sidewalks men and women moved unhur-
riedly. Did they ever think of their city's history?' (*AS*, 74). This
question frames the section and, while Phillips comes face to face
with ghosts of the past, Liverpool's history remains as silent
as its river: 'I walk up to the Cunard building and can see that
carved into its façade are the names of the major ports in the
world that this huge shipping company has done business with

over the years. The word "Africa" leaps out at me. Ships to Africa ... Behind me the Mersey lies silent' (*AS*, 80–1). Reminders of Liverpool's role in the slave trade are, quite literally, carved into the city's buildings, yet the past is still extensively silenced and ignored: 'It is disquieting to be in a place where history is so physically present, yet so glaringly absent from people's consciousness. But where is it any different?' (*AS*, 93).

If similarities can be detected between Naipaul's works and Phillips's *The Atlantic Sound*, a more distinctly similar precursor to Phillips's text is Ferdinand Dennis's 'travelogue about black Britain', *Behind the Frontlines* (1988).[63] Dennis also visits Liverpool and comments on the silence surrounding the slave trade: 'The city's museum has only a minor exhibition on the slave trade. Situated to the right of the entrance, it is easily overlooked by visitors. Its size and location hint at a desire to sanitise Liverpool's history, to purge the records.'[64] Dennis implies that the exhibition, apparently created in order to remember the slave trade, may actually enable a wilful forgetting, or 'purging' of this past. In *Making the Black Atlantic* (2000), James Walvin similarly comments on the apparent ease with which slavery, as something that happened overseas, was conveniently forgotten in Britain's slaving ports:

> What lay behind the rise of Bristol and Liverpool? ... Despite periodic reminders – returning slave ships, planters coming 'home' awash with their slave-based wealth, the occasional black servant/slave in London or Bristol – the slave system was out of sight and, too often, out of mind.[65]

Again, we should note Walvin's caution in employing the term 'home', suggesting, like Phillips, that black people have not been the only ones liable to hesitate before referring to Britain as their home. Phillips also sees firsthand that Liverpool's wealth is quite literally 'out of sight'; on entering the Town Hall, for example, he encounters the utter excesses of its interior:

> I discover the building to be a truly spectacular repository of marble, crystal, oil paintings and gilt. I pad my way from one room to the next, feeling increasingly glutted

with the visual evidence of excess, until I finally succumb
to a strange feeling of disgust. (*AS*, 83)

This wealth is something Phillips had written about in *The
European Tribe* (1987), declaring: 'Your eyesight is defective.
Europe is blinded by her past, and does not [understand] the
high price of her churches, art galleries, and architecture.'[66] The
necessity of understanding the past is a key point for Phillips; in
particular, comprehending how Britain's ostentatious architec-
tural displays have been funded. As he states in *A New World
Order*, 'History is contained in buildings. Their names mean
something. We have clues to our past, our present and even
some idea of our future if we study buildings and their origins'
(*NWO*, 306–7). It would seem, however, that the dominant view
encountered by Phillips in Liverpool is a drive to look away from
evidence of the slaving past.

Stephen tells him that a Liverpool councillor wanted to
rename one of the city's streets, 'The Goree', as 'Lottery Way'
because he felt the name to be '"embarrassing" because it referred
to the infamous island off the coast of Senegal where a slave fort
… was located' (*AS*, 78). The attempt to erase or rewrite Liverpool's 'embarrassing' slaving past links to the proposed 'renova-
tion' of slave 'castles' in Ghana, which Phillips discusses with
the 'renowned Ghanaian Pan-Africanist' Dr Mohammed Ben
Abdallah. Phillips proffers that this may be 'seen as a process of
literally and metaphorically whitewashing history' (*AS*, 118),
and also suggests that 'by calling them "castles" and equating
them with kings and queens and the Eurocentric tradition, the
African is not facing the reality of what these places really mean'
(*AS*, 121). In a related way, by proposing to rename 'The Goree',
Liverpudlians can also be seen as not facing the reality of their
city's history and the source of its prosperity. Again, connections
are traced by Phillips in seemingly unlikely places, though in
this case, Liverpool and Ghana are linked by their involvement
at two separate, but connected, points of the triangular trade.

While in Liverpool, Phillips also encounters reminders of
the city's connection through the slave trade to Charleston in
the United States, which assumes its place at the third point of

the triangle. Like Liverpool and Ghana, Charleston is a place that may try to ignore, but cannot entirely erase, the prominence of slavery in its past. Not far from Charleston is Sullivan's Island, 'an eerie and troubled place … Having crossed the Atlantic in the belly of a ship. An arrival. Here, in America. Step ashore, out of sight of Charleston. To be fed, watered, scrubbed, prepared. To be sold' (*AS*, 207). Phillips searches for the 'pest houses' which held arriving slaves; where, he tells us, 'over 30 per cent of the African population first landed in the North American world' (*AS*, 207). However, this proves a fruitless task: 'Of the many people that I have asked, nobody seems to know exactly where the pest houses were located, and of course nobody has thought it necessary at least to speculate and mark a place with a monument or plaque' (*AS*, 207). Phillips seems disappointed to find no fixed marker pinpointing the location of the pest houses; it would initially seem that in Charleston, as in Liverpool, the past of slavery is forgotten. However, although lacking a 'monument or plaque', Charleston perhaps provides a glimmer of hope, as Phillips finds that here there is an attempt to remember:

> in this city which 'processed' nearly one-third of the African population who arrived in the United States, a popula-tion who were encouraged to forget Africa, to forget their language, to forget their families, to forget their culture, to forget their dances, five young black women try to remember … Their sinewy bodies weave invisible threads that connect them to the imagined old life. (*AS*, 213)

As I have suggested, the past is unavailable, hence Phillips's care to mention that the 'old life' is an 'imagined' one, but this act of imaginative remembrance is clearly important in the face of enforced forgetting. Out of this act comes a vision of black and white people celebrating together: 'White men and women dancing to the rhythms of Africa in the street behind the United States Customs House. History smiles … Ghosts walking the streets of Charleston. Ghosts dancing in the streets of Charleston' (*AS*, 213). The 'ghosts' that walk and dance in the streets suggest, again, the continuing legacy of slavery and, rather like the diasporic chorus with which Phillips ends *Crossing the River*, here too we have a vision of a connection between black and white people, remembering and acknowledging a shared past. Perhaps Charleston, in its communal celebration, provides a tentative answer to the question posed earlier by Phillips. To recap, he commented that Liverpool's history is 'physically present, yet ... glaringly absent from people's consciousness' and asked, 'But where is it any different?' Phillips may feel that the citizens of Sullivan's Island have been neglectful in failing to mark the location of the 'pest houses', but Charleston's street celebration offers an alternative means of acknowledging this past.

Charleston, it would seem, has come a long way from the time of Judge Waring, who was ostracised by the white people of the town for his determination to secure the vote for black men and women. Waring was ultimately forced to leave, realising that 'It was simply too burdensome to be among those who openly hated you in a place you called "home"' (*AS*, 205). This section acts as a reminder that black diasporan people are not alone in experiencing alienation and unbelonging. In *A New World Order*, Phillips writes that his own 'continued sense of alienation in a British context is hardly original. The roots are racially charged, but others have felt similarly excluded on grounds of class, gender or religion' (*NWO*, 308). As Siddhartha Deb quite rightly states in his review of the book, therefore, Phillips 'is not interested in confining the experience of estrangement to just one racial group ... he makes the suggestion that the dialectic of familiarity and alienation has expanded to encompass all of humanity'.[67]

Crossing the River cautioned us that 'there is no return'; similarly, in *The Atlantic Sound*, although Phillips retraces the journey his parents made from the Caribbean to Britain by boat when he was an infant, it is both the same and different: 'For me this will be no Atlantic crossing into the unknown. I fully understand the world that will greet me at the end of the journey' (*AS*, 4). His years of habitation in Britain ensure that, for Phillips, the journey is to a familiar place:

> Beyond the captain is Britain. On this bleak late winter's morning, I am happy to be home. As I look at the white cliffs of Dover I realize that I do not feel the sense of nervous anticipation that almost forty years ago characterized my parents' arrival, and that of their entire generation. (*AS*, 16)

The time spent away from Britain seems to have created what is to be a rare moment in Phillips's writing; on returning to Britain he admits that he is 'happy to be home'. There is, in this unembellished phrase, none of the usual hesitancy surrounding the word 'home', normally signalled by his use of inverted commas. While, physically, he takes the same journey as his parents, his understanding of Britain renders it utterly different.

The impossibility of returning to the past runs contrary to the belief at the core of the Pan-African movement in the necessity of returning 'home' to an idyllic past:

> Not long after the first slave ships set sail from the West African coast, the idea that those of Africa, and those of African origin 'overseas' somehow constituted a family – albeit a family with a broken history – took hold. The idea was seized upon with a particular enthusiasm by those 'overseas' … There was engendered in their souls a romantic yearning to return 'home'. (*AS*, 113)

However, the Pan-African 'family' is not available to all; Phillips is informed by Dr Abdallah that the responsibility for the slave forts is the diasporan's: 'For us, they do not mean the same thing as they do for you people.' As Phillips responds, 'So much for Pan-Africanism, I thought. "You people"?' (*AS*, 118). Far from a family, therefore, there is a clear distinction made by Dr Abdallah between Africans who reside in Africa, and people of the African diaspora who live elsewhere. In calling this section of the book 'Homeward Bound', Phillips's pun on the word 'bound' suggests that a reliance on the notion of returning 'home' can be highly restrictive, or even enslaving.[68]

The 'romantic yearning' for home may be thought of in relation to Avtar Brah, who claims in *Cartographies of Diaspora* (1996) that home is always, for diasporans, a place of the imagination, rather than a real entity: 'On the one hand, "home" is a mythic place of desire in the diasporic imagination. In this sense it is a place of no return, even if it is possible to visit the geographical territory that is seen as the place of "origin".'[69] Home, Brah suggests, may be desirable but, as an imaginary location, is forever inaccessible. Furthermore, in the attempt made by the Pan-Africans to 'return home', they appear to 'forget' slavery. For example, the Panafest guide 'omits to point out the two female dungeons, each of which could accommodate up to one hundred and fifty slaves, or the male dungeon which often held upwards of a thousand slaves' (AS, 135). Gilroy writes about slavery as 'the site of black victimage and thus of tradition's intended erasure. When the emphasis shifts towards the elements of invariant tradition that heroically survive slavery, any desire to remember slavery itself becomes something of an obstacle'.[70] Again, this would seem to correspond to Bhabha's notion of the 'continuist, accumulative temporality of the pedagogical', but Gilroy identifies a danger in this behaviour:

> slavery becomes a cluster of negative associations that are best left behind … Blacks are urged, if not to forget the slave experience which appears as an aberration from the story of greatness told in African history, then to replace it at the centre of our thinking with a mystical and ruthlessly positive notion of Africa that is indifferent to intraracial variation and is frozen at the point where blacks boarded the ships that would carry them into the woes and horrors of the middle passage.[71]

Gilroy proposes then, that the 'negative associations' of slavery are often discarded, so that African history becomes arrested at the point of embarkation onto the slave ships. This tendency towards leaving slavery behind is evident at the Panafest but, as Phillips has suggested, there is a comparable desire in Liverpool to 'forget' its slaving past, provoking Stephen's comment: 'Liverpool people don't want to acknowledge their own history. They don't want you to know what built this town' (AS, 79). In writing about Liverpool and Ghana, Phillips draws some interesting, and perhaps surprising, comparisons – most notably, between the British 'mythology of homogeneity' and the Pan-African movement's aligned emphasis on historical continuity and racial separation. At a ceremony at the Panafest, Phillips records:

> Just in case the white people in the audience are not feeling alienated enough [the black poet] states the 'fact' that this is not a place for white people. The blonde woman flushes red and slowly leads her confused Ghanaian husband and even more confused son away from the scene. (*AS*, 177)

As in Britain, it seems that identity in Ghana is predicated on exclusions; the white woman is made to feel uncomfortable, just as black people have been made to feel unwelcome in Britain – though, due to slavery and colonialism, the histories of the countries are entwined. Phillips is, however, careful to make no judgements upon the people he encounters; re-examining slavery is not only about blame or retribution. Nor is it about solely black history; slavery, he reminds us, has involved white and black people. The mixed-race son, like Greer, is the result of this intertwining of black and white people and histories. Where, Phillips seems to ask, do mixed-race people belong in a world that is based on rigid Manichean divisions? His non-fiction arguably aims to fragment a polarised vision of slavery as 'black history', in favour of a shared understanding which invites people of differing races to take responsibility for the past of slavery. In *A New World Order*, Phillips writes about his initial reaction to Elmina Castle: 'I was coming face to face with a part of my Atlantic history. It was disturbing, but I wished neither to look the other way, nor to romanticise the encounter. I wished simply to understand' (*NWO*, 307). Unlike the Britons and Pan-Africans who 'look the other way', Phillips refuses to ignore the slave past, or to turn it into something else by 'romanticising' it. Instead, as always, he cites the necessity of 'simply' understanding the slave past, though – as his multitudinous works testify – this task is anything but simple.

The necessity, it would seem, is for a delicate balance between remembering and forgetting. Phillips writes that, 'On coming face to face with our history the vexing questions of belonging and forgetting rise quickly to the surface. And near-cousin to the words "belonging" and "forgetting" is the single word, "home"' (*NWO*, 307).[72] In order for black Britons to feel 'at home' within the UK, he implies, it is essential to remember the past and to acknowledge the impact of slavery upon Britain. This notion of remembering runs contrary, however, to the British amnesia which denies the history of habitation of black people within Britain in order to construct a racially homogeneous national identity. Bhabha's notion that forgetting is instrumental in 'remembering the nation' is also relevant in relation to the attempts made by Pan-Africans to 'forget' the reality of slavery.[73] For Pan-Africans, as for white Britons, forgetting, or distorting, the history of slavery and colonisation enables the construction of a national history and identity as continuous, unbroken and homogeneous.[74]

Although the desire to return home to retrace one's 'roots' is integral to the Pan-African movement, ultimately it is revealed by Phillips to be an inadequate metaphor when dealing with diasporan, and therefore plural and changing, identities. Gilroy has also claimed that the notion of roots is perhaps unfitted to people of the diaspora, and that 'routes' could be a more useful term:

> Marked by its European origins, modern black political culture has always been more interested in the relationship of identity to roots and rootedness than in seeing identity as a process of movement and mediation that is more appropriately approached via the homonym routes.[75]

This is a central motif in Phillips's writing – rather than embarking upon a quest for static 'roots', in *The Atlantic Sound* he instead traces diasporan identities by outlining the routes of the slave trade. In following these watery paths across the Atlantic, one cannot overlook the centrality of the sea in Phillips's imaginings. While Gilroy's concept of the 'Black Atlantic' differs widely from Phillips's 'Atlantic Sound', for reasons I shall explain in a moment, Gilroy remains useful here in examining the historical legacy of the Atlantic. He has written that the 'history of the black Atlantic', which has been 'continually crisscrossed by the movements of black people – not only as commodities but engaged in various struggles towards emancipation, autonomy, and citizenship – provides a means to reexamine the problems of nationality, location, identity, and historical memory'.[76] Gilroy makes an important point, in stressing that the Atlantic Ocean should not only be thought of in relation to the middle passage. It also has positive connotations for black diasporan people in encouraging critical thinking about identity, belonging and memory. Phillips diverges from Gilroy, in that his 'countless millions' include white as well as black people; hence, while Gilroy's book is called *The Black Atlantic*, Phillips's *The Atlantic Sound* has lost the racial specificity. However, like Gilroy, he too utilises the ocean as a 'means to reexamine the problems of nationality, location, identity, and historical memory', and it is ultimately the centre of the Atlantic Ocean that Phillips cites as the crossing point, or intersection, of these interconnected ideas.

In his play *Where There is Darkness* (1982), Phillips's protagonist Albert, who – like Phillips – was born in the Caribbean but migrated to Britain, asks: 'Why is it that the sea always sounds so fucking guilty? Whispering like it knows something but is not going say nothing.'[77] The guilt mentioned here could be seen as a testimony to the legacy of slavery; the silence attesting to the reluctance within Britain to acknowledge or discuss its slaving past. The significance of the sea in *The Atlantic Sound* is evident from its title but, if the sea sounds guilty to Albert, Phillips's 'Atlantic Sound' is no longer a guilty whispering, and nor is it the silence of the Mersey. Instead, in his exploration of a range of diasporan identities at key points across the Atlantic, the 'sound' Phillips hears, as he journeys across the water, is the polyphonic voices of the diasporic 'many-tongued chorus of the common memory' found at the close of *Crossing the River*.[78]

In *A New World Order*, Phillips takes the proposed significance of the Atlantic further in suggesting that, as an African/Caribbean/British diasporan subject, his true 'home', and the place where he wishes to have his ashes scattered, is in the middle of the Atlantic Ocean: 'this watery crossroads lay at the centre of a place that had become my other "home"; a place that, over the years, I have come to refer to as my Atlantic home' (*NWO*,

304).[79] George begins her book with a quotation from bell hooks that seems appropriate at this point: 'At times home is nowhere. At times one only knows extreme estrangement and alienation. Then home is no longer just one place. It is locations.'[80] Phillips's Atlantic home is also borne of a reconciliation to the idea that home is 'no longer just one place'. Instead, he offers a plural version of home, which corresponds to his notion of diasporan identities as shifting and ever-changing: 'These days we are all unmoored. Our identities are fluid' (*NWO*, 6). At the end of *A New World Order*, he pauses to contemplate his destiny:

> Whenever I stand on the ramparts of Elmina Castle and gaze out at the Atlantic Ocean, I know exactly where I come from. I can look to the north and to the west and see the different directions in which I have subsequently journeyed. And, on a clear day, I can peer into the distance and see where I will ultimately reside. (*NWO*, 309)

Phillips stands quite literally on his past and, as one of Said's 'people who simply don't belong in any culture', also at the intersection or 'crossings over' of journeys and identities. However, on a clear day – that is, when the 'cloud of ambivalence' surrounding identity has temporarily lifted – it is the future, and not the past, towards which he gazes. It is also, less optimistically, towards death that he looks. To recap, unlike Hall's positive celebration of the fluidity of diasporan identity, Phillips's crossroads emanate from a discussion about where his ashes should be scattered. By citing the middle of the ocean as his 'home', his is not a practical solution to the problems of diasporan identity. Slavery, he suggests, has created the difficulties of identity and belonging experienced by non-white people in Britain in the early twenty-first century, but Phillips is unable to propose a practical or realistic alternative to British identity which might alleviate some of these difficulties, and a perpetual unbelonging thwarts his attempts to resolve the 'conundrum of "home"'.

David Dabydeen and the ethics of narration

If V. S. Naipaul's work provided an interesting point of comparison for Caryl Phillips's non-fiction, then the importance of Naipaul – as an Indian-Caribbean writer – is even greater to Dabydeen. Dabydeen has described the protagonist of his novel *Disappearance* (1993) as embodying 'a Naipaulian rationality, detachment and ironic manner'.[1] Indeed, this novel bears an uncanny resemblance to Naipaul's *The Enigma of Arrival* (1987), in both tone and subject matter, of a man arriving from overseas (Guyana, in *Disappearance*, and Trinidad in Naipaul's novel) to a Britain haunted by its imperial past. However, Naipaul's often negative views of the Caribbean and its people mean that he remains for Dabydeen, as for Phillips, a complex and problematic figure. Statements like, 'a combination of historical accidents and national temperament has turned the Trinidadian Indian into the complete colonial, even more philistine than the white',[2] have led Dabydeen to admit: 'The novels I've written so far are forms of wrestling with Naipaul, the revered and despised Indian, the revered and despised father figure.'[3] As mentioned in Chapter 1, Naipaul's apparent disinclination to write about the past of Indian indenture is also significant for Dabydeen, who has returned to this past in his novel *The Counting House* (1996) and poetry collections *Slave Song* (1984) and *Coolie Odyssey* (1988).

David Dabydeen's first collection of poetry, *Slave Song*, is a tongue-in-cheek exploration of plantation life in nineteenth-century Guyana. It was awarded the Commonwealth Poetry Prize and the Quiller-Couch Prize and has generated a great deal of critical attention over the last twenty-five years, much of which is concerned with Dabydeen's use of creole to reflect the harsh realities and 'latent eroticism of the encounter between black and white' in Guyana during this time.[4] His poem 'Song of the Creole Gang Women', for example, illustrates his attempt to capture the monotony of field work:

> Wuk, nuttin bu wuk
> Maan noon an night nuttin bu wuk
> Booker own me patacake
> Booker own me pickni.
> Pain, nuttin bu pain
> Waan million tous'ne acre cane.[5]

In his endnotes to the poem, Dabydeen explains that, although it represents the women's 'cry against the sun and against white society', the poem is equally 'the cry of sexual frustration and the cry for sexual relief',[6] and it would seem that, in this collection, sexual desire has become enmeshed with the frustrations of plantation work. In addition, in the above quotation Dabydeen refers to the British company, Booker, who owned sugar estates in Guyana and, in 1969, created the Booker Prize. As he wryly notes in his Introduction to *Slave Song*, 'Bookers are involved in English literature (the Booker Prize) as well as in the real exploitation of literature's Noble Savage. They foster the illusion while at the same time profiting from the reality.'[7] This twinned concern with the exploitation of non-white people as slaves or labourers on the plantations and, in less obvious ways, through literature or art, is particularly evident in his long poem 'Turner' (1994) and novel *A Harlot's Progress* (1999), two of the works examined in depth in this chapter.

Written while he was an undergraduate at the University of Cambridge, *Slave Song*'s extensive introduction and critical endnotes, he tells us, were partly a 'literary joke': 'I referred twice in *Slave Song* to T. S. Eliot, because Eliot had also joked and provided a kind of spoof gloss to *The Waste Land*'.[8] At the same time, Dabydeen cites two more serious reasons for the endnotes; first, he claims they arose from his belief that, if creole is to be taken seriously as a distinct and separate language, it needs to be translated and, secondly, from Dabydeen's desire to be both 'the critic and the artist together in one book'.[9] In these poems, Guyana is the scenery for Dabydeen's exploration of the human subconscious, and it would seem that the poems' content cannot be separated from his use of creole, as he explains: 'the theme I had, which was eroticism, allowed me to adventure with language and "pervert" it'.[10] This convergence of form and content enables his most extreme exploration of what Dabydeen has elsewhere called the 'pornography of Empire'.[11] In his poem 'Nightmare', for example, a white woman dreams of being raped by her black servants:

> Waan gang sweat-stink nigga
> Drag she aff she bed
> Wuk pun she
> Crack she head
> Gi she jigga
> Tween she leg![12]

These poems – characterised by his (male and female) narrators' fantasies of rape and sexual violence – may be a deliberately uncomfortable read, but it is hard not to hear in this early collection Dabydeen's subsequent cynicism voiced in his poem 'Coolie Odyssey' concerning readers' interest in his work, now that 'peasantry is in vogue'.[13] In this later poem, Dabydeen explores what he sees as his presumed readers' consumption of 'exotic' poetry:

> [We] confess the lust of beasts
> In rare conceits
> To congregations of the educated
> Sipping wine, attentive between courses –
> See the applause fluttering from their white hands
> Like so many messy table napkins. (*CO*, 13)

'Coolie Odyssey' may be read alongside Graham Huggan's questioning in *The Postcolonial Exotic* (2001) of the strategic marketing of specific postcolonial literature according to its perceived 'exoticism'. As Huggan asks:

> What role do exotic registers play in the construction
> of cultural value, more specifically those types of value
> (re)-produced by postcolonial products and (re)presented in
> postcolonial discourse? How are these exoticisms marketed
> for predominantly metropolitan audiences – made avail-
> able, but also palatable, for their target consumer public?[14]

Dabydeen exhibits a high degree of playful self-consciousness
regarding matters of register and audience – as his slave narrator
of *A Harlot's Progress* is all too aware, 'nigger does munch and
crunch the English'[15]– and his continued uneasiness concerning
readers' apparently all-too-easy consumption of art and literature about slavery or Indian indenture is traced through the
works explored in this chapter.

The Counting House

In 'Coolie Odyssey', Dabydeen's narrator records the journey
– both literal and figurative – from the UK back to Guyana in
order to attend a funeral:

> Three airplanes boarded and many changes
> Of machines and landscapes like reincarnations
> To bring me to this library of graves,
> This small clearing of scrubland.
> There are no headstones, epitaphs, dates.
> The ancestors curl and dry to scrolls of parchment
> They lie like texts
> Waiting to be written by the children
> For whom they hacked and ploughed and saved
> To send to faraway schools. (*CO*, 12)

For Dabydeen, as a descendant of Indian indentured labourers,
these Guyanese graves contain the ancestors who 'lie like texts
| Waiting to be written'. In his collections of poetry *Slave
Song* and *Coolie Odyssey* and the novel *The Counting House*,
Dabydeen assumes the onerous task of imaginatively recreating
their stories, as theirs is a past under-represented in both historical and literary accounts. The problems involved in trying to

articulate the absence of the Indian indentured labourers render it a fraught and difficult attempt, and this, of necessity, is an undertaking assigned to the realms of the literary – within the 'library of graves' their bodies already lie 'like texts', or 'curled parchment'. The magnitude of the task of rewriting indentured history is complicated by the scarcity of historical evidence and the difficulty of representing the subaltern subject.[16]

As Gayatri Spivak writes in her essay 'Subaltern Studies: Deconstructing Historiography' (1985), 'The radical intellectual in the West is either caught in a deliberate choice of subalterneity, granting to the oppressed either that very expressive subjectivity which s/he criticizes or, instead, a total unrepresentability.'[17] Spivak suggests that the choice is between inadequate representation of the subaltern, or the silence of unrepresentability; the very language and means of articulation employed by the Western intellectual will always be incommensurate with subaltern experience. Dabydeen stands in this compromised position; educated – and currently residing – in Britain, he too can be viewed as a 'radical intellectual in the West' facing this dilemma. In 'Coolie Odyssey', the italicised 'voice' of his ancestors warns him:

> *Is foolishness fill your head.*
> *Me dead.*
> *Dog-bone and dry-well*
> *Got no story to tell.*
> *Just how me born stupid is so me gone.*
> Still we persist before the grave
> Seeking fables. (*CO*, 12)

The absence of historical information or markers like headstones leads to Dabydeen's inability to trace the 'truth' of the Indian indentured labourer. Everything is 'fable' and nothing appears concrete or certain. Hence, he is compelled to imagine this past, aware that the history of the indentured labourer can be neither trusted nor recovered. Dabydeen's work suggests that, rather than the absence of a story to tell, it is perhaps more accurate to posit the inadequate means of either accessing or expressing the stories of these Indian indentured ancestors, without falling into the trap of speaking for the subaltern subject.

In *The Counting House*, Dabydeen presents us with what history books cannot; he imaginatively recreates lives illustrative of what he calls 'the madness of [the] existence' of indentured life.[18] Set in what was a highly volatile period of the nineteenth century, *The Counting House* is the tale of Rohini and Vidia, Indians of different castes who marry and, persuaded by the rhetoric of British recruiters, travel to Plantation Albion in Guyana as indentured labourers to escape the poverty of their village in India. Once there, however, they discover it is not the land of riches that they had been promised, and their relationship slowly unravels as Rohini, like the black ex-slave Miriam, becomes the mistress of the plantation owner Gladstone, and soon falls pregnant by him. Miriam, in turn, faces continued resentment and anger from her partner Kampta for her sexual and physical abuse at the hands of Gladstone and, fearing that the offspring of Rohini and Gladstone would seek to inherit the plantation, Miriam – using money stolen from Vidia – has Rohini's child aborted. While the fates of Miriam and Rohini remain undetermined at the close of the novel, Vidia, who chooses to return to India, dies undertaking this journey.

Plantation Albion, in fact, is based upon a real plantation in Guyana; Dabydeen mobilises historical facts in order to write his tale, though does not confine himself to fact alone. Indeed, the scant remains of the lives of the Indian labourers in Guyana suggest this would be a particularly difficult task. Dabydeen records in the prologue that, upon visiting the ruins of the counting house, just 'three small parcels of materials survive as the only evidence of the nineteenth-century Indian presence' (*CH*, xi–xii). Among these remains are wage details, letters and other fragments around which he structures his novel:

> The contents of the third parcel are a cow-skin purse, a child's tooth, an ivory button, a drawing of the Hindu God, Rama, haloed by seven stars, a set of iron needles, some kumari seeds, and an empty tin marked 'Huntley's Dominion Biscuits', its cover depicting a scene of the Battle of Waterloo. (*CH*, xii)

In the prologue, alongside the inventory of surviving objects and historical 'facts' about Indian indentured labour, Dabydeen also quotes from plantation owners Gladstone and Fielding, who are known only by their surnames. Gladstone states that 'No account of coolie experience can ever be complete for they are the scraps of history' (*CH*, xi). Indeed, like the absent headstones of 'Coolie Odyssey', it is not from the historical archive that Dabydeen will take his inspiration, but from these 'scraps' or debris of the past. These are the otherwise discarded aspects of plantation slavery deemed of insufficient worth to chronicle; the subaltern history that cannot readily be reclaimed.

Fielding, on the other hand, on requesting to know the grievances of, presumably, his workers, comments:

> a hundred Negro and Indian voices arose, vying against each other to tell a story, like crabs in a sack seeking escape by clambering over each other. I called upon them to speak in turn, assuring them that I would give each story equal weight and benign consideration, but my words fell on deaf ears. I mounted my horse and departed, leaving the loudest to bully the rest into silence. (*CH*, xi)

Not only do the labourers' words fall upon deaf ears, but Fielding also leaves the scene, and so avoids taking responsibility for the situation. We might read his actions as indicative of the avoidance by some white Britons to be accountable for Britain's involvement in the slave trade and subsequent period of indenture by 'forgetting' this past. Furthermore, this quotation introduces the notion that, in the competition between the voices of African and Indian workers, only the 'loudest' have been heard. In some ways, therefore, the role played by African slaves in the Caribbean has arguably eclipsed the part played by Indian indentured labourers. In *India in the Caribbean*, Dabydeen claims that 'Scholarly research has been focussed overwhelmingly on the African dimension, and in the resulting Afro-centric view of the Caribbean, the Indo-Caribbean is relegated to a footnote'.[19] In *The Counting House*, via the medium of the novel, he ensures that both African slave and Indian indentured labourer are given the chance to 'speak in turn'.[20]

The epilogue to *The Counting House* provides a concluding confirmation that this novel is grounded in the precarious realm of fact. We learn that, while Miriam's grave 'cannot be found' and Kampta was fictional, Gladstone was the uncle of British Prime Minister William Gladstone, though even here Dabydeen does not confine himself to fact. While Gladstone, as a white plantation owner, has been included in accounts of British history, he too has become a figure about which little is now known. As the epilogue informs us:

> Two biographies appeared in the early twentieth century, both now out of print. An engraved portrait of him as the personification of Neptune, by the English marine artist Richard Campion, was once in the collection of the Victoria and Albert Museum, London; it can no longer be traced. (*CH*, 179)

I propose that this 'disappearance' of Gladstone is linked to the British denial of slavery, where little evidence remains of the role of white people in the history of this past (an exception to this claim, of course, can be found in the contribution made by British abolitionists, which stands relatively well documented). Gladstone, as a sugar-plantation owner, is a part of Britain's history that some Britons would rather forget.

There is, in addition, a twist in this tale: in his creation of the character of Gladstone, Dabydeen veers quite substantially from historical fact. Dabydeen has already told us that Gladstone was William Gladstone's uncle, and Kampta informs us that Gladstone was 'only orphan boy when they remove him from England and make him proprietor of the plantation' (*CH*, 142). However, the Guyanese plantation owner John Gladstone was, in fact, William Gladstone's father, not his uncle. The plantation was not bequeathed to him as an orphan, but instead, in 1803, John Gladstone took out a mortgage on a sugar estate.[21] Further, he was the first plantation owner to use indentured labourers, having obtained permission from the President of the Board of Control for India and the Secretary of State for the Colonies to begin an Indian emigration scheme; the first arrivals of Indian indentured workers were known as the 'Gladstone Coolies'.[22]

History books would suggest, then, that John Gladstone was very much an active participant in both the sugar-plantation trade and Indian indenture system, rather than, as Kampta suggests, an orphan who had no choice but to assume the role bequeathed to him. Further, while the book is set largely in 1860, Gladstone had in fact withdrawn completely from the sugar-plantation business by 1845.[23]

The reasons for this adaptation of historical facts I shall debate in a moment, for Dabydeen's poetic licence does not end here. If he has altered the history of Gladstone, this is accentuated in the case of Fielding. Evidence would suggest that there was no plantation owner in Guyana by this name, and Dabydeen therefore goes further than just manipulating historical facts; he goes as far as to 'quote' from the fictional Fielding. Any intended pun on 'field' (plantation) aside, I would argue that this is a form of literary joke. Dabydeen's choice of surname recalls both Henry Fielding and his brother, John. While the former association highlights the relationship between literature and Britain's overseas exploits, where money to fund Britain's artists and writers during the eighteenth and nineteenth centuries was all too often generated by the slave trade,[24] Sir John Fielding's *Extracts from such of the Penal Laws, as Particularly relate to the Peace and Good Order of this Metropolis* (1768), is especially relevant for its articulation of fears concerning the immigration of black people to Britain in the eighteenth century. In contrast to Phillips's close reliance on the historical archive in parts of *Cambridge* or *Crossing the River*, therefore, Dabydeen takes a more subversive approach to history. In his 'alteration' of historical 'facts', he not only indicates that history is not to be trusted, but also dares to distort what has been previously taken as historical 'truth'. In so doing, Dabydeen demonstrates a deliberate irreverence towards – almost vandalisation of – received history, seemingly in part born of the insubstantial portrayal of Indian indentured people in representations of this past. This disrespect is illustrative of his contempt for standard history and an attempt to refute its authority. In Dabydeen's bold defacing of historical fact we can detect a desire to force readers to confront the limits of historical knowledge: the past of the indentured labourer, he suggests, can only be accessed through the imagination. In presenting his readers with a collage of fragments – objects, historical details and fictional content – Dabydeen's novels are playfully constructed out of his irreverent readings from debris of the past of the Indian indentured labourer.

Spivak provides a useful example illustrating the inter-related nature of literature and history when she writes in 'A Literary Representation of the Subaltern' (1987):

> Those who read or write literature can claim as little of subaltern status as those who read or write history. The difference is that the subaltern as object is supposed to be imagined in one case and real in another. I am suggesting that it is a bit of both in both cases.[25]

Raising the point that literature and history both rely on the imaginary – something especially pertinent to my reading of Dabydeen's novel – there is a resemblance between history and literature as Spivak renders them. Her positing of the continuum between the subaltern as real (an object of repre-sentation) and as imagined (a product of representation) can be read as an articulation of the space where *The Counting House* exists between the real and the imaginary. The difficulty of being able to reconstruct the past of the Indian indentured labourer from the fragments found by Dabydeen is best illustrated in the novel by Kampta's birth certificate: '"Father's name: Unknown, deceased." "Mother's name: Unknown, deceased." ... "Date of Birth: Unknown." "Distinguishing marks: None." Everything is none or unknown or deceased, except my name in big-big writing, K-A-M-P-T-A' (*CH*, 78). So little is known about the past of the Indian indentured labourer that the blanks can only be imaginatively filled, recalling 'Coolie Odyssey' and the indentured labourers' lack of headstones or markers. The incon-sequentiality of the indentured labourer is echoed throughout the novel in Rohini's repeated complaint of 'I want more', to which finally Miriam provides an answer:

'I want more, Miriam, than button and biscuit tin.'
'That is all there is,' I say. (*CH*, 169)

Miriam's firm response reminds us that, like Rohini, Dabydeen has to make do with what is available. While he may utilise all the surviving evidence to provide a realistic basis for his novel, ultimately, imagination is the only means available to add cohesion to these fragments and create a story from the remains. At the same time, Dabydeen is all too aware of the impossibility of rebuilding such ruins – reflected in the novel's oscillation between the real and the imaginary. He struggles with the need to say more about the past of the Indian indentured labourer, but has to leave history in order to do so, turning instead to the imagination.

As Fielding's quotation suggested, there is more than one force of oppression in the past of Indian indentured labour. This notion finds its strongest articulation towards the end of the novel, where Miriam tries to assert her authority over Rohini by portraying herself as a storyteller with the power to determine the outcome of their tale. She aligns this role with her grandfather's position as an inscription carver for the Gladstone family's tombstones; a pertinent reminder that, unlike the Indian indentured labourer, for whom there are no headstones, epigraphs or dates, the members of the plantation-owning families have ornate markers validating and historicising their existence.

Miriam's grandfather, however, was specifically forbidden from using the Latin himself – it is a borrowed language only: 'She remembered her grandpa coming home with a bruised mouth because a big word he had acquired from some gravestone had slipped out in the presence of a whiteman who took his learning as a sign of arrogance' (*CH*, 109). Unable to read the inscription on the gravestone of 'old Gladstone' ('Sunt lachrimae rerum'), Miriam's crude interpretation of its meaning renders it comic and negates its power as a symbol of both learning and authority. Her attempts to translate the words also serve as a reminder of what cannot be read. The past, like the Latin, can only be guessed at or reinterpreted:

> Sunt is like scunt. Lachrimae sound like old Mrs Gladstone's
> name and Rerum is rear up, what preacherman does call
> resurrection. So the old scunt Lachrimae will break wind
> and break stone and walk the land when Kingdom come,
> and nigger once more will scatter at her footstep. (*CH*, 108)

Miriam reads the Latin as a comic resurrection, and the bawdy
register suggests a language not normally admissible to history.[26]
Her disrespect for members of the Gladstone family appears to
reflect Dabydeen's irreverent engagement with historical figures
and facts. Miriam's creativity when faced with the unreadable
Latin can be seen as corresponding to Dabydeen's own imaginative persistence 'before the graves', when faced with the limitations of the historical. Both are engaged in a process of creative
and imaginative translation of fragmentary relics in order to
create a space in which to imagine the past of the indentured
labourer or African slave.

Like the indentured labourers on the plantation, Miriam
is oppressed by her role as an ex-slave. She is also, however,
involved in the process of silencing that Dabydeen is concerned
about:

> Albion is *we* land, *we* man and *we* story and *I* tell it how
> *I* want. I start the story and I kill it so *you*, Rohini, hush
> and listen, for you is only a freshly-come coolie. When *I*
> give you freedom to talk, then you talk, but I can wave my
> chisel any time and interrupt you and take over the story
> and keep it or throw it away. What right have you to make
> story? What right have you to make baby for Gladstone?
> Albion is a nigger, we slave and slaughter here, Albion is
> we story, and you coolie who only land this morning best
> keep quiet till you can deserve to claim a piece. (*CH*, 170–1)

For 'story', we can read 'history'; Miriam believes that she has
some autonomy over the future, and can either write what she
wishes or, in a move which makes baby and story analogous,
'throw it away'. Dabydeen also divides the novel into three parts,
named Rohini, Kampta and Miriam. Miriam's is the only section
to be narrated in the first person, so Dabydeen bestows upon
her an authority not granted to his other characters. We could

see Miriam's belief in her dominance as corresponding to the notion that histories of plantation slavery which focus on the African slave have tended to eclipse the indentured labourer – encapsulated by the idea that slavery is 'black history'. Miriam tells Rohini that the plantation, its history, and Gladstone belong to her. Yet, for all her victory over Rohini, and belief that Plantation Albion is her story, Miriam ultimately remains powerless. So, while she envisages speaking to defend Kampta in his trial for theft from Gladstone, she is all too aware of her lack of influence:

> I raise my hand from the crowd to talk back. Magistrate take one look at my armpit as I raise my hand high above my head, and he sniff like magistrate them does sniff to show scorn ... The tall and short and plain middle of the story is that he ignore me. (CH, 159)

This moment exposes a particular problem of subaltern representation, with Miriam's well-founded concerns that she will not be heard. Elsewhere, she adds: 'I want to explain but who will listen?' (CH, 159), 'if I did talk Creole sense, who will listen?' (CH, 160). It is not only important who speaks, but how they are received or listened to. In A Critique of Postcolonial Reason (1999), Spivak writes of the disappearance of the 'figure of the woman', where,

> Between patriarchy and imperialism, subject-constitution and object-formation, the figure of the woman disappears, not into a pristine nothingness but into a violent shuttling that is the displaced figuration of the 'third-world woman' caught between tradition and modernization, culturalism and development.[27]

Miriam finds herself also disappearing 'into a violent shuttling', caught in an unstable – and violent – period between slavery and freedom. Despite the end of slavery, Miriam is not yet free, and is all too aware that this will take time to achieve. As Miriam takes over the story, she reveals that she cannot, after all, determine the outcome, and Rohini's fate remains unresolved: 'I wipe the sleep from my eye but still can't see what will happen to Rohini' (CH, 177).

By the end of the novel, therefore, we see Miriam's disappearance in her realisation of her powerlessness and continued enslavement (and the epilogue's stark information that her grave cannot be found). Yet, she does not vanish to the extent that Rohini does, in her rapid descent into madness, making 'mad-people parcels' for her unborn children (*CH*, 177). The last word of the 'story' belongs to Miriam (though the subject is Gladstone), reinforcing the notion that Indian indentured history has been overshadowed by the history of black people on the plantations.

Of the various fragments found by Dabydeen in the counting house, one in particular is invested with an importance that far exceeds its original function. The empty biscuit tin is now paradoxically full of meaning:

> [Vidia] watched [the biscuit tin] sullenly, wishing she hadn't brought it to his home. It was as if Gladstone had visited unexpectedly and caught him in the midst of his poverty ... All his intimate belongings would suddenly be exposed for what they were – meagre coolie goods. Gladstone's gaze would strip him of ambition, revealing him to be a coolie less than man. (*CH*, 151)

We should note the power of the unspoken; it is Gladstone's imperial gaze (via the unusual medium of a biscuit tin), rather than his words, that unsettles Vidia and leaves him 'less than man'. The biscuit tin, as both a possession of Gladstone and in its depiction of the Battle of Waterloo, may be read as a sign of British imperialism. In her book *Interpreting Objects and Collections* (1994), Susan Pearce also examines an item linked to the Battle of Waterloo; this time, a military jacket worn by Lieutenant Henry Anderson. Pearce notes that Waterloo was seen at the time as 'embodying bravery, loyalty, worthy self-sacrifice and national pride, so that its events became proverbial and all contact with it ... was lovingly cherished'.[28] It would seem that – in its guise as 'national pride' – the battle came to represent British imperialism. To read the tin as being just a sign of Empire is, however, to only read part of its meaning. Rohini is wrong to suppose Vidia lacks the ability to understand the significance of the tin:

> Vidia now attempted to compromise her, thrusting the tin-can at her as if it was a measure of her worth. The tin-can was for *him* to fill with his mean coins; she brought it for *him* to gape stupidly at its picture of war, knowing that he could never understand its meaning; the best he could do was to bury it from sight under the calabash tree. (*CH*, 154)

Vidia's resentment of the item is increased by the fact that it was a token from Gladstone to Rohini, and its depiction of battle serves as a reminder of his hopeless contest with Gladstone for Rohini. He attempts to remove from view the picture, as a continued visual reminder of both imperialism and his failure to prevent Gladstone from 'winning' his wife: 'Vidia examined the biscuit tin that Rohini had brought home, then placed it back on the shelf, upside down so that the picture on its lid was hidden' (*CH*, 148). Vidia's actions could also be read as a refusal to embrace the imperialist iconolatry of the tin; his removal of the object is a rejection of white imperial control.

The fact that the biscuit tin – marked 'Huntley's Dominion Biscuits', and manufactured for a British market – is among those objects described by Dabydeen as 'the only evidence of the nineteenth-century Indian presence' emphasises that the histories of all those involved in this past are inextricably entwined; the history of the Indian indentured labourer cannot be disassociated from that of the ex-slave or, in this case, the history of the plantation owner. We see again the problem facing Dabydeen of subaltern representation, where a British tin is included as evidence of Indian indentured experience. If the biscuit tin were only to be understood as a symbol of Empire, the Indian once more fails to leave a 'distinguishing mark' on history.

The collection of objects found in the counting house can be read as the surviving fragments of a neglected and inaccessible past. These 'meagre coolie goods' come to represent the lives of those who did not count; those written out of history books, and those that were 'empty-handed'. The notion of being 'empty-handed' occurs frequently in this book; the most striking example arises in Miriam's admission: 'For spite I scrape the gilt off the page edges of [Gladstone's] books with my fingernails until I come to see the folly of my hand, gloved in gold, yet empty' (*CH*, 164). This phrase reveals the illusionary nature of riches (the proverbial notion that all that glitters is not gold), suggesting that what appears valuable may, in fact, be worthless. Arguably, for Dabydeen, the reverse of this proverb is also true. The pieces found in the counting house – epitomised by the empty biscuit tin – have, like the past of the indentured labourer, been overlooked by historians of slavery and deemed to be of little value. Instead, Dabydeen illustrates that these items are important traces of the indentured past, which he uses to reconstruct the lives of his Indian indentured ancestors. In counting the indentured labourer, therefore, he both counters received history and attends to a neglected and piecemeal part of Britain's past of slavery. By problematising – and ultimately rejecting – the historical, Dabydeen refuses to accept the authority of history. In so doing, he frees the Indian indentured labourer from the constraints of a historical representation which adamantly claims to be 'all there is' to say about this past.

'Turner'

In his book on visual representations of slavery, *Blind Memory* (2000), Marcus Wood writes of the memorial function of J. M. W. Turner's painting *Slavers Throwing Overboard the Dead and Dying, Typhon Coming On* in the following terms:

> Turner's monument to the slave trade is a monument without names, which at least inaugurates the act of mourning. Turner's memorial does not submerge the slaves beneath an unrelenting grandeur but combines the sublime and the ridiculous. He puts the elements in mourning yet his natural world contains many elements, including gaiety and humour.[29]

Turner's painting was first exhibited at the Royal Academy in 1840. Its representation of drowning slaves, thrown overboard a slave ship, has been the subject of much debate, both at the time of its first public display and in more recent years, featuring most notably in the work of Paul Gilroy, as well as in that of Wood.[30] It is, for Hugh Honour, the 'only notable painting of the middle passage' and, indeed, the debate surrounding the picture has become, in many ways, as significant as the painting itself.[31] John Ruskin's summary of the painting in *Modern Painters* (1843), for example, has become infamous:

> I believe, if I were reduced to rest Turner's immortality upon any single work, I should choose this. Its daring conception, ideal in the highest sense of the word, is based on the purest truth, and wrought out with the concentrated knowledge of a life; its colour absolutely perfect, not one false or morbid hue in any part or line.[32]

His account has become as well known as Turner's picture, if not more so; as James Hamilton notes in his book, *Turner: A Life* (1997), Ruskin's comments became 'effectively, a surrogate for the painting for more than fifty years'.[33] Further, Ruskin's description, in which the slave is relegated to a footnote, was the apparent motivation for Dabydeen's poem 'Turner'.

Ruskin's footnote was an explanation for the epithet 'guilty' before mentioning the ship: 'She is a slaver, throwing her slaves overboard. The near sea is encumbered with corpses'.[34] Yet, despite the drowning slaves, it is perhaps surprising that Ruskin should note no 'morbid hue' in the painting; instead, he suggests it is 'dedicated to the most sublime of subjects and impressions ... – the power, majesty, and deathfulness of the open, deep, illimitable sea'.[35] It would seem that his comments have become characteristic of a tradition of reading Turner's painting which is unseeing of the jettisoned slaves. I intend to explore the mid-nineteenth-century reception of Turner's work before moving on to examine Dabydeen's own poetic reaction to, and representation of, the painting. It is important to examine some of these early contexts because Dabydeen's poem addresses not only Turner's painting, but also the tradition of criticism surrounding this work. I argue that his characterisation of Turner as both a slave-ship captain and paedophile is, in fact, prompted by the artist's attempts to deny black people an active role in nineteenth-century Britain through his portrayal of the drowning slaves. As will become clear, Dabydeen's poetic response to the painting not only rejects *Slavers*, but questions more generally the way in which black people have been represented in visual art – a concern previously voiced in his books on William Hogarth. Instead of promoting a visual representation of slavery, Dabydeen indicates in 'Turner' through the metaphor of blindness that a textual approach might be a more helpful way of thinking about this past. This move has important implications for Wood's suggestion of the suitability of Turner's painting as a monument to the slave trade.

Even twentieth-century writing about Turner's painting has overlooked its involvement with slavery. Graham Reynolds, for example, writes in his book *Turner* (1969) that

> There is no more majestic or terrifying instance of the wind and sea as elemental and destructive powers in all Turner's work. The red of the sunset reflected in the stormy waves becomes merged with and synthetized [*sic*] into the blood of the victims, and the ship itself, silhouetted against the storm, acquires something of the mythical quality of the ghost ships which haunt maritime imaginations.[36]

Reynolds's brief description – eerie in its echo of Ruskin's – also sees the 'elemental' wind and sea as the painting's focus, rather than its 'victims', whose blood is so skilfully 'synthetized' with the sunset. The ghost ship is an interesting choice of image, with regard to the way in which ghosts, or reminders of slavery, continue to 'haunt' not only maritime imaginations. Also, if the ghost ship has a 'mythical quality', then so too has the slave ship. As Wood writes, the engraving *Description of a Slave Ship* – the cross-section of a slaver detailing the positioning of Africans within the hold – became 'one image in which ... slave ships were to be memorialised through the centuries and across continents'.[37] In a related way, Turner's painting has also achieved a kind of a mythical status; not only in terms of being a 'monument' to the slave trade, as Wood argues, but also because of the sheer amount that has been written about it.

Although both Ruskin and Reynolds pay scant attention to the ship as a slave ship, and almost none to the slaves, it would seem that one of the reasons behind Turner's choice of subject matter was the publication in that year of the second edition of Thomas Clarkson's *History of the Rise, Progress, and Accomplishment of the Abolition of the Slave Trade*, along with Thomas Buxton's book *The African Slave Trade*, which was serialised in *The Times*.[38] It would appear that Turner has taken as his subject matter the jettison of slaves from the *Zong* in 1781.[39] As mentioned in the preceding chapters, this incident also proved to be the inspiration for Fred D'Aguiar's novel *Feeding the Ghosts* (1997), which I explore in Chapter 4 – evidence to suggest that the events aboard the *Zong* have become, like the painting, 'mythical': critical to contemporary debates about how to remember slavery one and a half centuries since its abolition.

The *Zong*'s captain, Luke Collingwood, apparently acted in order to claim insurance for the slaves, which the insurers refused to pay. In the ensuing court case he suggested that, in addition to the epidemic, there was also insufficient water aboard the vessel. As Thomas Clarkson records, however:

> It was proved ... that no one had been put upon short allowance; and that, as if Providence had determined to afford an unequivocal proof of the guilt, a shower of rain fell and continued for three days immediately after the second lot of slaves had been destroyed, by means of which they might have filled many of their vessels with water, and thus have preserved all necessity for the destruction of the third.[40]

Turner's subtitle for the painting of '*Typhon Coming On*' would suggest that he accepted this claim of imminent rainfall. Yet Clarkson, unlike Turner, does not attempt to represent the middle passage: 'here I must observe at once, that, as far as this part of the evil is concerned, I am at a loss to describe it ... Indeed every part of this subject defies my powers'.[41] Clarkson therefore acknowledges the inadequacy of language to convey

the horror of the middle passage. In debating the inappropriateness of describing or representing this journey I shall, of
necessity, borrow from the work of Holocaust theorists in order
to explore an area which has, on the whole, been neglected by
those writing about Britain's involvement in slavery.[42] While
retaining an awareness of the considerable discrepancy between
the Jewish experience and what writers like S. E. Anderson have,
however uncomfortably, called the 'Black Holocaust', theorists
of the Jewish Holocaust may offer a parallel in terms of the difficulty of remembering or memorialising a mass genocide.[43] Ziva
Amishai-Maisels, in *Depiction and Interpretation: The Influence
of the Holocaust on the Visual Arts* (1993), voices an important
question concerning the execution of such a task: 'How does
one combine the artist's pleasure in the act of creation with the
horrific subject matter which is the source of the creation?'.[44]
This question also seems to be at the heart of much of the
debate surrounding Turner's depiction of the middle passage.
As Dabydeen writes in his preface to 'Turner': 'The intensity
of Turner's painting is such that I believe the artist in private
must have savoured the sadism he publicly denounced'.[45] For
Dabydeen, then, it is certainly possible that Turner may have
enjoyed creating his depiction of the jettison.

    In one of the few essays tackling the subject of memori-
alising slavery in Britain, Alex Tyrrell and James Walvin have
stated:

> Britain's involvement in slavery was being remembered
> in and around the persons of the eminent abolitionists as
> they were depicted in what was literally a sacred site – one
> that the British Establishment had set aside for the venera-
> tion of the great and the good in the nation's history ...
> The critical fact that Britain had been the key slave-trading
> nation prior to abolition had to be sought elsewhere if it
> was sought at all.[46]

As I argued in Chapter 1, the emphasis on British slavery abolitionists has not been confined to monuments alone; standard
accounts of British slave history have been similarly keen to
play up the role of abolitionists as a means of detracting from

Britain's heavy involvement in instigating and perpetuating the slave trade. Wood has also claimed that 'There is no adequate monument or memorial to the slave trade in Britain' and therefore posits that Turner's painting performs this function.[47]

However, if *Slavers* is, for Wood, a memorial to the slave trade, then it is necessarily a retrospective depiction: Turner finds his subject matter in the preceding century by focusing on the case of the *Zong*. In my opening chapter, I mentioned James Procter's caution against the dangers of looking at the past when it acts as a decoy for embracing the present or facing the future. To reiterate, Procter claims:

> it needs to be considered to what extent the renewed focus on and manufacture of a black British past might also form part of an escape from or evasion of the black British present/future. How much easier is it to embrace the past … than to attend to the messy, unsettled politics of the 'here-and-now'?[48]

Turner's painting, created at a time when slavery had ended in the British Caribbean, also 'embrace[s] the past'. Arguably, *Slavers* deliberately points to the previous century in order to detract attention away from the then current position of black people within Britain. In so doing, Turner represents black people in a way that perpetuates an imagery of powerlessness and suffering, or what Paul Gilroy has called 'Slavery [as] the site of black victimage'.[49] In this reading of the painting, the chains that float somewhat unconvincingly on the surface of the water make explicit the enslaved status of the drowning, and the hands reaching up from Turner's waves (an overlooked aspect of the work) can be seen as correlating to the imploring hands of slaves depicted in abolitionist images, reaching out for salvation to the white audience. In order to explain my claim that his depiction of 'black victimage' was, in fact, painted in an attempt to evade the post-emancipation role of black people in mid-nineteenth-century Britain, some historical context is imperative.

In the last decades of the eighteenth century there was a steady stream of black people – mainly from America – into

Britain, especially in the years following the American War of Independence. Despite the Sierra Leone project of black 'repatriation', a significant proportion of black people remained in London.[50] Ron Ramdin writes in *Reimaging Britain* that, while this population may have declined in the nineteenth century, the struggles of black people

> now merged into a larger movement, with the black slave increasingly being used as an argument against 'white slavery' in Britain. It should therefore not surprise us that between 1800 and 1850 black leaders were accepted as playing an essential part in the vanguard of the radical movement.[51]

Evidence of the role played by black people in this vanguard may be found in the Cato Street Conspiracy of 1820, a response to the Peterloo massacre of 1819. One of the leaders of the group – who schemed to murder the members of the Cabinet – was William Davidson, ironically a black cabinet-maker living in St Marylebone. Turner could therefore be seen to be directing attention away from the continuing alignment between working-class radicalism and a potentially dangerous notion of black radicalism by deliberately portraying black people as helpless and suffering victims. As a monument to forgetting the black person's role in contemporary Britain by concentrating on the past, Turner's painting motions Homi Bhabha's claim that 'Being obliged to forget becomes the basis for remembering the nation'.[52] *Slavers* is arguably an attempt to 'forget' the presence of black people in Britain and their growing political consciousness – in order to maintain a racially homogeneous sense of nation – by portraying them as helpless victims, reliant on white benevolence.

Ruskin was all too aware of Turner's deliberately 'forgetful' portrayal. His interest in a picture which was, it would seem, firmly in place (if anachronistic) within the imagery of British slavery abolition has confused critics, but I would suggest that his later role in supporting Governor Edward Eyre in the Morant Bay Rebellion in Jamaica of 1865 is telling. On Eyre's orders, more than 400 rebelling black Jamaicans were killed, another 600 were flogged, and at least 1,000 homes were burnt.

The Eyre Defence Committee, which was supported by Ruskin, ensured the case against Eyre was dropped. John Berger has argued that

> Oil paintings often depict things ... which in reality are buyable. To have a thing painted and put on a canvas is not unlike buying it and putting it in your house. If you buy a painting you buy also the look of the thing it represents.[53]

The slave was, until seven years previous to Turner's painting, quite literally 'buyable', but what Ruskin seemingly gained in his acquisition of the picture in 1844 was 'the look of the thing it represent[ed]' – black people objectified in an image of powerlessness.[54] Turner's painting may seem to be comfortably located within a visual rhetoric of abolitionist work, but its date of composition is vital in challenging this positioning. While taking on a familiar abolitionist subject matter, by composing his picture at a date not only seven years after the abolition of the British slave trade, but almost sixty years after the events aboard the *Zong*, Turner's painting perpetuates the representation of black people as suffering victims at a time when they strove to rid themselves of that image.

There are different schools of thought on Turner, but while some are more benevolent towards him, others – including Dabydeen – believe that his painting 'in the sublime style' depicts the slaves as 'exotic and sublime victims' (*T*, xi, x). The meaning of 'sublime' has changed over centuries, but Andrew Wilton begins his book *Turner and the Sublime* (1980) with a quote from Ruskin, in which he defines it: 'Anything which elevates the mind is sublime ... Sublimity is, therefore, only another word for the effect of greatness upon the feelings – greatness, whether of matter, space, power, virtue, or beauty'.[55] It would seem that, for Ruskin, Turner's painting is a fine example of this; to recap, he ends his description in *Modern Painters*: 'the whole picture [is] dedicated to the most sublime of subjects and impressions ... – the power, majesty, and deathfulness of the open, deep, illimitable sea'.[56] Once again, Ruskin sees in Turner's painting a depiction of the sea first and foremost, not the act of jettison.

It is perhaps fitting, if Turner's painting is, for Wood, 'paradoxical, abstract, difficult',[57] that Dabydeen's poem should also be, in Karen McIntyre's words, a 'complex and elusive work'.[58] 'Turner' is a long poem of forty pages, divided into twenty-five sections. Its narrator – a slave drowned by the slave-ship captain Turner in the Atlantic – is joined by a stillborn child thrown overboard some time later, also by Turner. Descriptions of the underwater world are interspersed with 'memories' of a pre-slavery Africa in a blend of time past and present.[59]

In writing 'Turner', Dabydeen is looking at much more than the subject of the canvas. He arguably returns to this past in order both to question Turner's depiction of the middle passage and to think about the continued invisibility of slavery in Britain's history. In 'Turner', Dabydeen raises the issue of the absence of a memorial to this past:

> What sleep will leave me restless when I wake?
> What mindfulness that nothing has remained
> Original? There could have been some small
> And monumental faith. Even the leper
> Conserves each grain of skin, the aged
> Grin to display a tooth sensuously
> Preserved in gum, memorial to festivity
> And speech that mocks the present and the time
> To come.[60]

This passage gestures towards a discussion of memorialisation. While it suggests, first, the notion that nothing in art is original, with a slight syntactical alteration it becomes: 'nothing has remained [that is] original'; everything, therefore, has to be invented. This is an important point, which I shall return to in a moment. While there are other things capable of acting as 'memorials' – Dabydeen chillingly cites skin and teeth – nothing remains as a visible monument to the history of slavery. He also foregrounds the contention that a monument is undeniably backwards-looking; it mocks not only the present, but also the future. James Young writes in *The Texture of Memory* (1993) that 'the aim of memorials is not to call attention to their own presence so much as to past events *because* they are no longer present. In this sense, Holocaust memorials attempt to point immediately beyond themselves'.[61] Turner's painting also points 'immediately beyond' itself; this is most clearly signalled by its anachronistic subject matter which has attracted much attention in late twentieth-century criticism. As we shall see, Dabydeen questions the assumption that memorials might be helpful ways of thinking about the past of slavery; as well as 'mocking' the present, he suggests that an accurate monument to the slave trade may be irrevocably flawed by the morbidity of the subject matter.

As I have mentioned, part of Dabydeen's motivation for writing 'Turner' was Ruskin's footnote, which 'reads like an afterthought, something tossed overboard' (T, ix).[62] In the poem, the child too is 'tossed overboard', and the narrator writes that 'What was deemed mere food for sharks will become | My fable' (T, 1). The subject of the poem is, therefore, the slaves. Rather than focusing on the sea or slave ship, Dabydeen ensures the drowning slaves are the central concern, no longer merely a jettisoned footnote or afterthought.

Dabydeen logically starts his poem with a beginning – the birth of a child. The infant, however, is stillborn – providing the opening word. Turner's painting is also an act of creation upon the subject of death; Dabydeen arguably suggests the inappropriateness of trying either to redeem or compensate for slavery by means of a national memorial or through art by indicating that any attempt to memorialise this past will be thwarted, or stillborn. The past of slavery is characterised by death; even a creative response to it, like Dabydeen's poem, will still necessarily centre on this fact. Illustrating his belief in the macabre nature of art composed on the subject of death, in 'Turner' the underwater world is correspondingly transformed and decaying corpses become beautiful:

> The sea prepares
> Their festive masks, salt crystals like a myriad
> Of sequins hemmed into their flesh through golden
> Threads of hair. The sea decorates, violates. (T, 9)

If the meaning of 'sublime' has altered with time, I would suggest that Jean-François Lyotard's redefinition of the term is particularly apt with regard to Dabydeen's poem. In an essay entitled 'The Sublime and the Avant-Garde' (1984), Lyotard describes the sublime as alluding 'to something which can't be shown, or presented'.[63] He writes that, for Immanuel Kant,

> The aesthetics of the sublime is still more indeterminate: a pleasure mixed with pain, a pleasure that comes from pain. In the event of an absolutely large object – the desert, a mountain … or one that is absolutely powerful – a storm at sea, an erupting volcano … the faculty of presentation, the imagination, fails to provide a representation corresponding to this Idea. This failure of expression gives rise to pain, a kind of cleavage within the subject between what can be conceived and what can be imagined or presented.[64]

If we return to 'Turner', we can see in Dabydeen's quotation a corresponding combination of 'pleasure mixed with pain, a pleasure that comes from pain' in its conflation of horror and beauty, as the sea 'decorates [and] violates' the corpses of the drowned. Recalling Clarkson's struggle with describing the middle passage, the 'failure of expression' of which Lyotard writes can be seen as the problem facing Dabydeen: how to represent a past that is arguably beyond representation? Furthermore, the sea assumes the role of Turner in decorating its subjects; elsewhere Dabydeen's narrator writes that it has

> Painted me gaudy, dabs of ebony,
> An arabesque of blues and vermilions,
> Sea-quats cling to my body like gorgeous
> Ornaments. I have become the sea's whore,
> Yielding. (T, 14)

The sea, like Turner, displays and exploits a powerless, fetishised body, or objectified 'other'. It paints and adorns the slaves, but it is in order to better sell and exploit them; the narrator is, after all, 'the sea's whore'. Dabydeen makes clear the link between the exploitation of slaves through slavery and through visual art – Turner's depiction of the 'beauty' involved in the drowning of slaves ensured the painting was saleable and, in so doing, sold not only a painting but also an image of slavery and black victimhood. In Dabydeen's poem, the relationship between Turner's depiction of the slaves and the narrator's position as an exploitable commodity or 'whore' is made explicit. Wood's opening comment that Turner's 'natural world contains many elements, including gaiety and humour' has its parallel in Dabydeen's sea world, which mixes elements of horror and humour: 'these depths, where terror is transformed into | Comedy' (T, 21). Dabydeen captures in these lines Turner's potentially comic rendering of a horrific subject matter. Earliest viewers of the work seemed unsure of how to respond to *Slavers*, not knowing whether the depiction was supposed to be comic or tragic.[65]

Unafraid of challenging representations of the most hallowed of English figures, or what Dabydeen refers to as 'taking on an English icon and "blackening" it',[66] he rewrites the artist as not only a slaver but also a paedophile. By transforming Turner into a slave-ship captain, Dabydeen suggests that the artist has profited out of the slave trade by selling pictorial representations of it. In also portraying him as a paedophile, Dabydeen accentuates the exploitation involved in this process. Turner's power over the boys is evinced not only in his sexual abuse of them, but also in his linguistic control:

> we repeated in a trance the words
> That shuddered from him: *blessed, angelic,*
> *Sublime.* (T, 38)

Like the artist Turner's 'sublime' picture (in Ruskin's sense of the word), which attempts to elevate the jettison of slaves into a sublime subject, this extract shows the captain's 'love for boys' being raised into a heavenly pursuit, rather than remaining a tale of slavery and child abuse. Turner's ejaculation of words makes a clear link between power, sex and language; all arguably part of the 'pornography of Empire'. The sexual exploitation of the boys by Turner suggests that, for Dabydeen, the artist's representation of the slaves is also an act of sexual violation.

In suggesting that Turner's representation of slavery may be exploitative, the poem questions the ways of looking at the past of slavery. In addition to Turner's 'forgetful' portrayal, Dabydeen highlights the ineffectiveness of visual art as a medium for exploring this past. If visual art is a way of looking, then Dabydeen suggests in his poem that the past of slavery should not be gazed at. The narrator records:

> simple deities of stone
> And wattle, which Turner vandalised
> With a great sweep of his sword in search
> Of his own fables. (*T*, 30)

The artist Turner also 'vandalises' slavery in searching for his own fables of black powerlessness and victimhood. He is exposed as a scopophile, whose pleasure emanates from looking at, and painting – and hence exploiting – the slaves, or objectified 'other'.[67]

The art on the slave-captain's walls implies a link between visual art and the debauched 'truth' that lies behind – or, in the case of Dabydeen's captain, in front of – the painting: 'we lay freely in his bed, gazed at | Pictures on his wall' (*T*, 23). Ironically, the enslaved narrator lies 'freely' in Turner's bed, studying landscape paintings, suggesting that such images are also not 'free' from the past of slavery. It should not be forgotten where the money used to fund Britain's art from the mid-sixteenth to the mid-nineteenth century was generated, often from the slave trade. In the poem, an analogy can be found in Turner's position as slave-ship captain, which earned him the money to purchase the rural depictions of England with which he decorates his cabin walls. Dabydeen implies that people have been blind to the money that funded art; behind the great works produced in Britain lies the money of the slave trade – the invisible past behind a visual medium. Turner's painting differs from many pictures created in this period, in actually depicting the slave past, yet it too hides a reality: the growing black presence in the radical movement of Britain. While Turner's painting is, necessarily, centred around the voyeuristic act of looking, it is equally a painting that looks away; his waves of pigment attempt to veil, or submerge, the political role of black people in Britain in the mid-nineteenth century. Dabydeen suggests in 'Turner' that, in order to critically examine slavery, it is first necessary to evaluate the ways in which this past has previously been looked at, remembered and forgotten.

Instead of a visual response to slavery, Dabydeen indicates the necessity of a textual creative exploration of this past. His turning away from J. M. W. Turner's kind of vision is one which leads him from seeing to imagining. Hence, in his poem, the blindness of the narrator also provides a space of darkness in which to create. Although the child jolts 'memories', these are imagined. The example of the broken jouti necklace exemplifies the necessity of such invention; the separated beads are illustrative of the rupture of history, and of slaves from Africa. Like the beads, cultures, families and villages are torn apart:

> in the future time each must learn to live
> Beadless in a foreign land; or perish.
> Or each must learn to make new jouti,
> Arrange them by instinct, imagination, study
> And arbitrary choice into a pattern
> Pleasing to the self and to others
> Of the scattered tribe; or perish. (*T*, 33)

The alternatives are to live without culture, die, or learn to reinvent this culture and past. There is no precedent in the arrangement of the beads, and they cannot be reassembled as they were before. Dabydeen's conviction in the inability of reconstruction contrasts with the views of Edward Kamau Brathwaite, who has claimed in *Folk Culture of the Slaves in Jamaica* (1970) that 'The slave ship became a kind of psychophysical space capsule, carrying intact the carriers of [a] kind of invisible/atomic culture.'[68] Instead, Dabydeen does not, in the example of the jouti necklace, suggest this kind of 'intact' transference. Unlike Brathwaite's belief in the African person's 'potential of reconstruction', Dabydeen underscores the necessity of invention and the deployment of imagination in thinking about the history of the African slave. The past, he indicates, cannot be reconstructed – the necklace is shattered. In 'Turner', there are repeated reminders of the impossibility of return; its ending a catalogue of what cannot be recovered. There is no access to this history, but there is the possibility of taking the seeds of this memory, represented by the beads, and creatively revising the past.

Dabydeen insists upon the importance of the role of imagination in naming: the child is called 'Turner' after his father, but the names of everything else are invented. The narrator cites the distinction between what can be 'seen' (remembered) and what has to be imagined:

> I have made
> Names for places dwelt in, people forgotten:
> Words are all I have left of my eyes. (*T*, 14)

Although *Slavers* is reprinted at the start of 'Turner', Dabydeen's poem – as a written, rather than visual, depiction of slavery – invites the reader to employ imagination in challenging the authority of the visual. In addition, in 'Turner', Dabydeen also uses 'seeing' to mean 'remembering'; as he writes from a late twentieth-century position, memories of the past of slavery are unavailable to him – all he has to hand, therefore, are words with which to imaginatively explore this past. Like Dabydeen, for whom actual remembrance of slavery is impossible, his eyeless narrator also cannot 'see' – or remember – the past, but he is able to imagine with careful use of words both a past and present. In privileging a textual expression of the past over a visual approach, 'Turner' offers a different kind of remembering which does not involve gazing at the past of slavery. In *Memoirs of the Blind* (1990), Jacques Derrida writes:

> Now if tears *come to the eyes*, if they *well up in them*, and if they can also veil sight, perhaps they reveal, in the very course of this experience, … an essence of the eye … For the very moment they veil sight, tears would unveil what is proper to the eye. And what they cause to surge up out of forgetfulness, there where the gaze or look looks after it, keeps it in reserve, would be nothing less than the *alētheia*, the *truth* of the eyes, whose ultimate destination they would thereby reveal.[69]

Derrida suggests that tears are important precisely because they inhibit the eye from seeing, and it is from this blindness that the 'truth' of the eye originates, thereby enabling a different kind of vision. Critical of Turner's portrayal of the middle passage, Dabydeen raises the notion that a visual representation is not necessarily the most helpful, or sensitive, way of exploring the past of slavery. Instead, he offers a different kind of 'truth' which moves from a visual to an imaginary perception – a veiled, yet truthful, eye.

Wood has called *Slavers* a 'monument' to the slave trade, but Dabydeen offers a very different reading of the painting. In 'Turner' he presents an imaginative exploration of the past of slavery which not only rejects Turner's painting of the jettison of slaves, but also the tradition of visual depictions of this past. For Dabydeen, the Derridean 'ultimate destination' of the eye does not reside in voyeuristically gazing at the past of slavery. Instead, as I have suggested, he posits a desire to move away from vision towards an imaginative, textual, re-vision of the ways in which we think about the slave trade. 'Turner' ultimately offers a way of remembering which, if deliberately 'blind' to the past of slavery, is forward-facing towards a black British future.

A Harlot's Progress

Dabydeen's novel *A Harlot's Progress* takes its title from a series of prints of 1732 by William Hogarth. Dabydeen is not the only author to have been inspired to write by these pictures, as Frederick Antal notes in his book *Hogarth and His Place in European Art* (1962):

> His cycles, deeply rooted in English middle-class thought and closely connected with its theatre, were immensely popular; they were continuously plagiarised, put into verse (authorised and unauthorised) and commented on; they inspired books and pamphlets and were, in their turn, adapted for the stage.[70]

Their theatricality is immediately striking; each plate is a scene in the ironic 'progress' or, rather, decline of the harlot, beginning with her arrival in London and culminating in her death from venereal disease. Dabydeen accentuates his book's relationship to these images by providing details, or fragments, of the prints at the start of each of the nine sections of his book. Though this is a novel less directly preoccupied with art and artists than his poem 'Turner', he remains both fascinated and worried by the continued production and reception of representations of black people into the twentieth century. As Mungo, the eighteenth-century protagonist of *A Harlot's Progress*, predicts, 'Centuries from now, when your descendants think of a Negro, they will think of a pimp, pickpocket, purveyor of filth' (*HP*, 273).

Hogarth's work has been a lasting subject of interest to Dabydeen, inspiring his doctoral thesis and books *Hogarth's Blacks* (1985) and *Hogarth, Walpole and Commercial Britain* (1987)[71] and, fourteen years after the publication of his first book on Hogarth, Dabydeen returns to the area in his novel *A Harlot's Progress*. Unlike other eighteenth-century artists who used black people as 'mere background figure[s]', Dabydeen claims that 'Hogarth's sympathy for the nobodies, for the lower orders of society, extends to a sympathy for black people … This hitherto little-known sympathy of Hogarth's greatly increases our appreciation of the radicalism and deep humanity of the artist.'[72] In Hogarth's series, the black servant appears in just one of the six plates, but is accorded a narrative centrality by Dabydeen. *A Harlot's Progress* is the tale of Mungo (also named Noah and Perseus), an African captured into slavery by the notorious Thomas Thistlewood, at the hands of whom he suffers both physical and sexual abuse, and is brought to Britain. He is prepared for sale by a washerwoman named Betty, and sold at a coffee-shop auction to Lord Montague. Following Lady Montague's illness – and her husband's uneasiness at having him in the house – Mungo runs away to assist a Jewish quack doctor, Mr Gideon, and ends his days 'treating' – in reality, poisoning – diseased prostitutes. There, he meets the dying Moll Hackabout, the central character of Hogarth's study. The text, mainly narrated by Mungo, begins some thirty years after the publication of Hogarth's prints. Now an old man, Mungo is reluctantly speaking his tale to Mr Pringle from the Abolition Society, in return for basic necessities.

Slave narratives were instrumental to the abolitionist movement. As Paul Edwards and David Dabydeen argue in *Black Writers in Britain 1760–1890* (1991):

> Personal survival and advancement apart, the literate black contributed directly to the liberation of his fellow Africans. Black autobiographies and testimonies formed an essential weapon in the arsenal of the Abolitionists who were mobilising public opinion against the slave trade ... Black people had moved from being packed 'like books upon a shelf' aboard the slave ship, to being authors.[73]

This passage – which borrows John Newton's analogy between slaves and books – also indicates, however, the way in which slaves were, like books, read and consumed by an audience. Slave narratives may have been instrumental in the abolitionist cause, but they were part of a process of representing black people which was not devoid of exploitation. In *A Harlot's Progress*, Mungo struggles with the ethics of narrating his story and, in so doing, arguably trades places with the harlot of the title. Dabydeen also suggests in this novel that the 'essential weapon' mentioned above may include economic power; it is disclosed that Mungo's narrative would bring, alongside personal glory for Mr Pringle, 'great dividends for the Committee for the Abolition of Slavery' (*HP*, 3).[74]

Upon completion of his narrative *Thoughts and Sentiments on the Evil of Slavery* (1787), (Quobna) Ottobah Cugoano feared that his words would soon be forgotten – 'to some what I have said may appear as the rattling leaves of autumn, that may soon be blown away and whirled in a vortex where few can hear and know'.[75] However, it would seem that there is an increasing relevance of the stories of these early 'black Britons' to contemporary society, where slave narratives have played an important role in claims of black people's legitimacy of habitation in

Britain. As James Walvin writes in *An African's Life: The Life and Times of Olaudah Equiano, 1745–1797* (1998):

> Equiano is more popular today than ever before. Pictures of Equiano festoon any number of dust-jackets, his face is used on posters to promote exhibitions and TV programmes. He has his own postcard issued by an English museum … It is worth reminding ourselves that, a mere thirty years ago, very few people knew who Equiano was. In the course of a generation, he has gone from anonymity to international fame: a best seller in Africa, North America and Britain.[76]

As he points out, Equiano has not always been seen as a significant figure to black people within Britain – it is particularly in the last thirty years that his relevance has been felt.[77] Walvin's book, published in 1998, comes exactly thirty years after Enoch Powell's 'Rivers of Blood' speech; I would contend that Equiano's burgeoning relevance in the thirty years following this moment arises from a need to understand the historical precedence for black habitation in Britain, in order to counter racist claims of the newness of the country's black presence. This need to understand the history of the black presence in the UK runs alongside an increasingly widespread identification in both Britain and North America with Equiano's articulation of the complexities of a diasporan identity. Also indicative of this late twentieth-century interest in early black Britons was the exhibition in 1997 dedicated to Ignatius Sancho at the National Portrait Gallery. The renewed interest in these historical figures inevitably poses a long-overdue corrective to the largely white history books of Britain and acts as a clear challenge to the amnesia typified by the speeches of Powell and Thatcher, which 'forgets' that these black figures ever existed.

While it would seem that there is a growing, and important, movement towards remembering the early black British presence, Dabydeen suggests – in his concerns about the reception of slave narratives – that such figures need to be remembered sensitively. The experiences of his narrator Mungo bear witness to the exploitation ingrained in the slave-narrative genre, whether at the hands of the abolitionist editor or voyeuristic reader. Dabydeen suggests in *A Harlot's Progress* that interest in these texts may be in part due to a morbid fascination or voyeuristic titillation at reading stories of bondage and cruelty exercised against black people. These concerns regarding the reception of slave narratives are central to the novel and something I shall return to in greater detail in a moment when we encounter the character of Lady Montague.

Although Dabydeen has called *A Harlot's Progress* 'a novel by Equiano', this is not a canonical engagement with the eighteenth century.[78] In narrating Mungo's story, Dabydeen chooses not to ventriloquise the voices of slaves like Sancho or Equiano, but rather writes the story of an unvoiced black presence. Mungo, at the same time, is a stereotyped figure; as Jack Gratus has noted, 'the black man as a figure of fun … [had] names by which he could easily be identified and placed like Sambo and Mungo'.[79] While perhaps alluding to a particular 'type' of black man, Dabydeen refuses to be drawn into 'speaking for', or ventriloquising, the voices of actual slaves like Equiano or Sancho – figures already heavily over-represented. Dabydeen suggests through his character Mungo the ways in which slave narrators have, in 'speaking' their stories, also been spoken for. There are constant reminders in the novel of what Mungo's readers will or will not tolerate, and he has economical reasons for his adherence to matters of audience – as he informs Ellar, 'They can refuse to buy my book, and I'll starve' (*HP*, 256).

Mungo is, therefore, uneasy with his British readership, all too aware of the constrictive form of the slave narrative and fearful of 'alienating his readers' (*HP*, 256). His exasperation with the silenced and servile role expected of him is illustrated in his encounter with another black servant, named Saba, whom he strikes. Despite his apparently anglicised stance – intimated by his position as a slave narrator – Mungo is not willing to be comfortably 'assimilated' within Britain, whereas Saba 'was a Reynolds' black, and behaved accordingly' (*HP*, 220).[80] Here, not only does Mungo suggest that the black servants featured in portraits by Sir Joshua Reynolds were afforded considerable status by their depictions, but also he rather scathingly hints that such servants were accordingly mild-mannered or servile. In his poem 'Dependence, or the Ballad of the Little Black Boy (On Francis Wheatley's *Family Group and Negro Boy* painted in the 1770s)', Dabydeen also writes about the positioning on the margins of the black servant in Francis Wheatley's painting *Family Group in a Landscape*:

> While painterman splash, drip, dip, rearrange
> And produce picture marvellously strange
> How fair they seem and full of grace
> Benevolence and love spread upon each face
> And me at the edge typical of my race
> Holding back the urine the hurt and disgrace.[81]

In paintings such as these, which featured a black servant alongside his or her white owner, often the black figure functioned not only as a status symbol, but also in contrast to the whiteness of the master or mistress, as Dabydeen's narrator recognises.[82] Unlike Wheatley, Reynolds was, in fact, listed as a subscriber to Cugoano's *Thoughts and Sentiments on the Evil of Slavery*, indicating that he was sympathetic to the abolitionist cause.[83] Dabydeen's attack on Reynolds is therefore part of a wider questioning of the reception of representations of black people in art and literature. His suggestion that Reynolds expected black people to be servile is in keeping with the particular type of representation found not only in the works of artists like Wheatley or Reynolds, but also in slave narratives. Slave narrators had very carefully constructed identities and Mungo wrestles with the problems and complexities of reinvention, both of his own identity and past and that of his African tribe.

In his continued critical reappraisal of the genre, Dabydeen also proposes that the authors of slave narratives may not be who they purport to be – we see the heavy-handed role of abolitionists, as 'editors', in shaping the narrative:

> the book Mr Pringle intends to write will be Mungo's portrait in the first person narrative. A book purporting to be a record of the Negro's own words (understandably corrected in terms of grammar, the erasure of indelicate or infelicitous expressions, and so forth). (*HP*, 3)

The use of 'portrait' reinforces the novel's connection to art and to visual representation, as befits a book based on a series of engravings. In indicating the artistry behind Pringle's representation of Mungo, Dabydeen also suggests a certain way of looking at his slave narrator. Like J. M. W. Turner's heavily loaded representation of black people in *Slavers*, Pringle constructs a particular type of representation of Mungo. His role in the narrative is, therefore, that of an artist, 'resolv[ing] to colour and people a landscape out of his own imagination' (*HP*, 3). Also like Turner, this process is not devoid of voyeurism or exploitation – a point I shall return to in due course.

The 'ghost writing' of Mungo's narrative has a historical precedent; it has been suggested that Cugoano, for example, was not the actual author of his book, and concerns have also been voiced over the 'authenticity' of Equiano's narrative.[84] Pringle's proposed role in shaping Mungo's tale serves as a reminder that it is unwise to assume that slave narratives were actually representative of slaves – the slaves 'writing' their tales were inevitably anglicised, and often had much assistance in constructing their stories. This context is relevant when thinking about Walvin's claim that Equiano was 'the first spokesperson for the Afro-British community', and recalls Spivak's articulation of the problematics of subaltern representation.[85] Dabydeen is aware of the insufficient means of articulating this past, yet is compelled to try to do so; to reiterate Spivak's words, he is arguably caught between 'granting to the oppressed either that very expressive subjectivity which s/he criticizes or, instead, a total unrepresentability'.[86]

The heavy-handed 'editorial' presence in the narratives of slaves is, then, another indication of the ways in which these authors have been spoken for, or represented. While Mungo's considerable rhetorical abilities would negate the need for Pringle's corrections, Mungo is equally aware of the expected register of a slave and so conceals his linguistic and rhetorical skills from him, a reminder that 'peasantry' was then, as of now, 'in vogue' (*CO*, 9). In depicting the methods by which Mungo is prevented from fully narrating his own story – bound by conventions of form and readership – Dabydeen reveals the problematic nature of the slave-narrative genre; his figure is silenced even as he struggles to represent himself. One might make a comparison between Mungo's struggle for self-representation and the ways in which Equiano and Sancho have been represented – for example, as figureheads for black Britain – to recall Walvin's words: 'Pictures of Equiano festoon any number of dust-jackets, his face is used on posters to promote exhibitions and TV programmes'.

While there may be a tendency to view slave narrators as being representative of black people in the eighteenth century, as Walvin has suggested, he has also been clear to point out that Equiano and Sancho 'were not *typical* of other blacks in London; both were well known, had caught the imagination, and both were literate'.[87] Although these men have come to be seen as representative of the eighteenth-century black presence in London, it is important to remember that their very literacy which brought them fame also differentiated them from other black people in Britain at this time. Mungo is presented by Dabydeen as being similarly problematic because – like Equiano and Sancho, or Phillips's Cambridge – he is an anglicised black, commenting on his fellow slaves: 'After a while I ceased feeling pity at their distress, my original mood giving way to an acceptance of the nature of things. Being heathen, it was inevitable that they would perish in irrelevant numbers' (*HP*, 49). We can compare this quotation to the letter written by Sancho on 18 July 1772:

> I thank you for your kindness to my poor black bretheren – I flatter myself you will find them not ungrateful – they act commonly from their feelings: – I have observed a dog will love those who use him kindly – and surely, if so, negroes, in their state of ignorance and bondage, will not act less generously.[88]

Sancho's comparison of his 'poor black bretheren' to dogs is not dissimilar to Mungo's comments about 'heathen' slaves. In both cases, the narrator makes explicit his difference from those he describes and, in so doing, internalises eighteenth-century assumptions about the supposed inferiority of black people. By exposing the constructed and performative nature of identity and anglicised manner of slave narrators, Dabydeen questions the degree of authority invested in them as representatives for black Britain. In the first volume of *Slavery, Abolition and Emancipation* (1999), dedicated to black writers of the Romantic period, Sukhdev Sandhu and David Dabydeen note that Equiano came from a slave-owning family and, once free, 'purchased slaves whose back-breaking work he oversaw on a Central American plantation'.[89] Like Phillips's Cambridge or Dabydeen's Mungo, it appears that actual slave narrators were often problematic figures.

The reference in the earlier quotation by Edwards and Dabydeen to the diary of the infamous slave owner turned abolitionist, John Newton – with slaves packed 'like books upon a shelf' – has further resonance in *A Harlot's Progress*, when Dabydeen compares both Thistlewood and, obliquely, Pringle to Newton. In drawing a comparison between Newton and Pringle, Dabydeen interrogates the virtue of abolitionists, suggesting that the move from slavery to abolition is a process of 'conversion' that can work either way:

> Perhaps I should not make such a trial of his Christian soul and convert him to the ways of slavery. I watch his fingers bunch into a secret fist, as if he would cuff me for my rebelliousness … The pen is in [his hand] as if waiting to sign a warrant for my arrest, or my sale. (*HP*, 7)

Pringle is, it would seem, as capable of being a slave owner as an abolitionist, the pen able to sign Mungo's sale as much as write his tale – or, indeed, that in writing his tale, Pringle is also 'selling' Mungo. Pringle's sexual exploitation of the slave narrator leads Mungo to conclude, 'He makes me feel like a strumpet whose performance is undeserving of his coin' (*HP*, 178). Mungo's literal and metaphoric 'whoring', alongside his centrality in the novel, intimates he is the 'harlot' of the novel's title. In comparing Thistlewood's literal whoring of Mungo to Pringle's metaphorical prostitution of him, Dabydeen proposes there may be reason to worry about the enslaving and exploiting nature of the slave-narrative genre and the indulgence of pornography lurking within such tales. It should come as no surprise, therefore, that Mungo also feels exploited by Hogarth's portrayal: 'Once I was affordable only to the very rich, a slave worth countless guineas, but because of Mr Hogarth I was possessed, in penny image, by several thousands' (*HP*, 274). Mungo is thus whored by Hogarth, as well as by Pringle, indicating that eighteenth-century representations of black people in Britain may well have been fatally compromised by form.

In addition to Pringle's heavy-handed control of the narrative, much of Mungo's tale is fabricated, indicating a continuing resistance to narrating his story: 'Memory don't bother me, that's why I don't tell Mr Pringle anything. I can change memory' (*HP*, 2).[90] Mungo refers to his 'mind's inventiveness' (*HP*, 41) – his memory is 'invented' both necessarily (to compensate for what he has forgotten) and wilfully (to ensure Mr Pringle hears the story he wants). Cathy Caruth writes in the preface to her edited book *Trauma: Explorations in Memory* (1995) that, for people who have experienced a traumatic series of events, 'To cure oneself – whether by drugs or the telling of one's story or both – seems to many survivors to imply the giving-up of an important reality, or the dilution of a special truth'.[91] It is possible to view Mungo's resistance to telling his story to Pringle as a similar reluctance to relinquish an 'important reality' – a desire to 'hoard the past and squirrel on it through miserable seasons' (*HP*, 2).[92] For Mungo, however, the construction of the book also entails a more deathly outcome:

> the book is no more than a splendidly adorned memorial and grave. To speak is to scoop out substance, to hollow out yourself, to make space within for your own burial, so I have kept in things as bulwarks against death. I have kept silence before the nib and gravedigger's spade of Mr Pringle. (*HP*, 34–5)

In this quotation, Mungo portrays writing as a preparation for death. Silence is shown to be far from passive, but a survival tactic, or 'bulwark against death', which simultaneously signals Mungo's defiance at Pringle's expectations of him.[93] Without physical memorials to slavery, Mungo appears to propose that books about this past may act as monuments to the trade. However, he suggests that the slave is destroyed in narrating his tale, which raises the important question: what is lost in the act of narration? I would suggest, borrowing Spivak's terminology, that in narrating his story, Mungo is subsequently killing the subaltern figure.

Mungo's inventiveness leads to a contradictory tale. The mark of 'TT' on his forehead, for example, is, variously, a sign of evil made by the Headman of his tribe (*HP*, 19), a sign tradition-ally used to brand women's hands for failure to produce children (*HP*, 30), representative of the bush (*HP*, 31), a sign present at birth (*HP*, 33), a coming-of-age sign (*HP*, 65), and Captain Thistlewood's brand (*HP*, 66). 'Truth' is unavailable in this text – what matters is the way in which the past is invented, manip-ulated and bought – for as Lord Montague comes to realise, 'Truth itself was hostage to the designs of stockjobbers, another commodity changing hands at a price' (*HP*, 199).

Much as in *The Counting House* and 'Turner', Dabydeen has once again drawn on existing historical sources to shape this novel. The sign 'TT', for example, was indeed the brand of Thomas Thistlewood, a slave owner who came to Jamaica in 1750. On 3 January 1758, he wrote in his journal that he had acquired from Savanna la Mar a silver brand 'TT', which he soon made use of.[94] Thistlewood was a notoriously cruel and sadistic punisher of slaves, and in *A Harlot's Progress*, Dabydeen also makes him responsible for the jettison of slaves aboard the *Zong*, the subject matter of his poem 'Turner'. Thistlewood therefore becomes representative of the worst atrocities of slave owners or captains and also, like Dabydeen's Turner, has a predilection for young African boys.

Mungo's rebellion against the form of the slave narrative encompasses his refusal to demonise Thistlewood or create the kind of representation Mr Pringle wants to hear about: 'Mr Pringle's version of Captain Thomas Thistlewood is untroubled. Captain Thistlewood is a demon and I his catamite' (*HP*, 75). As Elizabeth Kowaleski Wallace writes, in this novel Thistle-wood is marginally more than just a 'pederast taking masochistic pleasure from the body of a boy slave'; he is provided with 'a complex, if perverted, psychology. In particular, Thistlewood reverently worships a mythical lost Albion'.[95] He is, indeed, especially sensitive to the changes to England, largely ushered in by the flourishing slave trade – he tells Mungo to 'forget the land' (*HP*, 69), but strives to take his own advice.[96] England in the mid-eighteenth century is not the homeland he wishes to remember, barely recognisable due to the effects of slavery and early industrialisation, in which Thistlewood, of course, played a vital part. The art on his cabin walls is, therefore, an escape from an increasingly polluted and corrupt England to an idyllic pre-industrial pastoral vision of the country – also depicted in the paintings on the slave-ship captain Turner's walls. In Thistlewood's nostalgia for a lost England, however, we find the idea of a deliberately forgetful past and a refusal to take responsibility for the slave trade which has altered and shaped England beyond recognition. Like the connection Dabydeen makes in 'Turner' between Britain's eighteenth- and nineteenth-century art and the slave trade that funded these works, the pastoral images favoured by Thistlewood are also intimately connected to this past, and bear witness to the 'pornography' of slavery that is enacted before them.

To Thistlewood, slaves are ultimately animals, and the slave ship is a deathly ark. Mungo ironically compares this to Hogarth's prints of animals being mistreated:

> You, English, inhabitants of a country distinguished for its adoration of pets and charity to the lesser breed, will know the tempest of emotions that overcame my Captain. You have the nightmare of Mr Hogarth's genius, in his series of prints, *Scenes of Cruelty*, to stir you to patriotic rage. (*HP*, 50)

Again, like his questioning of the motivation behind Turner's representation of the slave-ship jettison, Dabydeen questions why Hogarth would want to paint – and people would want to own – these images. While Hogarth apparently created these pictures of cruelty 'with the hope of in some degree correcting that barbarous treatment of animals, the very sight of which renders the streets of our Metropolis so distressing to every feeling mind', Dabydeen suggests a more sinister reason for their acquisition.[97] It is intimated in *A Harlot's Progress* that Hogarth's audience takes a sadistic pleasure from looking at images of cruelty, and also from being chastised for their transgressions – by extension, the motivations of the reader of slave narratives are also brought into question. Mungo notes that, 'to ensure that his book sells, he will not repel his readers by calling them necrophiles' (*HP*, 257), articulating once more the notion that there is something voyeuristic and underhand about the reader's expectation of what lies within the narratives.

As if to clinch this suggestion of the potentially improper reception of these texts, Dabydeen includes in his novel a depiction of the voyeuristic reader in the character of Lady Montague. While Dabydeen's Thistlewood amply demonstrates the 'pornographic' reaches of Empire, therefore, he is not the only white Briton in *A Harlot's Progress* to harbour sadistic desires towards Mungo. Alongside the violence of servants Jane and Lizzie towards Mungo, his action in striking Saba has a profound effect on Lady Montague, making her think of the jettison of slaves:

> There was no denying the pleasure – an inexact word, but she could think of no better – in following the news of the massacre … Her imagination, so bounded by her surroundings, found sudden release in the descriptions of sharks feasting on men's flesh; men bound and chained, unable to resist or to retaliate with the violence glimpsed in [Mungo's] violent utterance, violent act. (*HP*, 222)

Restricted by her position as a wealthy woman in eighteenth-century Britain, Lady Montague yearns for the sadomasochistic violence she reads in the sensational descriptions printed in the newspaper reports. This is a clear articulation of her 'fantasy of domination, bondage and sadomasochism' and can be aligned with what Kobena Mercer has referred to in *Welcome to the Jungle* (1994) as the 'certain ways in which white people "look" at black people and how in this way of looking, black male sexuality is perceived as something different, excessive, Other'.[98] The means by which Lady Montague achieves a temporary 'release' is, therefore, in perusing descriptions of bondage and violence specifically directed towards black people. However, this will remain a short-lived freedom; the sadism will be once more restricted, or 'bound', in being edited from Mr Pringle's narrative. As Mungo complains: *'a Lady is not ever improper, and if she is, it can never be in print'* (HP, 226).

In contrast, Mungo is all too aware of what Mr Pringle *does* want to hear about; like Lady Montague, he craves the sensational or pornographic, pandering to his abolitionist readers' desire to hear of 'evil' slavers and innocent slaves. However, while 'All or part of Mr Pringle's conception of [Mungo's] Progress is, or may be, true,' Mungo writes,

> I will not move you to customary guilt, gentle reader, even though you may crave that I hold up a mirror to the sins of your race. You will reward me with laurels and fat purses for flagellating you thus, especially should I, with impoverished imagination, evoke for you the horror of the slave-ship's hold, the chained Negroes, their slobbering, their suffocation, their sentimental condition. (HP, 70)

Again, there is a sadomasochistic element in the inversion of the dynamics of slavery, with slave narrators 'flagellating' the white readership. The detail of 'impoverished imagination' is particularly telling; Dabydeen provides us with descriptions of the slave-ship hold, but these are some way from portraying a 'sentimental condition'. For example, we learn that 'When the ship pitched in a sudden rough sea, the chains tightened and cracked their ankles, spines and elbow joints. Sometimes arms and legs and heads were wrenched clean off, and their torsos rolled freely about the ship' (HP, 48). Declining to censor his narrative, Mungo provides us not with a sentimental description, but a gruesome one, refusing to edit or gloss it as part of his continuing resistance to the slave-narrative genre.

Like Thistlewood, who becomes representative of all slave-ship captains, Mungo is also at one level representative of all slaves, due to the very nature of slave narratives – their rarity ensures that they are taken to represent millions unable to voice their own stories:

In the faraway plantations of the West Indies, in the barracoons of the African coast, I have rebelled, stabbed, poisoned, raped, absconded, and sought escape by killing myself and my offsprings. In return I have been strangled, flogged to death, roasted alive, blown away and lynched. (*HP*, 244)

In a narrower sense, on Mungo is bestowed the task of speaking for his village, a burdensome enough responsibility – he records that he 'grew melancholy with the realization of how they had burdened me to utter for them. Only my voice survived the general hum of pain' (*HP*, 59–60). There may be a comparison to be made between Mungo's struggle with his identity as a black spokesperson and Dabydeen's burden of how to represent the past of slavery. Mercer writes about what he calls the 'burden of representation' experienced by black artists:

When artists are positioned on the margins of the institutional spaces of cultural production, they are burdened with the impossible task of speaking as 'representatives,' in that they are widely expected to 'speak for' the marginalized communities from which they come.[99]

We can see in Mercer's argument the problematic expectation that a marginalised black artist or writer should be a representative or spokesperson for his or her race. As Equiano has become a spokesperson for black Britain, it would seem Mungo is also a reluctant representative of his village. Dabydeen perhaps indicates the danger of loading the eighteenth- or twentieth-century writer with these onerous expectations.

Mungo's burden is augmented by the knowledge that he must remember the villagers 'in the best light' (*HP*, 60), a responsibility with which he particularly struggles:

Kaka's sores still gleamed. He was the same, accompanied by the same flies. His head was as comically big. He was the same stinking nigger as when I pelted him with stones. Nor did Ellar's limbs straighten, howsoever I willed them to elegance. (*HP*, 62)

In thinking about Mungo's attempts to beautify the other

villagers, it is perhaps useful to recall Dabydeen's poem 'Turner'. Like Dabydeen's suggestion that J. M. W. Turner has beautified the middle passage journey in order to sell his painting, Mungo ironically attempts to transform the violence of slavery into a 'sublime' depiction (using Ruskin's sense of the word) in order to appeal to his voyeuristic readers: 'Kaka's head is a palette of colours. … Rubies of congealed blood hang from his ears. Here and there, glimpses of clean white bone exposed by the Captain's cuff subdue the viewer's eye, necessary foil to the decorative richness which threatens to overwhelm' (*HP*, 97). Mungo's over-aestheticised description, with the 'rubies' of blood and 'decorative richness' of bone, can be understood to be a heavily ironic comment on the need to decorate the 'truth' of slavery, and an additional sign of his continuing reluctance to conform to the limits of the slave narrative.

Ellar, however, cuts through this attempt at a sublime portrayal. When Mungo tells her: 'I was praising you, I was saying that in spite of all you remained beautiful within', Ellar succinctly replies: 'But I didn't … Outside I was covered in my own shit, and inside too' (*HP*, 256), reiterating that there was nothing sentimental about slavery. Her words fall at the other end of the spectrum, suggesting a refusal to embellish the truth. Her lack of concern for matters of audience poses an equally stubborn challenge to the slave-narrative form. In this section of the book, Ellar has been dead for some time and is now a ghostly part of Mungo's psyche as he wrestles with the different approaches to the representation of his, and his village's, past. Her words recall those of the ancestor in 'Coolie Odyssey', and the historical basis of the works of Dabydeen examined in this chapter suggest his own compulsion to 'persist before the grave | seeking fables' (*CO*, 12). The kind of fictional re-imagining of the past of slavery undertaken by both Mungo and Dabydeen may be both 'fable' and burdensome, but is nonetheless necessary when faced with an absence of historical accounts concerning either indentured labourers or African slaves. Dabydeen recognises the compulsion to look at this history, despite the problems inherent in his attempt to imaginatively explore this past.

Mungo soon realises that, ultimately, if he is to survive, he must overcome the guilt both of having survived thus far and of having done so by submitting to exploitation. *A Harlot's Progress* therefore explores the necessity of learning to surmount guilt; Mungo relates to Betty the untainted countryside's ability to do just this,

> telling her stories suckled from Captain Thistlewood, of Sparrowhawk and Owl, of Thistle and Cowslip and Penny-royal, their ancient fame and magical properties which survive the guilt that makes men murder men, and build their shining governments of the damned. (*HP*, 150)

While we might think of the burden of guilt surrounding Thistlewood's pastoral images in his cabin, the end of this passage paraphrases Guyanese poet Martin Carter's words in his poem 'After One Year': 'Men murder men, as men must murder men, | to build their shining governments of the damned.'[100] In the same year that Dabydeen published *A Harlot's Progress* he also edited a new edition of Carter's *Selected Poems* – poems largely written to signal his discontent with the colonial government of mid-twentieth-century Guyana. In Gemma Robinson's words, Carter 'was among a dissatisfied generation of colonial people who would resist the life that had been mapped out for them by the British Empire', but despite the apparent differences in subject matter between the two works, connections can be traced, culminating in Dabydeen's paraphrasing of the last two lines of Carter's poem within the text of his novel.[101] This intertextuality draws *A Harlot's Progress* not only firmly into the twentieth century, but also into a correlation with Guyanese politics and the struggle for freedom, suggesting a wider application of notions of enslavement and liberation.[102] Men, of course, were quite literally murdering men in the course of slavery – the jettison of slaves by Collingwood, or 'Thistlewood', is a particularly blatant and brutal example. The money from the trade was benefiting not only the merchants but also the government, enabling the construction of Britain's sixteenth- to nineteenth-century 'shining governments of the damned'. Also, as Robinson notes, Carter's poems are first and foremost about resistance. So, too, I have argued that in *A Harlot's Progress* we see Mungo's repeated resistance to the life and genre 'mapped out for [him] by the British Empire' in his refusal to conform to Mr Pringle's desired narrative and to his white readers' pornographic demands – indicating that resistance is an essential component in the continuing survival and struggles of black people in both Britain and its former colonies.

The link to Carter's work is not, however, the only twentieth-century connection in the novel. Dabydeen has commented in an interview with Mark Stein that *A Harlot's Progress* 'has a black character as the narrator, so it's England from eighteenth century [*sic*] black eyes. But of course it has resonances of today; it's eighteenth century only in form'.[103] Published just over fifty years after the arrival of the *SS Empire Windrush*, Dabydeen's novel dwells in the eighteenth century, but also points to a more recent mid-twentieth-century British past. One of these resonances includes Thistlewood's forgetful England, which can be aligned with the historical forgetfulness of those Britons who view the *Windrush* as the first black British arrival. However, arguably the most important resonance for Dabydeen concerns the ongoing reception of representations of black people within Britain.

While Dabydeen's novel serves as a necessary reminder of the eighteenth-century black presence in London, it also illuminates the problems and complexities behind slave narratives. It cautions us that such works have to be taken in context as products of the abolitionist movement and that the slaves 'writing' these tales were severely restricted by issues of form, readership and editors. It also reveals the perversion behind such tales, and the danger of a pornographic response to their publication. His book imaginatively adds the motivation and thoughts behind the slave narrative – the irritation at problems of editing, register and tone, for example, all suggest the complexity of Dabydeen's slave narrator. Mungo's frustration at the limits or checks forced upon him by the genre also indicate the ways in which slave narrators often have been 'spoken for', and represented, as

Sancho has lamented, 'From Othello to Sancho the big – we are either foolish – or mulish – all – all without a single exception'.[104]

In the genre of the slave narrative, the 'pornography of Empire' had found a form that simultaneously bound the narrator while flagellating the reader; writing at a time when slavery was still legal, slave narrators found that these chains had yet to be loosened. Black people were exploited by more than just slavery in the eighteenth century – slave narrators were appropriated for different causes; used to advertise and promote museums or books, overtly constructed and over-represented. However, the twentieth-century casting of slave narrators as icons may be seen as another form of enslavement, in stripping these early black Britons of their complicated humanity. As Sandhu and Dabydeen write, it is vital to recognise the flaws of slave narrators in order to 'move beyond an uncritical celebration of the books which the likes of Cugoano and Sancho – both of them caustically perceptive literary critics – would themselves deride'.[105] While recognising the continuing importance of these figures to twentieth-century Britain, Dabydeen suggests in *A Harlot's Progress* that it is imperative to acknowledge their complexities in order to begin lightening their burden of representation.

Fred D'Aguiar and the memorialisation of slavery

Like David Dabydeen's poem 'Turner', examined in the last chapter, Fred D'Aguiar's novel *Feeding the Ghosts* (1997) is based upon the story of the slave ship *Zong*, from which, in 1781, one hundred and thirty-two slaves were jettisoned. However, in D'Aguiar's novel the slave ship continues to haunt the present and, as the transhistorical narrator comes to realise, while the *Zong* still rides upon the waves, and its spectral jettisons recur, it is uncertain where blame lies, or whether it should be attributed at all:

> Men, women and children are thrown overboard by the captain and his crew. One of them is me. One of them is you. One of them is doing the throwing, the other is being thrown. I'm not sure who is who, you or I.[1]

Like Caryl Phillips, D'Aguiar rejects a retributive view of the past of slavery and, like Dabydeen, he struggles with the problems of representing this past. He also shares these authors' concerns with the historical record pertaining to the slave trade, and has written about the issues involved in examining accounts of received history when returning to this past:

> My first awareness of history was of my place in it as the descendant of slaves. In history, stories of blackness always limited the humanity of blacks to something less than whiteness. Slavery and poetry pulled in opposite directions since poetry could never be enslaved and a slave could never really remain a slave and be a poet, not if poetry meant liberation or at least a freedom of thought unhindered by any material circumstance even if born out of it.[2]

D'Aguiar seems particularly aware of his slave ancestry and chooses not to adopt a historical approach to this past, due to the 'limited humanity' offered to black people. Instead, poetry – and perhaps literary creativity in general – can be seen as an appropriate mode with which to try to achieve a new understanding of the past of slavery. History provides D'Aguiar with a starting point – the events of the *Zong*, for example, offer him a place from which to begin exploring this past.

I suggest in this chapter that D'Aguiar is deeply troubled by the act of writing about the memory of slavery, and asks how we are to remember this past a century and a half after its abolition and in the absence of witnesses. In my reading of D'Aguiar's first novel, *The Longest Memory* (1994), I will interrogate, via Jacques Derrida's essay 'Plato's Pharmacy' (1968), the distinction between memory (*mnēmē*) and remembering (*hypomnēsis*).[3] D'Aguiar proposes two alternatives for the representation of counter- and collective remembrance of slavery: first, a literary *hypomnēsis*, or imagined remembrance of this past, and, secondly, the body as a receptacle for remembering. However, neither offers an uncomplicated form of remembrance, and he is unable to offer a third, and perhaps less troubling, way of remembering the past of slavery.

The long poem *Bloodlines* (2000), in some ways, is D'Aguiar's most challenging text, especially in relation to the portrayal of available roles for women. Like *The Longest Memory*, *Bloodlines* demonstrates his concern with the problem of the *pharmakon* – for Derrida, both remedy and poison – and is a deliberate attempt to avoid augmenting the continuum of neo-slave narratives.[4] Marianne Hirsch has coined the term 'postmemory' as a way of explaining what she calls the belated 'memories' experienced by those who did not directly witness traumatic events.[5] Postmemory, as Hirsch uses it, is applicable to what she calls the 'second generation' of trauma witnesses; that is, the children of Holocaust survivors. This is not, therefore, a term referring to *mnēmē*, or living memories; as Hirsch adds, the name 'postmemory' is intended to indicate 'its secondary or second-generation memory quality, its basis in displacement, its belatedness'.[6] Given the temporal distance between slavery and the present, postmemories of this past can only ever be belated. *Bloodlines* can be seen as enacting a postmemorialisation of the past of slavery; in D'Aguiar's texts, postmemory arguably extends the scope of *hypomnēsis* to include those exiled from the concept of the body as a receptacle of remembering. The postmemorialisation of slavery, however, is ultimately revealed to be a dispiriting state which precludes a redemptive text or any affirmative conclusions in works addressing this past.

As mentioned in previous chapters, in referring to a theorist like Hirsch who is more commonly associated with writing about the Holocaust, I do not wish to minimise the differences between this more recent past and that of slavery. However, those who write about the Holocaust usefully provide a vocabulary with which to explore notions of trauma, memory and forgetting, which are also, as D'Aguiar shows, important issues to address in terms of the legacies of the slave trade. He is particularly interested in the recursive nature of trauma and can be seen as searching for new idioms in which to express the integral painfulness of slavery. As we shall see, D'Aguiar's texts expose his profound struggle to suggest ways of remembering slavery which do not either beautify or re-traumatise the past through recollection.

D'Aguiar's works propose a gloomy outlook on the transformative potential of writing about slavery. He offers a sombre view of this past and its continuing legacies; his works suggest a bleak picture of British and American societies, as unalterably based on racial distinctions. Such racial polarisation, he contends, feeds the continuity of what he refers to as '*this past, this present, this future, this slavery*', or slavery's longevity.[7] It is his unfaltering belief in the unending nature of slavery that leads to the apparent pessimism of his works.

The Longest Memory

In 'Plato's Pharmacy', Derrida outlines the transformative moment of writing in which memory (*mnēmē*) is supplanted by 'reminding' or remembering (*hypomnēsis*):

> The boundary (between inside and outside, living and nonliving) separates not only speech from writing but also memory as an unveiling (re-)producing a presence from re-memoration as the mere repetition of a monument ... The 'outside' [begins] ... at the point where the *mnēmē*, instead of being present to itself in its life as a movement of truth, is supplanted by the archive, evicted by a sign of re-memoration or of com-memoration. The space of writing, space *as* writing, is opened up in the violent movement of the surrogation, in the difference between *mnēmē* and *hypomnēsis*.[8]

Although 'writing is *given* as the sensible, visible, spatial surrogate of the *mnēmē*', Derrida argues, like speech, memory is immediately lost to writing by the archival act of remembering.[9] Memory is 'supplanted by the archive' of writing, and hence exchanged for what he terms 're-memoration' and 'com-memoration'; once written, the text stands as an inconstant monument to the memory. The notion of writing as 'com-memoration' is mportant, therefore, in signifying something that has passed; the no longer 'living' memory is memorialised in writing. Derrida's thoughts on the memorialisation of memory through writing have provocative implications for the challenge of remembering slavery, especially for black writers in Britain who – writing more than a century and a half since slavery was abolished in Britain – are also 'outside' of slavery and therefore have only *hypomnēsis*, or a monumentalised form of remembrance, available to them.

It is important to note that Derrida describes memory as being unveiled. Memory is – to be accurate – 'an unveiling (re-)producing a presence'. The veil might be thought of as signifying the threshold between the moment once passed, to which the memory corresponds, and the present moment of remembering. Derrida's cautious phrase, '(re-)producing a presence' indicates that memory is the repeated production of the past.

Remembering or 're-memoration', on the other hand, is the 'mere repetition of a monument' – that is, the act of remembering points to the memory that has passed, but it is the monument, or replica, that repeats; remembering is unable to directly access (or re-produce) the memory. There can, of course, be no access to the past, so memory and remembering are, importantly, both reproductions; one of an event, one of its monument. The notion of a veil between the moment and memory may also be effective in suggesting the diaphanous border between the past and the present, where the past is partitioned from the present and therefore inaccessible, but tantalisingly visible.

This summary of Derrida's essay stabilises for a moment some very unwieldy terms, without denying their complexity. The distinction between *mnēmē* and *hypomnēsis* is not inflexible or concrete; the notion of a veil may be useful in thinking about the permeability of the border here, too. Derrida's notions of *mnēmē* and *hypomnēsis* are valuable to readings of D'Aguiar's works. For example, as mentioned, *Feeding the Ghosts* revisits the story of the slave ship *Zong*. To anticipate momentarily this novel, we see through the main character Mintah that memories can be involuntarily triggered. In the following extract, D'Aguiar suggests that traumatic memory can be prompted by the most unlikely of things:

> a savannah will start to tumble bundles of bracken across its flat face and suddenly, through some trick of the light and heat, it will tremble into a seascape and that bracken will become tossed into a sea current and this one-hundred-and thirty-second body will have to be a witness again.
> (*FG*, 4–5)

Mintah, a traumatised survivor of the slave ship *Zong*, was not deliberately remembering the past aboard the ship; in fact, she consciously tries *not* to remember. In the above passage, she was experiencing *mnēmē*, or the re-production of a memory – the *Zong* is re-produced in front of her as she gazes at the savannah. The involuntary nature of memory thus differs from *hypomnēsis*, or the intentional remembering of the past, which does not open ready access to memory but rather supplants memory with an act of remembering. Her journal, which records her time aboard the slave ship, is an example of *hypomnēsis*, so is a monument to – rather than a re-experiencing of – the traumatic past. It is through writing her journal, or 'remembering' the past of the *Zong*, in fact, that Mintah, paradoxically, hopes to forget. She writes as an attempt to purge herself of recollections of the *Zong* and so forget the traumatic past, but her act of *hypomnēsis* fails to exorcise the trauma and she is unable to forget. D'Aguiar seems to suggest that, although it is painful for Mintah to recall the events aboard the ship, it is morally necessary to remember the deaths. Her counter-remembrance of the events aboard the *Zong*, however traumatic for Mintah, is important in challenging the received historical remembrance of this past, represented in *Feeding the Ghosts* by the slave-ship captain's version of events. Mintah wants to forget but, D'Aguiar suggests, we need to remember. This problem would seem to be the crux of his work – whether we can remember without trauma, or if there can be transformative remembrance of the past of slavery.

This example from *Feeding the Ghosts* goes some way to clarify the difficult relationship between *mnēmē* and *hypomnēsis*, but 'Plato's Pharmacy' is of even greater use to the understanding of *The Longest Memory*; in particular, in examining the ways in which Whitechapel, an elderly male slave, attempts to forget the traumatic past but, like Mintah, fails to escape both the trauma of *mnēmē* and that of remembering or *hypomnēsis*. D'Aguiar ultimately suggests that remembering may be agonising, but it is vital; as we see in the character of Chapel, Whitechapel's son, not remembering slavery has deathly consequences.

I wish to extrapolate Derrida's distinction between *mnēmē* (memory) and *hypomnēsis* (remembering), though as I have indicated, these are not opposing states. As we have seen in the works of Phillips and Dabydeen, exploring imaginatively the past of slavery arguably enables a perspective with which to evaluate the present (and the continuing legacies of slavery) and envisage the future. For D'Aguiar, exploring the past of slavery is primarily an issue of memory and remembrance, and *The Longest Memory* can be seen as interrogating the space of the 'violent movement' between the two states. D'Aguiar contends with the problem of how to remember the past of slavery in a way that does not reproduce official remembrance; his text gathers a range of imagined responses to the slave past – some representing received remembrance, others portraying counter-remembrance. While he and Derrida are both interested in the modes of memory and remembering, therefore, D'Aguiar's concerns are with the literary, rather than philosophical, contexts for remembrance.

Derrida's distinction between *mnēmē* and *hypomnēsis* also has particular relevance with regard to the title of D'Aguiar's novel. While *The Longest Memory* is about the vagaries of memory and 'the longest memory' of slavery – that is, a collective recalling of this past – it does not pertain to be 'a memory' of this past, or a singular imagined slave narrative. We have already seen that memory, in Derrida's terms, is 'an unveiling (re-)producing a presence', whereas remembering or 're-memoration' is best thought of as the 'mere repetition of a monument'. Writing, he argues, 'does not answer the needs of memory, it aims to the side, does not reinforce the *mnēmē*, but only *hypomnēsis*'.[10] Those who write sell 'the signs and insignia of science: not memory itself (*mnēmē*), only monuments (*hypomnēmata*), inventories, archives, citations, copies, accounts, tales, lists, notes, duplicates, chronicles, genealogies, references. Not memory but memorials'; *hypomnēsis* rather than *mnēmē*.[11] Writers, therefore, offer written documents which may claim to record memories, but these are '*not memory, but memorials*'. Writing as memorialisation is helpful when thinking about how to remember or commemorate the past of slavery. D'Aguiar's novel, one could argue, is therefore mis-named; its story is not the memory of a moment of slavery but an imagined remembering of, or repeating monument to, the slave past.

In *Time Passages: Collective Memory and American Popular Culture* (1990), George Lipsitz writes that 'counter-memory' is

> a way of remembering and forgetting that starts with the local, the immediate, and the personal. Unlike historical narratives that begin with the totality of human existence

> ..., counter-memory starts with the particular and the
> specific and then builds outward toward a total story ...
> Counter-memory forces revision of existing histories by
> supplying new perspectives about the past.[12]

Of course, what Lipsitz refers to as 'counter-memory' would,
in Derridean parlance, be better called counter-remembrance;
it concerns remembering the past, rather than the moment of
memory. Counter-remembrance may be thought of as remembrance which runs contrary to the standard account of history, or
received remembrance. In the novel, the counter-remembrance
projected by Whitechapel, Chapel, Cook or Lydia suggests an
alternative to the version of received history, represented by
The Virginian, which claims that slaves are 'quite literally, not
like us. They do not feel what we feel'.[13] The plurality of narrative viewpoints by people normally excluded from the historical
archive of slavery (for example, illiterate slaves and women)
indicates D'Aguiar's imagined 'new perspectives of this past'.
The absence of living witnesses to slavery necessitates an imaginative approach to counter-remembrance of this past.

D'Aguiar's novel is a fabricated collection of memories
concerning a slave plantation in Virginia, and does not attempt
to sound 'historical' by replicating nineteenth-century linguistic
registers.[14] Unlike *Feeding the Ghosts*, it is not closely inspired
by historical records; instead, in this book, D'Aguiar turns
towards an imagined 'archive' of remembering. Elsewhere, he
has argued that

> Each generation inherits an anxiety about slavery, but the
> more problematic the present, the higher the anxiety and
> the more urgent their need to attend to the past. What the
> anxiety says is quite simply that the past is our only hope
> for getting through this present. So we return to memory,
> imagined and real, fanciful and mythical, psychological
> and genetic.[15]

D'Aguiar not only addresses the need of each generation of
black writers in Britain to return in their works to the past of
slavery in the face of troubled present times, but also suggests
that 'memory' is a viable entry point into that past and may

take different forms – ranging from 'imagined' memory of the kind experienced by Mintah, to 'genetic', or inherited, collective remembrance.[16] Again – although he uses 'memory' as a kind of all-encompassing term in his example above, he refers chiefly to remembering, or *hypomnēsis*, rather than *mnēmē*. While he can create imagined memories for his characters, 'real' *mnēmē* pertaining to the past of slavery is not available to him and, arguably, is involuntary triggered – not something to which we can, in D'Aguiar's words, 'return'. Psychological 'memory' in this context is probably most familiarly thought of as trauma – once again, direct trauma from slavery is unavailable to D'Aguiar. Instead, he explores the means of attempting to remember the past of slavery, but his particular anguish originates from the difficulty of how to remember this past without effecting retraumatisation.

The Longest Memory differs from the works we have so far looked at in its specific focus on American plantation slavery. It is a challenging text which defies any straightforward attempt at a plot summary – the story is revealed gradually and non-chronologically – or an easily drawn conclusion. These concerns notwithstanding, it is largely the story of Whitechapel, an old slave on the Whitechapel plantation in Virginia, with twelve daughters born of his first wife and a son born of his second – because of the practice of naming slaves after their owners, this child is also named Whitechapel. Not immediately known to the reader, Whitechapel Junior, or Chapel, is actually the biological son of the plantation overseer, Mr Sanders – or Sanders Senior – who raped Whitechapel's wife, known only as 'Cook'.[17] Following his mother's death, Chapel runs away and is brought back to the plantation by information provided by Whitechapel as to his whereabouts. Chapel is punished with two hundred lashes, dealt by his half-brother, Sanders Junior, which prove fatal. After we have learnt of Chapel's death, we discover that he has been conducting a relationship with the plantation owner's daughter, Lydia, and we realise their mutual love of literature and plans to run away together to the North – presumably the primary reason for his escape.

D'Aguiar's polyphonic novel acts as a reminder of the many voices of slavery. Chapters are narrated by Whitechapel, Chapel, Lydia, Cook, Whitechapel's great-granddaughter and Mr Whitechapel, the plantation owner, with diary extracts by Sanders Senior and editorials from *The Virginian* newspaper. The opening prologue of *The Longest Memory*, narrated by Whitechapel, is entitled 'Remembering', and the epilogue 'Forgetting' – suggesting the delicate balance required in negotiating the two positions. It is morally necessary for readers today to remember slavery but, in order to survive day-to-day living, it is also, for Whitechapel, necessary to forget. The last page suggests that only with death can forgetting come: 'I must sit down. No, lie down. Rest these eyes, tired of trying not to see. Rest this mouth. Stop tasting the sourness there. Forget. Memory is pain trying to resurrect itself' (*LM*, 138). The past, for Whitechapel, is too painful to remember: 'Don't make me remember. I forget as hard as I can' (*LM*, 2). In these passages, Whitechapel refers to both memory and remembering as being traumatic. *Mnēmē*, as Mintah also found, can be thought of as 'pain trying to resurrect itself', but the pain involved in acts of remembrance leads Whitechapel towards the attempt to forget. *Hypomnētic* remembrance is not painless, and can be dangerous, not only because of its potential for retraumatisation, but also because monuments of *hypomnēsis* may unproductively pave the way to forgetting. By 'fixing' remembrance in a monument, living memory is evicted, and stasis – the repeated production of the monument – begins, echoing Andreas Huyssen's claims that monuments may 'stand simply as figures of forgetting, their meaning and original purpose eroded by the passage of time'.[18] Like the diaphanous distinction between *mnēmē* and *hypomnēsis*, remembering and forgetting should not be viewed simply as opposites. Remembering slavery may be important, but it is not, D'Aguiar suggests, easily conducted; an act of remembrance can erode, rather than expose, its existence.

Yet, in *The Longest Memory*, remembering is shown to be vital, not just to the courtship of Lydia and Chapel, which I will come to in a moment, but also in relation to Sanders Junior, who kills Chapel because the recent past concerning his father and Cook was not known or remembered by all:

> You see, no one was to talk about it. And with time it sank to the bottom of everyone's minds. My father died, your father, Whitechapel's wife. It seemed all the people who were directly involved to whom it was important and painful were dead along with the shame, with the exception of Whitechapel. (LM, 34)

Living memory (or *mnēmē*) is only available until the last witness dies – D'Aguiar therefore suggests that there exists a compelling need to pass on the stories of the past as counter-remembrance (*hypomnēsis*). The above comment that 'no one was to talk about it. And with time it sank to the bottom of everyone's minds' can be seen as being applicable to Britain's past of slavery, though slavery does not, of course, like any other trauma, necessarily stay 'dead' because not discussed.

D'Aguiar indicates the need to write about, and hence confront, the past of slavery in order to avoid the fulfilment of Whitechapel's claim that 'The future is just more of the past waiting to happen' (LM, 1). With Whitechapel's death, the 'living memory' of slavery also dies, but the section narrated by one of his great-granddaughters suggests that the collective counter-remembrance of this story continues. As the great-granddaughter prepares Whitechapel's body for burial, she recalls the ways in which he was ostracised by the slave community following his son's death: 'What form of reasoning could have convinced Grandfather his son would be safe? I have wanted to ask him every day since, imagining I could defy the ban to speak to him' (LM, 128). As she recognises, this social exclusion meant Whitechapel became a ghost: 'He is a ghost we all see and ignore because he killed his only son' (LM, 126). D'Aguiar suggests that acts of remembering are perpetuated or passed on through stories told about the past of slavery. In including this chapter within the novel, he reveals the modes of survival of counter-remembrance. *Mnēmē*, or living memory, ends with the last survivor of an event, but can be superseded by collective counter-remembering or *hypomnēsis*. As I have already intimated, the challenge, of course, is how to ensure that these remembrances are truly acts of counter-remembrance. Acts of remembrance can be exploitative; D'Aguiar's apparent desire to create an imagined counter-remembrance of slavery stems from this problem of received remembering.

At this point, it may be helpful to explain how D'Aguiar's opposition to received remembering can be illustrated by *The Longest Memory*. In this novel, the issue of trying to understand the slave past is vital. As Mr Whitechapel tells Sanders Junior and his Deputy: 'My fury will not result in revenge. You must understand' (*LM*, 31), a notion reiterated by Whitechapel: 'It cannot now be undone, only understood' (*LM*, 137). Mr Whitechapel, talking to Sanders Junior about the death of Chapel, tells him that 'There is simply too much history between us all to justify what you did last night. Too much. What began as a single thread has, over the generations, woven itself into a prodigious carpet that cannot be unwoven' (*LM*, 33). Here, history does not mean a recorded chronicle of the past, but suggests an interwoven connection of lives; like the woven carpet, slavery has lead to the inextricable intermingling of black and white people. This notion is reaffirmed by Whitechapel's statement that 'I would need another life. No, several lives. Another hundred years. No, more, to unravel this knotted mess' (*LM*, 136–7). Whitechapel's 'knotted mess' is, however, arguably a more suitable analogy than that of a woven carpet. The latter suggests not only a coherent pattern, but also neatly minimises the violence typically engendered in the 'weaving' or sexual relationships between black and white people in the United States in the early to mid-nineteenth century. As the 'history' to which Mr Whitechapel refers was actually the rape of Cook by Sanders Senior, 'history', as suggested here, becomes a euphemism for rape and exploitation. This metaphor can be read in two ways; first, and more literally, D'Aguiar appears to propose that an accurate history of slavery in the United States must record acts of rape and exploitation. Secondly, and perhaps more provocatively, in the absence of such a 'truthful' examination of this past, history can be seen as metaphorically 'raping' black people through their continual exploitation and (mis)represen-tation. The unsuitability of the official remembrance of slavery (whether in Britain or the United States) indicates the necessity of counter-remembrance, as proposed by D'Aguiar.

The notion of 'too much' history is vital. In *Feeding the Ghosts* the narrator confides: 'All the knowledge has done is to burden me' (*FG*, 229) and, in *The Longest Memory*, D'Aguiar also raises the unsettling problem of what to do with the histor-ical legacies of slavery; how to respond to knowing 'too much' about this past. As history, for him, is exploiting, he probes the issue of how else to remember the past of slavery. In *The Longest Memory* D'Aguiar attempts to posit an imagined counter-remembrance of this past, which avoids adding to the received remembrance of slavery.

D'Aguiar, then, is uneasy about the way in which slavery is written about and remembered. A clear examination of Chapel's relationship with books in *The Longest Memory* will be helpful in further illustrating his concerns, as Chapel's troubled relation-ship with literature may be seen as indexing D'Aguiar's anxieties about writing. Literature may be, for D'Aguiar, the most appro-priate medium with which to explore the past of slavery but, given his reservations about received forms of narrative, it is perhaps unsurprising that he portrays Chapel as experiencing a troubled relationship with written texts. Alternately delighted and tormented by the books he discovers, Chapel's unease with literature is echoed by 'Plato's Pharmacy'. Derrida writes about Plato's portrayal of Socrates as being entranced by the *'pharmakon'*, which he defines as 'the drug: the medicine and/or poison'.[19] The *pharmakon* therefore pivots in its meanings, and its particular attraction as a 'drug' for Socrates is all too evident, as Derrida ventriloquises:

> you seem to have discovered a drug for getting me out ...
> A hungry animal can be driven by dangling a carrot or a
> bit of greenstuff in front of it; similarly if you proffer me
> speeches bound in books (*en biblios*) I don't doubt you can
> cart me all round Attica, and anywhere else you please.[20]

The changing meaning of *'pharmakon'* is also significant in suggesting the danger of his addiction, as Derrida explains: 'this "medicine," this philter, which acts as both remedy and poison, already introduces itself into the body of the discourse with all its ambivalence. This charm, this spellbinding virtue, this power of fascination, can be – alternately or simultaneously – beneficent or maleficent.'[21] Socrates finds the *pharmakon*/text to be both beneficial and damaging; spellbinding but dangerous.

We see a similar oscillation in Chapel's relationship with books – on the one hand, they entrance him, and it is through literature that he begins to love Lydia. Chapel, having watched Lydia reading on several occasions, is taught to read by her:

> she opened the rose

> She called a book and moved my finger over
> The words as she sang them: I heard a choir. (*LM*, 59)

As she reads to him, Chapel experiences a moment of epiphany, suggesting the significant powers of the *pharmakon*/text. Its powerful attraction is part of the danger of writing. In addition, the description of the *pharmakon* as a philtre – implying its potency as an aphrodisiac – is appropriate to Chapel's conflation of illicit sex with Lydia, and literature.

Yet, writing as a *pharmakon* also brings him sorrow through his self-awareness of the racially based limitations placed upon him during the time of slavery:

> I asked her to what use I could put reading and writing.
> She said I was the son of slaves and it was forbidden

> For a slave to know how to write and read.
> I said it was a mighty waste of a good head.

> She reminded me that I took a pledge
> Not to tell a soul. I watched her and felt grudge. (*LM*, 60)

Paradoxically, later Chapel is silenced the moment he finds, in learning to read and write, a voice. Not content with devouring the books from the library, his aspirations are to be a poet. His section of the novel is therefore the only non-prose part, mainly narrated in rhyming couplets, which corresponds to his love of classical verse. Alongside Chapel's resentment towards Lydia comes his chastisement from Mr Whitechapel, when he happens upon Chapel and Lydia reading together:

> He drew his belt, signalled me to bend and shout
>
> At my peril. As he lashed, he spoke. Do not,
> I repeat, do not let me ever catch you reading
>
> Again. (*LM*, 61)

Chapel immediately 'disguises' his voice; his couplets markedly contrast with the 'slave' register he adopts when chastised:

> Yes master.
> I am sorry
> ...
> I am ungrateful;
> A wretch,
> Who deserves
> To be a slave. (*LM*, 62)

For Chapel, as for Socrates, then, the *pharmakon* is the text – both remedy and poison. Books provide the means of temporary escape from, and transformation of, his reality as a slave; yet, to return to D'Aguiar's earlier metaphor, like the transient beauty of a rose, his literacy soon provokes the 'maleficent' reprimand from Mr Whitechapel. His chastisement acts as a stark reminder of Chapel's slave status and of the danger of the *pharmakon*. I outline Chapel's difficult relationship with literature in order to suggest that D'Aguiar makes a greater point about the problem of writing about the past of slavery – like Chapel, he is compelled to write, yet is aware of the problems of doing so. Writing about slavery is compelling – it is important to address this past and remember, but the danger is not only (as Dabydeen identifies) that one might read received books about slavery in a problematic way, but that writing may imitate received remembrance which has little to do with the experiences and voices of slaves. It is vital that Chapel chooses to write in a standard verse form and that he aspires to write poetry like his literary heroes Shakespeare and Milton; this kind of replication of received forms of expression or remembrance is precisely what

D'Aguiar wants to avoid in writing his texts. Instead, he aims for a counter-remembrance which does not aim to replicate official *hypomnēsis*, hence his novel comprises plural, conflicting narratives and non-chronological sections.

Derrida outlines another role of the *pharmakon* helpful to this reading of D'Aguiar's novel; namely, in the beautification of the dead:

> The *Republic* also calls the painter's colors *pharmaka* ... The magic of writing and painting is like a cosmetic concealing the dead under the appearance of the living. The *pharmakon* introduces and harbors death. It makes the corpse presentable, masks it, makes it up, perfumes it with its essence.[22]

The *pharmakon*/text here functions as a kind of mortician – preparing and masking the corpse for presentation. There are certain comparisons to be made with books that write about the dead, in the way that any novel returning to the site of slavery must. Arguably, the attempt to represent the past of slavery will always be unsavoury – its primary concern (as Dabydeen's Mungo found) is with making the dead palatable to an audience. When applied to *The Longest Memory*, this concern with the *pharmakon* can be seen as part of the larger issue of the ethics of representation – raising the question of how exactly to write about the 'dead' past of slavery. D'Aguiar's novel exposes his anxiety about his role as a writer engaging in the past of slavery: the problem of how to write about slavery without sanitising this deathly past. Derrida argues that all writing exists or 'plays' within the simulacrum: 'writing *has* no essence or value of its own, whether positive or negative. It plays within the simulacrum. It is in its type the mime of memory, of knowledge, of truth, etc.'[23] Writing, as remembering, can only mimic memory – it is, we recall, a monument to the moment of memory. D'Aguiar refuses, however, to produce a *pharmakon* of slavery by attempting to 'conceal the dead under the appearance of the living'. His text may be a kind of simulacrum of remembering, but it is self-consciously so, and it is categorically *not* a simulacrum of a slave narrative. Instead, D'Aguiar's disinterest in replicating slave registers, the different genres and conflicting narrative viewpoints, the non-chronological sections and newspaper editorials all suggest not only a 'hydra-headed' polyphony, but also a conscious desire to reveal the artificiality of the text.[24] In *The Longest Memory* D'Aguiar gathers together imaginary received and counter-remembrances of slavery, which are often conflicting and necessarily biased. The (fictional) newspaper editorials from *The Virginian* represent received remembrance, and the suitability of this version as the official, colonial, remembrance of the past of slavery is challenged by the accounts of those normally excluded from received history, and whose stories can therefore be thought of as counter-remembrance, such as those by Whitechapel or Lydia. D'Aguiar's use of form resists the beautifying confection of officious remembrance.

The other mode of *hypomnēsis* suggested by D'Aguiar's text is a counter-remembrance articulated on the body. Like literature, this form of *hypomnēsis* is also a problematic means of counter-remembrance due to the exclusivity of inherited remembrance. In 'Nietzsche, Genealogy, History' (1971), Michel Foucault provides us with a terminology for the physical inheritance of past experience. Writing about Friedrich Nietzsche's term *Herkunft* (defined by Foucault as 'stock or *descent*'), he notes that 'The body – and everything that touches it … is the domain of the *Herkunft*. The body manifests the stigmata of past experience'.[25] Furthermore, for Foucault, effects of experience are such that the body is 'a volume in perpetual disintegration'.[26] If we look at *The Longest Memory*, the human body as a disintegrating text is most convincingly suggested by the way in which Whitechapel's body 'wears' his experiences in the form of a transformed counter-remembrance: 'Memory rises to the skin then I can't be touched. I hurt all over, my bones ache, my teeth loosen in their gums, my nose bleeds' (*LM*, 2). D'Aguiar uses 'memory' rather than 'remembrance' here – I shall explain in a moment why his use of memory at this point is appropriate. As a slave, Whitechapel is largely excluded from the history of slavery and, unlike his literate son, is also denied the means of writing his own past or story. Without more usual means of narrating, his counter-remembrance is imprinted onto his body: 'The bags under my eyes are sacks of worries, witnesses of dreams, nightmares and sleep' (*LM*, 3). This alteration of terms from memory to remembrance requires explanation, as *mnēmē* is transformed into *hypomnēsis* on Whitechapel's body. Derrida's notion of memory as living is helpful here; 'Memory and truth cannot be separated. The movement of *alētheia* is a deployment of *mnēmē* through and through. A deployment of living memory'.[27] Derrida suggests that *alētheia*, or 'truth', can only exist in living memory; it cannot, therefore, be subsequently narrated. Due to Whitechapel's advanced age and years of witnessing events on the plantation, he can be seen as embodying living memory of slave experience. As Mr Whitechapel tells Sanders Junior, living memory is a vital tool in countering amnesia; to be precise, 'Whitechapel's longevity and living memory' prevent the 'whole mess' of slavery from being forgotten (*LM*, 35). However, in the process of memory being inscribed, or 'written', upon his body – as wrinkles, lines and bags – the living memory, or *mnēmē*, is transformed into *hypomnēsis*. To recall Derrida's terms, in writing, memory or *mnēmē* is 'supplanted by the archive, evicted by a sign of re-memoration or of com-memoration'. In *The Longest Memory*, counter-remembrance becomes articulated as a discourse of the body, and D'Aguiar conceives of the body as being in opposition to books. Counter-remembrance of slavery is passed on through the collective remembering of generations – physically captured on the body and passed on through genealogy (as I shall indicate in a moment, this has provocative implications in terms of Chapel's biological parentage). This kind of remembering cannot be accurately reproduced or commemorated in books, linking to the problematic nature of the *pharmakon* or written text and its apparent potential for enslavement. The articulation of remembrance on Whitechapel's body has to be counter-remembrance; it is not consciously transcribed (unlike received remembrance), and cannot imitate official forms of remembrance. Like moments of *mnēmē*, this kind of involuntary *hypomnēsis* cannot be affected or voluntarily created and, as an expression of a slave's experience, it is necessarily at odds with received remembrance. Whitechapel, like Mintah, tries to forget what he has witnessed, but trauma is inscribed onto his body – it 'rises to the surface' of his skin. Like Mintah's journal, Whitechapel's body can be seen as a repeating monument to slavery (and an exteriorisation of the mental trauma of this past) which bears witness to the 'longest memory' or, more accurately, the 'longest remembering' of slavery.

The role of Whitechapel's body as a receptacle of remembering is contrasted by D'Aguiar with that of Chapel. Whereas the former slave's body functions as a physical manifestation of counter-remembering, Chapel's body moves from being initially a site of pleasure to a symbol of the danger of not remembering the slave past. His character is connected to transgression – both in terms of his exploration of literature and his mapping of the white slave-owning woman's body. As Lydia reports: 'Our hands explore each other's bodies in the dark. We carry on with our talk, memorizing each other's lines throughout' (LM, 93). The interconnection between literature and illicit sex is convincingly illustrated with the pun on memorising lines of poetry alongside the lines of the body, although, unlike his father, Chapel of course does not have the crucial lines of experience – the wrinkles that carry *hypomnēsis*. As the ownership of a slave's body resided with the master, Chapel's pleasurable use of his body suggests that it was already the site of rebellion long before he ran away. The removal of his body, and hence his labour, is a further rebellion or 'grand theft' from the plantation (LM, 107). Once recaptured, his body then becomes a spectacle of punishment, as Sanders Junior adamantly states: 'There is no way this nigger is not going to face the usual punishment for his crime. An example must be set' (LM, 24). If Whitechapel's body can be seen as bearing witness to the traumatic remembrance of slavery, Chapel's body is, correspondingly, the site of not remembering this past. As Whitechapel comes to realise, Chapel seems to lack this remembered past (or, to borrow Nietzsche's earlier term, he is revealed by *Herkunft*) because he is not, biologically, his son:

> I tell you everything I know, everything I see and hear and work out for myself, as a slave ... It should suit a son of mine, born a total slave. But not with your blood. What I say can never be enough for you. (LM, 135)

Only Whitechapel sees Chapel's identity as being problematised by his biological parentage. In the eyes of Sanders Senior and Junior, Chapel is, without doubt, a 'total slave'. Rejecting any filial ties, Sanders Junior confesses to the deceased Whitechapel, 'I am sorry about your son. Not my brother. I knew him only as the son of a slave' (*LM*, 130). The punishment administered to him by Sanders Junior upon his recapture can be seen as an attempt at reminding him of his 'place' as a slave. The whip reaffirms the notion that Chapel's body is owned by another, as Whitechapel recalls: 'I literally saw the boy surrender to that whip, those blows, the whole rhythm of lash, pause, lash and tense, breathe, tense. I saw it in his eyes. They looked at me, at us all, for one last time' (*LM*, 5). Finally submitting to the rhythm of slavery, as Chapel looks at his father and the surrounding slaves, his eyes reflect his sudden identification with them. In suggesting that Chapel's death has been caused by his lack of remembrance of the slave past, D'Aguiar indicates the problem of genealogical remembrance or *hypomnēsis* on the body. It is not available to all, and not remembering, as Chapel found, can be endangering.

The Longest Memory can be seen as exploring the diaphanous distinction between *mnēmē* and *hypomnēsis*, as well as highlighting the *hypomnētic* roles of counter- and collective remembrance in challenging historical accounts of the past of slavery and ensuring the past is not forgotten. If memory, as *mnēmē*, cannot be uncoupled from trauma and is, in any case, directly inaccessible or 'veiled' from the present, *hypomnēsis* perhaps offers a way of remembering this past. *The Longest Memory* offers two means of possible *hypomnēsis*, though D'Aguiar articulates the problems associated with both forms of remembering. Unashamedly artificial, the imagined counter-remembering offered by *The Longest Memory* implies that the novel can perhaps also be thought of as a kind of monument to remembering the past of slavery. However, this monument is irrevocably flawed. The notion that literature can unproblematically perform a *hypomnētic* function has been challenged with reference to the *pharmakon*, which revealed it to be an inadequate and potentially dangerous form of remembrance. At the same time, as the remembrance of slavery through genealogy and the body is unavailable to many, this vehicle for *hypomnēsis* can be seen as an equally troubled method of remembrance. This impasse renders *The Longest Memory* a perplexing text. While indicating the necessity of remembering the past of slavery, it is unable to offer a means of attaining a state of *hypomnēsis* without either enslaving or exiling those that hope to remember.

Feeding the Ghosts

In 'The Last Essay About Slavery', D'Aguiar contests the notion that slavery is a spectral 'condition of non-being'; instead, he claims that this is a past which 'still lives' within him:

> *This is a fact of my heritage. So how can it be over? How can it ever be conferred to a condition of non-being when it lived, still lives, in me? And not just in me. In the names of streets, in the graveyards, in the literature of public and private libraries, in the very architecture that stores these books, my records (at least of when I was born) are reminders of this past, this present, this future, this slavery.*[28]

It is precisely the wraithlike nature of slavery that, paradoxically, enables it to be simultaneously over and yet continuous. The public reminders of the ghostly legacies of this past in Britain's architecture and written records also testify to slavery's continuation into the present and envisaged future. Slavery may well have ended, but its legacies, such as racism, exist still as spectral mementos of this past.

D'Aguiar's novel *Feeding the Ghosts* examines one such ghostly legacy, recounting the tale of the slave ship *Zong*. Alongside the ill slaves jettisoned by the crew, in D'Aguiar's version, Mintah, who is healthy, is thrown overboard on the orders not of the captain, but of his first mate James Kelsal.[29] The motivation behind this order is her apparent 'insubordination' in questioning the jettisoning of sick slaves; another reason for Kelsal's reaction is revealed later on in the novel, when we learn that he had previously been shipwrecked and nursed to health at an African mission by Mintah. She manages to climb up a trailing rope back on board, and hides in the store cupboard, assisted by the sympathetic cook's assistant, Simon. Following a failed insurrection, instigated by Mintah, she is recaptured. The second part of the book details the ensuing court case, after the insurers refused to pay for the jettisoned slaves. Mintah's account of the voyage, written aboard the ship, is submitted by Simon as evidence of the crew's barbarity in throwing overboard slaves less ill than suggested by the captain, but is soon dismissed as an improbable 'ghost story'. The final part of the novel, set in 1833, sees Mintah living in Kingston, Jamaica, watching an emancipation parade. Now an old woman, surrounded by wooden carvings she has made of the slaves that were drowned, she – deliberately or accidentally – sets fire to herself and her house.

Feeding the Ghosts is framed by a prologue and epilogue which attest to the continuation of legacies of the slave trade: 'There is only the fact of the *Zong* and its unending voyage and those deaths that cannot be undone. Where death has begun but remains unfinished because it recurs' (*FG*, 230). D'Aguiar seems to suggest in this passage both the repetitive nature of trauma and that, by ignoring this past, we perpetuate the legacy of deaths aboard the *Zong*: a reminder that 'The *Zong* is on the high seas. Men, women and children are thrown overboard by the captain and his crew. One of them is me. One of them is you' (*FG*, 229). This notion is reinforced if we look at the way in which D'Aguiar responds to the epigraphs he chooses to preface his novel. One is taken from Derek Walcott's poem 'The Sea is History':

> Where are your monuments, your battles, martyrs?
> Where is your tribal memory? Sirs,
> in that grey vault. The sea. The sea
> has locked them up. The sea is history.[30]

This historicisation of the ocean is transformed in D'Aguiar's prologue to a more obvious statement explicitly linking the

Atlantic ocean with slavery: 'The sea is slavery' (*FG*, 3). The substitution of the word 'history' for 'slavery' reiterates the importance for D'Aguiar of slavery to the history of the Caribbean, though slavery is also a central concern of Walcott's poem:

> Then there were the packed cries,
> the shit, the moaning:
> Exodus.
> Bone soldered by coral to bone,
> mosaics
> mantled by the benediction of the shark's shadow.[31]

Following on from Walcott, in his association of history with slavery D'Aguiar also suggests that history is a form of enslavement. By excluding the voices of slaves, Britain's received historical remembrance of this past ensures slaves retain a subaltern and ghostly presence, represented in the novel by Mintah. Similarly, in the prologue of *Feeding the Ghosts*, D'Aguiar writes: 'Over three days 131 such bodies, no, 132, are flung at this sea. Each lands with a sound that the sea absorbs and silences. Each opens a wound in the sea that heals over each body without the evidence of a scar' (*FG*, 3). If, as he indicates, the sea 'is history', then history is guilty of concealing the past of slavery – it is precisely this kind of historical amnesia concerning British slavery that D'Aguiar writes against, choosing instead to represent this past through literature. In addition to answering received history's inadequate representation of slavery, there is also a need to counter the silence surrounding this past by expressing its trauma – as Mintah finds, silence can be painful. D'Aguiar suggests the pressing demands of slavery to be communicated, though he struggles to do so.

D'Aguiar has also chosen as an epigraph the opening line from Edward Kamau Brathwaite's poem 'Calypso': 'The stone had skidded arc'd and bloomed into islands'.[32] While several critics have spent time exploring the relationship between D'Aguiar's novel and Walcott's poem, the link to Brathwaite's poem has been neglected.[33] This poem of Caribbean island life is one in which plantation slavery is central:

The islands roared into green plantations
ruled by silver sugar cane
sweat and profit
cutlass profit
islands ruled by sugar cane.[34]

We are ironically told by the narrator that 'it was a wonderful time | a profitable hospitable well-worth-your-time'.[35] In addition to the 'cutlass profit' gained from the plantations, the captains carry:

receipts for rices
letters spices wigs
opera glasses swaggering asses
debtors vices pigs.[36]

Although Brathwaite's poem refers to slavery, conspicuous in their absence from this list are the slaves.[37] D'Aguiar, in contrast, is explicit about the cargo carried by the *Zong*. Brathwaite's poem explores Caribbean history before and during the slave trade, and into the twentieth century, alluding to post-war migration away from the region. In so doing, he traces the legacies of slavery into the present: this is also something, as we have seen, with which D'Aguiar is fascinated. While his focus in *Feeding the Ghosts* is specifically on Britain's involvement in slavery, he shares with Brathwaite the desire to expose the continuation of slavery's legacies into the twentieth century; for D'Aguiar, these are particularly evident in the perpetual evolution of racism.

The literary legacies of Walcott and Brathwaite are not the only intertextual connections in the novel. The way in which the story of the *Zong* has been retold is crucial in D'Aguiar's response to this past; this was an exceptionally publicised story in a history largely concealed from the eyes of the general public. Although Marcus Wood has described the middle passage as 'initially the primary site for the depiction of the trauma of slavery in terms of the problems it posed for the art and collective consciences of European and American societies', outside the perimeters of abolitionist discourse, there have been few literary attempts to represent the middle passage.[38] It would seem that there is something morally necessary, but aesthetically troubling, about creating art from the past of slavery. The works of the authors I have looked at which, with some frequency, return to the site of the middle passage, engage with the inherent problems of this quandary.[39] If contemporary authors are compelled, through the continuation of legacies of slavery, to return to this past, then the particular story of the *Zong* has had an unprecedented importance. As I argued in Chapter 3, the case of the *Zong* has become infamous – a true 'ghost ship' of mythic proportions.[40] The way the story of this ship has been used is important, as the myth surrounding the *Zong* can be seen as having played a vital role in the mystification of Britain's involvement in the slave trade. Ian Baucom writes in his aptly titled essay 'Specters of the Atlantic' (2001) that the story of the *Zong*

> acquired a good deal of notoriety in the late eighteenth and early nineteenth centuries. The massacre, recorded in the trial documents, the pages of the *Morning Chronicle*, and in one letter after another in Granville Sharp's set of transatlantic correspondences, was soon recounted once again by John Newton, Ottobah Cuguano [*sic*], and Thomas Clarkson.[41]

The names of prominent abolitionists – Sharp, Newton, Cugoano and Clarkson – indicate that the *Zong* had a significant effect on the course of slavery abolition. As Hugh Thomas writes, the case proved to be of importance for the future treatment of slaves: 'Such events as the massacre on the *Zong* had occurred before, but now there was much more concern about the question of slavery and there were now methods whereby protest could be articulated'.[42]

The many ways in which the story of the *Zong* has been recounted and represented suggests that D'Aguiar's imaginative re-telling adds to a long history of narrating this past. The case of the *Zong* was uncommonly shocking, even by eighteenth-century standards. It is, however, important to remember that the court case was concerned with assessing whether or not the captain was correct to jettison his property – it was not a murder trial, as slaves were considered to be cargo. It was not until 1796 that a ruling was made that slaves could not be viewed purely as merchandise, when a Liverpool slave merchant claimed insurance money for 128 slaves who had starved to death on an unusually long voyage. The case of the *Zong* became notorious in the nineteenth century because of its significant role in the cause of abolition. However, as suggested in Chapter 1, the success of this campaign has meant that Britain's involvement in the slave trade is primarily remembered (if at all) along these lines. Building on D'Aguiar's claim that 'the sea … heals over each body without the evidence of a scar', is the notion that, by emphasising its prominence in slavery's abolition, the history of the *Zong* ironically may well have become complicit in concealing Britain's role in the early stages of the transatlantic slave trade. Such are the mechanics of official forms of remembrance – something D'Aguiar attempts to avoid. The suggestion that mythologising the *Zong* enables its legend to obscure the early years of slavery can be seen as adding to D'Aguiar's difficulty of responding to this past. The (mis)use of the history of slavery in order to construct a fallacy that Britain ended, rather than instigated, the slave trade indicates another way in which the history of this past has been enslaving. As we saw in *The Longest Memory*, it is this dissatisfaction with received remembrance that leads D'Aguiar towards forms of counter-remembrance: arguably represented in *Feeding the Ghosts* by Mintah's carving.

The inadequacy of historical accounts of Britain's slave trade means that, although he may have based his novel on factual events, D'Aguiar does not limit his story by conforming to historical accuracy. Though his tale is inspired by historical records, his alteration of the captain's name from Collingwood to Cunningham is illustrative of his refusal to adhere to historical facts. Instead, he problematises received history, not wishing to add to received remembrance, or a way of writing about this past which distorts Britain's involvement in the slave trade. *Feeding the Ghosts* raises the particular question of what is to be done with the historical legacy of the *Zong*; as the narrator reveals in the epilogue, 'All the knowledge has done is to burden me' (*FG*, 229).

In the case of the *Zong*, therefore, the moment the slaves were thrown overboard they entered into history – used as propaganda in the war against the slave trade. D'Aguiar vividly suggests, in his continuing aquatic metaphor, that history has manipulated the past of slavery. When history *does* look at this past, he seems to argue, it violates the slaves in so doing:

> Sea refuses to grant that body the quiet of a grave in the ground. Instead it rolls that body across its terrain, sends that body down into its depths, its stellar dark, swells the body to bursting point, tumbles it beyond the reach of horizons and gradually breaks fragments from that body with its nibbling, dissecting current. (*FG*, 4)

The drowned slaves are consigned to the murky depths and rendered anonymous and untraceable by the devouring current. Unlike the *Zong*'s captain, whose existence was recorded in court proceedings and newspapers, and so remains a visible and verifiable presence in historical accounts, details about the slaves are scant – the number of slaves jettisoned is the extent of the information.[43] At the same time, the case of the *Zong* was pored over by abolitionists and historians – indicating in the previous passage a lack of respect for, and even violation of, the dead. D'Aguiar implies that the slaves jettisoned from the *Zong* have been used by these people in a way that prevents them reaching a 'quiet grave'. As we shall see, he is all too aware that his novel adds to the catalogue of retellings of this past and, while raising the problem that history may abuse the past of slavery, the slaves of *Feeding the Ghosts* are equally unable to rest peacefully by the novel's close.

If the *Zong* had become a well-known case by the early nineteenth century, by the twentieth century it had largely been forgotten. British twentieth-century ignorance concerning slavery is central to D'Aguiar's poem 'At the Grave of the Unknown African' (1992), in which he writes of the graveyard vandal: '*If he knew not so much my name but what happened to Africans,* | *he'd maybe put in an hour or two collecting his Heinekens*'.[44] The continued lack of awareness of, and refusal to recognise, the significant part played by Britain in the trans-atlantic slave trade amounts to a vandalisation of the past of African slaves. In *Feeding the Ghosts* D'Aguiar's imaginative recounting of the slave ship *Zong* works against this ignorance of the slave trade – specifically raising the profile of the events of 1781. D'Aguiar's poem 'Feeding the Ghosts', taken from *Mama Dot* (1985), also alludes to this missing and ghostly past of Britain's history of slavery: 'A solid absence, picturing the lost gold | Of El Dorado; the ruins of Great Zimbabwe'.[45] This brief and overlooked poem's articulation of the existence of ancestral 'ghosts' that haunt the present not only suggests the continu-ation, or legacies, of the past but also indicates a much earlier link between Africa and Guyana – widely believed to be the location of El Dorado – than that forged by the transatlantic slave trade. D'Aguiar intimates that thinking about and remem-bering the past is important in terms of challenging received remembrance. In his novel *Feeding the Ghosts*, he suggests that Britain's silenced slave-trading past is also a, perhaps ghostly, 'solid absence' against which he writes. By returning to the subject of slavery, he rouses and reanimates the ghosts, which can be seen as functioning as a metaphor for a traumatic past. D'Aguiar seems unable to offer a suggestion of how to examine slavery without enacting a recurring and traumatic haunting of this past; this is also precisely Mintah's predicament.

The novel's title immediately foregrounds the importance of ghosts, as remnants of the past, to the present, and the demands of the past to be remembered. The rhetoric of slavery's ghostli-ness can provocatively be read alongside the work of Theodor Adorno. In an essay entitled 'Meditations on Metaphysics: After Auschwitz' (1966), Adorno claims that, for Holocaust trauma victims, 'Thinking men and artists have not infrequently described a sense of being not quite there, of not playing along, a feeling as if they were not themselves at all, but a kind of spectator'.[46] The etymological closeness of the words 'spectator' and 'spectre' also evokes an otherworldliness or sense of 'other-ness' within society. In addition, he asserts:

> it is not wrong to raise the ... question whether after Auschwitz you can go on living – especially whether one who has escaped by accident, one who by rights should have been killed, may go on living ... By way of atonement he will be plagued by dreams such as that he is no longer living at all, that he was sent to the ovens in 1944 and his whole existence since has been imaginary, an emanation of the insane wish of a man killed twenty years earlier.[47]

While Adorno's articulation of the repetition of traumatic experience in the survivors of Auschwitz finds an unlikely resonance in *Feeding the Ghosts*, its emphasis on the recurring and haunting nature of trauma is particularly relevant to D'Aguiar's novel. In *Feeding the Ghosts*, the ghosts of the title are not only the slaves jettisoned by Collingwood and his men, but also slaves like Mintah who 'by rights should have been killed', but escaped death and are forever 'plagued by dreams' – held by the force and horror of their memories. This approach to Mintah may well explain why, as each slave is thrown into the water, she hears her name, not theirs: 'I asked the sick their names and heard mine instead. "Mintah," they seemed to say. Death' (*FG*, 213). This equation of her name with death signals not only her guilt for having survived, but also her inability to forget the fate that should have befallen her. Furthermore, as the narrator of her book, Mintah is described with some frequency as a ghost – a kind of spectator/spectre – her book being 'penned by a ghost, it seems, since the hand has not been produced here today in this court to prove its authorship' (*FG*, 169). D'Aguiar seems to suggest through his spectral figures that he is haunted by the legacy of the *Zong*; the absence of slave testimonies or narratives about this past ensures its slaves remain, like Mintah, ghostly presences. The demands of the past to be remembered in the present compel D'Aguiar to retell this story. The intention is for the past to be 'laid to rest' when told (*FG*, 230) but the novel proves this to be an unrealistic aim: once again, the problems of remembering slavery come to preoccupy the novel.

Ultimately, Mintah's account is dismissed, outweighed by the authority and presence of the captain's slave ledger: 'Which are we to believe? The captain's account or the ghost-written musings [...?]' (*FG*, 170). Her status as 'ghost' renders her not quite real or believable – the court, unable to conceive that a slave could create this text, assumes it has been 'ghost-written'. Adorno has similarly observed:

> The only trouble with self-preservation is that we cannot help suspecting the life to which it attaches us of turning into something that makes us shudder: into a specter, a piece of the world of ghosts, which our working conscious-ness perceives to be nonexistent. The guilt of a life which purely as a fact will strangle other life ... – this guilt is irreconcilable with living.[48]

As Adorno argues, the survivors of an event that killed many others discover their lives transformed into something unreal; they find themselves at odds with reality – a 'piece of the world of ghosts'. Borrowing this phrase, we can see that Mintah, as a spectre, also resides in 'the world of ghosts' – an in-between place, caught between past and present, present and future: 'I live in the past and dream in the future. The present time is nothing to me ... The sea keeps me *between* my life. Time runs on the spot, neither backwards nor forwards' (*FG*, 199). We can see in this suspension of time the corresponding notion – seemingly paradoxical – that slavery has ended, yet its effects continue – a reminder of '*this past, this present, this future, this slavery*'.[49] Arguably, Mintah's guilt also becomes 'irreconcil-able with living', despite her various attempts to deal with it: 'Ghosts needed to be fed. She carved and wrote to assuage their hunger' (*FG*, 222). These attempts include, alongside carving, planting trees and, in Maryland, she helps slaves escape north to freedom: 'For every one thrown to the sea I multiplied by two in Maryland when I acted as guide' (*FG*, 209).

Initially, writing her book is also part of Mintah's attempt to ease the guilt of having survived the middle passage, unlike so many of her fellow slaves, and becomes a form of testimony. Optimistically, she views this outpouring as an initial 'release' from witnessing and a means of forgetting:

> How much can anyone remember? The head cannot retain
> everything ... Most of what I do is not worthy of being
> stored in my head. Or it hurts too much to store it. So I let
> it go. I wrap it up like the respected dead and release it with
> a prayer or fling it unceremoniously like the disrespected
> living into a sea of forgetting. Writing can contain the
> worst things. So I forget on paper. (FG, 196)

The pain of remembrance suggests the necessity of forgetting –
something Mintah attempts to achieve through writing. She is
desperate for memorial, or *hypomnēsis* rather than *mnēmē*. We
can see the way in which all her memories are linked to events
aboard the *Zong*; she is unable to uncouple remembering from
trauma. When her written account is dismissed as a 'ghost-book'
(FG, 173), it becomes an unheard testimony which leaves her
unable to forget or 'jettison' what she has seen. As Dori Laub
has argued: 'if one talks about the trauma without being truly
heard or truly listened to, the telling might itself be lived as a
return of the trauma – a *re-experiencing of the event itself*'.[50]

The dismissal of her account from court is just one way in
which Mintah is prevented from narrating trauma. On board
the *Zong*, with the realisation that she cannot end the deaths of
her fellow slaves, and following an unanswerable question from
a fellow slave, Mintah is silent:

> 'Why are they throwing us away?' Mintah was being
> shaken. The imploring voice echoed in her with the same
> question but a little louder with each repetition and echo.
> A hand was attempting to untie her gag. Mintah moved
> her head away and shook off the hand. (FG, 41)

Mintah's actions suggest that silence is a typical response to
horror of this magnitude; such a hitherto unthinkable act renders
her unable to phrase a response. There is a gap here between
what needs to be expressed and what can be comfortably accommodated within the existing limits of language. Phrases which
exceed or transcend those limits necessitate the development of
new modes of expression. Because her previous attempt at writing
her story was discounted, rather than narrating her story again

in conventional ways she instead carves figures of those that were jettisoned: 'There are 131 of them. A veritable army' (*FG*, 209). Thinking back to Derrida's terminology, for Mintah, the figures act as a kind of *hypomnēsis*, or form of remembering the past of the *Zong* which is a repeated monument to the memory of this past, rather than the flashes of memory that characterise *mnēmē*. Mintah wants to forget the traumatic past, but her *hypomnētic* carvings, which act as a counter-remembrance to the received remembrance (or history) of the *Zong*, fail to arrest the pain. This may be because the repeating monument to the past enacted by *hypomnēsis* implies a sense of fixity. For Mintah, the trauma is frozen and endlessly repeating, held in motion by the memorialising form of *hypomnēsis*.

In his book on Charles Baudelaire and Paul Celan, *Remnants of Song* (2000), Ulrich Baer notes that

> Celan's unenviable and devastating task is to testify to a horrendous reality that no one ever wanted to experience or know. He had to find an adequate frame for representing what seems to exceed all known forms of comprehension and representation. Celan's historical burden of writing poetry after Auschwitz consists in the unprecedented challenge of representing an event *as* unrepresentable and *as* irremediably other.[51]

The above passage recognises the paradox of trying to represent an event which is 'unrepresentable'. Baer indicates that an inability to express what has been witnessed necessitates going beyond normal 'frame[s] for representing'. Part of Celan's approach therefore is to represent the event honestly as unrepresentable or 'other', pushing beyond the limits of representation. In a similar way, Mintah's sculptures also testify to the unrepresentable nature of the past of slavery, and are indisputably 'other' – illustrated by the unease with which they are regarded: 'The shape of each piece is pulled from the sea of my mind and has been shaped by water, with water's contours. People say they see a figure of some kind, man, woman or child reaching up out of the depths' (*FG*, 208–9). The uncertain reception of her carvings suggests that, as Mintah is going beyond limits of representation, her figures are difficult, ambivalent and complicated. As she notes, while people may appreciate what she does, they 'cannot keep such a shape in their homes. Such shapes do not quench a thirst. They unsettle a stomach. Fill the eyes with unease' (FG, 209).

Mintah is compelled, then, to try to carve the past, yet unable to exorcise the ghosts of the *Zong*. Carving is, for her, arguably a new medium for remembering what has happened, though this medium of carving is both successful and unsuccessful. The creation of her ghostly army permits Mintah to remember the events of the *Zong*, but ultimately fails in allowing her to forget. Instead, her carvings may be seen as enacting a retraumatisation; this seems to be the crux of her pain – she is unable successfully to transform *mnēmē* into memorial, or *hypomnēsis* by the acts of writing or carving. D'Aguiar's conviction that this is not, ultimately, a successful means of forgetting the trauma of the *Zong* is illustrated by the pessimistic ending of his story. As Mintah dies, she watches the 'dancing, leaping figures' as they are animated by the flames (FG, 226). The reanimated ghosts of the *Zong* suggest that the trauma of this past overcomes her attempts to 'forget'. The veil between memory and remembering is permeable; the trauma of *mnēmē* pervades her *hypomnētic* figures. Instead of permitting Mintah to forget the past of the *Zong*, her carving arguably feeds the trauma.

D'Aguiar's reasons for re-examining the past of slavery are clearly enunciated in 'The Last Essay About Slavery':

> I have tried to imagine without success a last poem, a last play, a last novel, a last song, about slavery: final acts of creativity in this given area that would somehow disqualify any future need to return to it in these forms. The will to write such a thing is itself a call for slavery to be confined to the past once and for all; for slavery's relevance to present anxieties about race to come to an end; to kill slavery off.[52]

D'Aguiar's imaginings are 'without success' – we may also think of the way in which Mintah is ultimately unsuccessful with her carvings. Both succeed in creating representations of slavery but are unsuccessful in carving or narrating definitive versions of this past, or 'exorcising' the ghosts of slavery, which would negate the need for successive renderings. *Feeding the Ghosts* cannot, therefore, be the last novel about slavery. The past of slavery requires, it would seem, continual revisiting in order to acknowledge its ghosts and so lay the past 'to rest'. D'Aguiar suggests that slavery cannot be 'over' while the spectre of this past lives on in him and other descendants of slaves and the force of its legacies continues to be keenly felt in current racial 'anxieties'. *Feeding the Ghosts* sees D'Aguiar attempt to engage with the spectres of the *Zong* in order to free its slaves, and him, from being defined by these historical legacies.

It remains, however, a contradictory novel which suggests that the past is 'laid to rest when told', yet acknowledges that the *Zong* is also 'on the high seas'. While D'Aguiar's novel raises the difficulty of what to do with the historical legacies of slavery, his ghosts feed not on history but on 'stories of themselves'. *Feeding the Ghosts* indicates the moral necessity of retelling the past of the *Zong* and, in the aftermath of history's failure, attempts to instigate new idioms in which to phrase the trauma of slavery. However, D'Aguiar is conscious that his text is caught in an impossible position: there is a need to express the painful past of slavery, but returning to this past arguably 'feeds' the ghosts and reawakens the trauma of slavery, illustrating the impossibility of 'forget[ting] on paper'. D'Aguiar seems painfully aware in this text that he cannot formulate a solution to this problem, when each *hypomnētic* retelling can also retraumatise. Slavery is not dead – partly because of ongoing racism, but also because remembering, though important, sees the perpetuity of the traumatic past in the repeating monument of *hypomnēsis*.

Bloodlines

> We joke about associating only with other couples … with an equal distribution of the two races between them. Our children. We stop. The words hang in the air. Two stars that

have dropped from the heavens to a point just above our heads and as bright as two suns. Our children. Yes. Our children. Several of them. (*LM*, 103)

Like the narrator figures of *Feeding the Ghosts* and Phillips's *Crossing the River*, the life of the central narrator of D'Aguiar's long poem *Bloodlines* has spanned centuries. In the course of the poem, he traces the evolving relationship between his parents. Faith, a black slave, was raped by Christy, a white son of a slave owner, but they gradually fall in love. The couple run away together, and are aided in their plan to move north by Tom and Stella, two ex-slaves in the Underground Railroad movement. Unfortunately, as Tom steers their boat across the river, they are ambushed and Christy and Faith become separated from Tom, whom they presume dead. They eventually find refuge in a barn, but a gang of white men happen upon them and, after repeatedly raping Faith and humiliating Christy, sell Faith back into slavery to Mr and Mrs Mason. Christy, captured for indenture, becomes a boxer. Faith dies shortly after giving birth to the narrator and Christy, unable to locate either Faith or his son, is buried a pauper. Meanwhile, Tom and Stella survive the years of the American Civil War and enjoy the book's only happiness. The narrator records his journeys to find his father and laments his inability to die, rendered animate by the continuing legacies of slavery.[53] Alongside the central narrator, chapters are also narrated by Faith, Christy, Mrs Mason, Stella and Tom. D'Aguiar deploys the ottava rima form throughout his text, a style appropriate to the nineteenth-century beginning of the tale.[54] As we shall see, his choice of form also has important implications for his concerns about the apparent 'vogue' of texts written about slavery.

Bloodlines is a much more problematic and morally challenging text than *The Longest Memory* or *Feeding the Ghosts*, particularly in relation to the portrayal of female roles. The above passage from *The Longest Memory* introduces the notion of the transformative power of sexual relations between black and white people: a premise devastatingly challenged in *Bloodlines*. Published six years after *The Longest Memory*, *Bloodlines* is characterised by a pervading cynicism regarding the potential of relationships between mixed-race couples. The optimism of the above passage, which shapes the stellar imagery of Chapel and Lydia's future hopes for children, is contrasted in *Bloodlines* with the mixed-race narrator; he is orphaned and alone, fruit-lessly searching for a place to 'belong' and subject to continuing racism and violence.

Towards the start of the poem, there occurs the rape at knifepoint of Faith – a moment critics have argued is not handled by D'Aguiar with due sensitivity or gravitas. D'Aguiar suggests in this passage the level of trauma experienced by Faith as she 'shut[s] her mind down' to her violation.[55] She does not, it is clear, yield willingly to Christy's assault. Yet, as Christy rapes Faith, D'Aguiar writes of 'her hate burning to love' (*B*, 6). In the midst of being raped, therefore, he suggests that Faith falls in love with her rapist. This seemingly untroubled shift of Christy's category from rapist to suitor arguably perpetu-ates the myth that women essentially enjoy the masochism of violent relationships.[56] Following Faith's later rape by the group of men, it is significant that Christy dreams of her 'in an orgy instead of her trials' (*B*, 73). The worrying suggestion that Faith 'chooses' Christy precisely because he uses force to subdue her seems to correlate to the notion of 'hate burning to love' and a deliberate confusion by D'Aguiar of the two states.

If the act of rape is not already dealt with in a contentious enough way in *Bloodlines*, it is further problematised by race; it is, specifically, the rape of a black woman by a white man. This adds a further, difficult, layer to the already problematic aspect of rape. The racist view of the apparently 'harlot' or sexualised nature of black women has been explored by a range of scholars. Frances Berry and John W. Blassingame, for example, have written that, until the last decades of the twentieth century, white men were 'fascinated' by black people. They note that black women featured in the majority of their fantasies, claiming that: 'The image of the black woman was that she was the most sensuous, exotic, mysterious, and voluptuous female in the world – the embodiment of passion'.[57] The apparent abundance of passion and subsequent dehumanisation of black women has also been examined by bell hooks, who writes in *Ain't I a Woman* (1981):

> The designation of all black women as sexually depraved, immoral, and loose had its roots in the slave system. White women and men justified the sexual exploitation of enslaved black women by arguing that they were the initiators of sexual relationships with men. From such thinking emerged the stereotype of black women as sexual savages, and in sexist terms a sexual savage, a non-human, an animal cannot be raped.[58]

In *Bloodlines*, the sexual exploitation of black women is shown to be institutionalised within the slave trade; as Christy's father tells him, Christy was expected to 'fuck as many as [he] liked' (*B*, 17). It is perhaps logical, then, that he at first apparently shares this view of Faith, imaging her to be initiating the 'relationship':

> when she locked eyes with his
> all he could think of was that she was there
> because she wanted him, making easy this
> thing he was always doing with a slave;
> the polar opposite of her motive. (*B*, 4)

Christy assumes that Faith, in hooks's terminology, is a 'sexual savage', although his advances are clearly unwanted. D'Aguiar's handling of the scene differs markedly from Phillips's sensitivity in writing about women or Dabydeen's bawdy, eighteenth-century tone. D'Aguiar seems in this text to write carelessly about his female protagonist and, as is to be expected, some reviewers have picked up on the book's apparent misogyny. Bruce King, for example, has argued in his review of *Bloodlines* that, 'We are to believe that a black slave raped at knifepoint by a lusty young white man will fall in love with him and he with her. It seems more like de Sade than the romantic tale that follows.'[59]

From the start of this text, then, important issues are raised, via D'Aguiar's portrayal of the rape of a slave, surrounding the ethics of writing about slavery; the most pressing being whether his writing ought to be categorised as exposing the 'pornography of Empire' or an act of de Sadean titillation, as King implies.[60] The narrator reports that, as a child, he was informed by other children:

> My mother was raped and I came along,
> that was the truth and I should confess
> and drop this love-match, love-child crap. (*B*, 50)

In this passage, D'Aguiar not only challenges the concept of 'truth' but illustrates that he is aware how the relationship could be viewed, arguably forestalling his reader's thoughts to desist in calling rape, 'love'.

In addition to D'Aguiar's concern raised in *The Longest Memory* that history may be seen to have been metaphorically 'raping' black people in its ongoing exploitation, I would suggest that his portrayal of rape in *Bloodlines* serves an important and threefold metaphorical purpose. First, D'Aguiar indicates through his long-suffering female protagonist – the aptly-named Faith – the inherent misogyny of slavery in nineteenth-century America. As mentioned, black women were persistently abused by white men on the plantations. *The Longest Memory*, of course, also included the violent rape of Cook by Sanders Senior, although, and less controversially, she failed to love Sanders Senior despite, or because of, her violation.

Secondly, hooks provides another possible explanation for D'Aguiar's handling of the scene in her comments about the 'devaluation of black womanhood'. She cites this devaluation as stemming from the aforementioned sexual exploitation of black women during the slave trade and suggests that it has been perpetuated into the twentieth century.[61] Referring to Susan Brownmiller's book about rape, *Against Our Will* (1975), hooks notes:

> While Brownmiller successfully impresses upon readers the fact that white men brutally assaulted black women during slavery, she minimizes the impact that oppression has had on all black women in America by placing it solely in the limited historical context of an 'institutionalized crime' during slavery.[62]

By confining the rape of, and violence towards, black women by white men to the past of slavery, hooks argues, writers like Brownmiller fail to address the continuing problem of violence against black women in the twentieth century. Like the continued devaluation of black womanhood, D'Aguiar's novel offers intimations of the things that extend from the time of slavery into the present day – such as racism, violence and sexism – the act of rape of black women by white men conflating all three elements. D'Aguiar's narrator is unable to die until the conditions of slavery end, reiterating D'Aguiar's argument in 'The Last Essay About Slavery' that there cannot be a last text about this past because slavery is not yet dead: '*This is a fact of my heritage. So how can it be over? How can it ever be conferred to a condition of non-being when it lived, still lives, in me?*'[63] The *Zong* is perpetually on the high seas: it is, D'Aguiar reminds us, 'the present, not slavery, [that] refuses to allow slavery to go away'.[64]

Bloodlines therefore sees a renewal of D'Aguiar's concerns with the continuation of slavery and, in particular, with the ongoing problem of racism in the twenty-first century as a legacy of this past. The narrator's existence captures this concern:

> So history greeted me. I am condemned
> to live an eternity, unless all the conditions
> that brought me into being somehow mend:
> I mean Slavery and all its ramifications
> marching unfazed into the new millennium.
> Everything that I see in countries and nations
> tells me this is true: Slavery may be buried,
> but it's not dead, its offspring, Racism, still breeds. (*B*, 150)

The conditions that brought him into being were slavery, of course, but also rape. Christy's rape of Faith therefore stands as a metaphor for slavery and an example of what D'Aguiar suggests was the prevailing engagement between black women and white men during the first half of the nineteenth century. Therefore, he can be seen as intimating that the violation of women has been perpetuated, like racism, into the twenty-first century:

[it] will always be the white man's way:

to take what he wants when he wants,
how he wants. (B, 5)

By indicating the continuation of this abuse via his 'timeless' narrator, D'Aguiar arguably avoids hooks's charges of confining this kind of violation of women to the historical past.

Thirdly, I want to suggest that much of the motivation behind the violent opening section of *Bloodlines* is derived from D'Aguiar's attempt to persuade his reader of the difficult nature of relationships between black and white people during the time of slavery and the ultimate failure of interracial love as a vehicle for transforming the legacies of this past. In *The Longest Memory*, the love and hopes of Chapel and Lydia for children as a method of healing the damage done by slavery were thwarted by Chapel's death. In *Bloodlines*, the relationship between black and white people is also ended through separation and provided with finality by the death of Faith. *Feeding the Ghosts* is no more optimistic about mixed-race relationships, suggesting that D'Aguiar feels these relations were difficult to sustain at this time. While D'Aguiar is interested in mixed-race relationships, or those that defied the norms of nineteenth-century America and Britain, he makes clear that these relationships are especially problematic and, in *Bloodlines*, uses rape as a way of suggesting their perpetually uneven footing. He implies the relationship between Faith and Christy is compromised by a fundamental inequality, inviting us to 'Picture those two if you can, arm-in-arm, | master and slave' (B, 18). Faith and Christy are unable to move beyond their historically prescribed roles in this text. The unsteadiness of their relationship is in direct comparison to that of Tom and Stella, who are portrayed as starting off on a more even level; both are ex-slaves and able to find happiness, despite hardship.

As the opening quotation from *The Longest Memory* suggested, utopian hopes for a harmonious future for black and white people are dashed in *Bloodlines*. D'Aguiar declines to provide a happy ending; the bond of love between Christy and Faith is unconvincing and, following their separation, Faith soon dies. D'Aguiar therefore refuses to transcend a relationship that began in violence; in so doing, he does not minimise the psychological damage enacted by rape, or make it (returning to the earlier metaphor), like slavery, something easily dismissed. This text deliberately withholds a happy conclusion. Faith pays the ultimate price for Christy's rape: it effectively kills her with the birth of her son, suggesting that, although the central characters make an attempt to forge a relationship together, ultimately, the violence and trauma cannot be transcended. We can see in this failure to provide positive conclusions to his texts the fatally dispiriting way in which D'Aguiar indicates the futility of attempts to transcend slavery via the idealisation of mixed-race relationships. He offers no hope that this is, or even should be, possible; we should not forget or minimise the damage perpetrated at the start of *Bloodlines*. The poem can be seen as being caught in a state of anguished postmemory, where postmemories of this past and the continuing legacies of slavery forestall a transformative counter-remembrance.

From such sordid beginnings, D'Aguiar proposes, only sadness can follow. The narrator is correspondingly troubled and leads a wandering, unfulfilled life. The narrator's itinerant sense of unbelonging can be attributed to his mixed-race origins, like Chapel in *The Longest Memory*, who also struggled with his role as a slave – unknowingly because of his dual-racial parentage. D'Aguiar's narrator in *Bloodlines* is a fitting emblem of the legacies of slavery because he embodies both 'sides' of slavery and is accordingly riddled with contradictions. He has inherited the plantation from Mrs Mason, yet, as born of a slave, feels he should work upon it. It seems that slavery has left difficult legacies:

> my immortal side bends all the rules
> that keep my slave side well versed
> in hard work, hoping to kill the soul
> by wrecking the body. I am master,
> slave and overseer bringing disaster. (*B*, 152)

The narrator's troubled position as 'master, slave and overseer' indicates the complexity of the legacies of slavery. D'Aguiar is questioning the simplicity and idealism of the transformative potential of love. From rapist to knight, slaver to abolitionist, later actions cannot, he implies in this text, be permitted to overshadow earlier ones. He also does not pander to the vogue for an affirmative story about slaves overcoming their oppression.

If *Bloodlines* is troubled at times by its author's use of rape as a means of suggesting the misogynistic and continuing nature of slavery, it is, at others, made increasingly difficult by its ottava rima form which requires a patient reading. The writing is so unwieldy in places that, towards the beginning, the narrator apologises for his anachronistic vocabulary: 'He would never have said hood, but wait, | he doesn't have to rhyme every other line' (*B*, 17). Although D'Aguiar's poetic talent has been questioned in reviews of this book, at the time of the publication of *Bloodlines* he was already an accomplished poet. I would suggest the awkward form of *Bloodlines* perhaps contains an implication for the way in which form and content can interact in examining the past of slavery. D'Aguiar has chosen a particularly difficult form in which to narrate his story – one which distorts and fragments his sentences and words. Depictions of rape, violence, racism and the poem's obtuse verse and faltering rhythm arguably collude to prevent an easy or enjoyable exploration of the past of slavery; D'Aguiar ensures, in his ungainly text, that it is not going to be comfortable for the reader.

A poetic form is also particularly helpful in allowing his narrator to move through centuries in a more condensed way and, after writing about the involvement of Britain and America in the slave trade in his novels *Feeding the Ghosts* and *The Longest Memory*, turning to poetry arguably further dissociates D'Aguiar from the simulacrum of the slave narrative. In my reading of *The Longest Memory*, I explored Chapel's oscillating relationship with literature; equally bewitched and ensnared by the text, which indicated D'Aguiar's own reservations about prose forms. *The Longest Memory* is adamantly not slave narrative simulacrum, and his choice of poetry for the genre of *Bloodlines* could be seen as an even more radical attempt to avoid the dangers of the slave narrative *pharmakon*.[65] The number of novels about slavery published in the last decade of the twentieth century reinforces Dabydeen's claims about 'peasantry' being 'in vogue'.[66] Writing about slavery in prose is a popular choice and, by writing in poetry, D'Aguiar therefore seeks to avoid the normalising propensity of prose or its ability to 'conceal the dead under the appearance of the living'.[67] The contemporary, self-conscious references of *Bloodlines* also ensure it does not attempt to imitate nineteenth-century poetry by slaves like Phillis Wheatley. As in *The Longest Memory*, in this text D'Aguiar does not attempt to offer a beautifying or transformative work about slavery.

The title of *Bloodlines* alludes not only to the act of writing, but also to the genealogical lines in the veins: the idea of collective memory, or remembering, carried by blood. I have already suggested that, in *The Longest Memory*, Chapel lacked a collective memory of slavery, which was soon brutally inscribed onto his body by the whip. D'Aguiar also explores this notion of inherited collective memory in *Bloodlines*:

> I am the lives of slaves. Every move
> I make obeys orders from an overseer.
> First he is a whip, a kick, a rude
> mouth, a fist and spit, yes sir, no sir. (*B*, 150)

Although not a slave, the narrator carries the 'lives of slaves' within him – indicating the perpetuation of experiences of slavery for those born of slaves; however, once again, to be accurate, this is remembering rather than memory. As mentioned earlier in this chapter, Hirsch's concept of 'postmemory' has a peculiar relevance to *Bloodlines*.[68] Postmemory is defined by Hirsch as the relationship between the experiences of those who have undergone trauma and their children, who 'remember' their parents' experiences as stories or images, though these 'are so powerful, so monumental, as to constitute memories in their own right'.[69] Ultimately, for Hirsch,

> Postmemory characterizes the experience of those who grow up dominated by narratives that preceded their birth, whose own belated stories are displaced by the stories of their previous generation, shaped by traumatic events that they can neither understand nor re-create.[70]

The life of D'Aguiar's narrator is dominated by the narratives of Christy and Faith and, as a result, he devotes his time to tracing his father and trying to come to terms with his ancestry as well as the larger past of slavery. The narrator appears to struggle with postmemories of slavery; this is also the challenge facing D'Aguiar. He is aware, in his disinterest in simulating slave narratives or poetry, that the past of slavery cannot be 're-created'. Rather than trying to do this, therefore, D'Aguiar attempts to understand slavery through *new* creation. However, the paralysing narratives of postmemories of slavery dominate *Bloodlines*, as D'Aguiar and his narrator are unable to relinquish the fundamentally incomprehensible and unsettling memories of this past.

Bloodlines, therefore, seems caught in what can be viewed as a sombre condition of postmemorialisation. Although conceptualised in relation to the children of Holocaust survivors, Hirsch is adamant that she does not wish 'to restrict the notion of postmemory to the remembrance of the Holocaust', and is clear in suggesting the wider scope offered by the term.[71] As Hirsch adds,

> It is a question of conceiving oneself as multiply interconnected with others of the same, of previous, and of subsequent generations, of the same and of other – proximate or distant – cultures and subcultures. It is a question, more specifically, of an *ethical* relation to the oppressed or persecuted other for which postmemory can serve as a model.[72]

Unlike *hypomnēsis* via the body, postmemory, as conceptualised by Hirsch, is not restricted to actual descendants of trauma, and therefore may be expanded to include the 'ethical' and multiple connections between twentieth- or twenty-first-century readers and the past of slavery. The postmemorialisation of slavery can be seen as a central concern in the work of Phillips, Dabydeen and D'Aguiar who grapple with the earlier 'narratives' and 'traumatic events' pertaining to the slave trade. Furthermore, Hirsch argues in 'Past Lives: Postmemories in Exile' (1996):

> Holocaust postmemory ... attempts to bridge more than just a temporal divide. The children of exiled survivors, although they have not themselves lived through the trauma of banishment and the destruction of home, remain always marginal or exiled, always in the diaspora. 'Home' is always elsewhere.[73]

This is, of course, the same conclusion D'Aguiar had reached in his poem entitled 'Home' in *British Subjects* (1993), in which he writes of the airport official 'telling [him] with Surrey loam caked | on the tongue, home is always elsewhere'.[74] The extended scope for postmemory suggested by Hirsch therefore has interesting implications for black writers within Britain who often struggle with the notion of 'home'.

As Hirsch continues, the 'condition of exile from the space of identity, this diasporic experience, is characteristic of postmemory'.[75] The exiled diasporic experience is arguably reflected within *Bloodlines* in the articulation of the narrator's condition of unbelonging:

> I have no one left on earth to speak of.
>
> ...
>
>   Only a gap big enough
> for me to spend the rest of my days
> between earth and sky, my cloudy head
> humming full of Slavery's towering dead. (B, 146)

We can see in this extract the difficulty of examining the past of slavery for D'Aguiar, with no living witnesses – just a 'gap' between present and past. Slavery cannot be ignored, however; the narrator's head 'hums' with the dead of this past. Hirsch signals that possibly the most taxing issue for those exploring art forms of postmemorialisation concerns the appropriateness of identification:

> The challenge for the postmemorial artist is precisely to find the balance that allows the spectator to enter the image, to imagine the disaster, but that disallows an overappropriative identification that makes the distances disappear, creating too available, too easy an access to this particular past.[76]

D'Aguiar employs various distancing effects in *Bloodlines* – rape, deliberately uncomfortable poetry, twenty-first-century references – many of the most perturbing features of the poem can be seen as methods of distancing the reader from the slave past. The twentieth-century references enhance the text's eschewal of slave narrative simulacrum, and the conspiring violent content and troublesome form further alienate the reader and point to D'Aguiar's intention to avoid an 'overappropriative' identification with this past. In refusing to provide an uplifting story about the potential of love between races as a means of overcoming slavery, *Bloodlines* does not offer an easy access into this past.

It is also important to be sensitive to the distance between the lives of slaves and the writers under examination in this book, in their admitted twentieth-century positions of privilege. As Dabydeen has commented in an interview: 'we have to be honest with the subject and say, "Really, it happened a long time ago to our ancestors"'.[77] British slavery was abolished more than one-hundred and fifty years ago, yet it is not a too-distant past, and is one which, for these three authors, requires continual revisiting and exploration. Hirsch identifies a similar desire to work through trauma in the work of Dominick LaCapra:

> He has distinguished between two memorial positions: acting out (melancholia) and working though (mourning). Acting out is based on tragic identification and the constitution of one's self as a surrogate victim. It is based on overidentification and repetition. Keeping the wounds open, it results in retraumatization. Working through, on the other hand, involves self-reflexivity, a determination of responsibility, some amount of distance.[78]

Melancholia, where the writer enacts a 'tragic identification' is the kind of position Dabydeen hopes to avoid in his call for honesty in writing about slavery. This concern is clearly shared by D'Aguiar and the notion of retraumatisation is also particularly crucial to his work. Characters like Mintah and Whitechapel are unable to escape retraumatisation by their memories of slavery. For the narrator of *Bloodlines*, retraumatisation occurs through the postmemory of his parents' past. The distancing effects utilised in *Bloodlines* create a necessary gap that indicates D'Aguiar's desire to elucidate the difference between his texts, which examine the slave past in an imaginative way, and slave testimony. This space enables him, in Hirsch's words, to attempt to 'work through' the past of slavery. As Dabydeen reminds us, we have perhaps moved on from this past. However, while the material position of black people in Britain and the United States has undoubtedly improved since the demise of the slave trade, we are left with lingering racial prejudices from this period which have not been entirely banished and continue to affect trauma. It would seem that D'Aguiar is unable to offer hope for this particular legacy of slavery ending. His poem attempts to work through the past of slavery, but he finds this is not entirely possible – there can, he affirms, be no final text yet about this past because slavery has not truly ended.

Such pessimism would seem to be contrary to received readings of texts about slavery that seek to identify messages of hope from the struggles of protagonists. In her essay '"Where Else to Row, but Backward?" Addressing Caribbean Futures through Re-visions of the Past' (1999), Paula Burnett examines six Caribbean texts which explore the past of slavery, including *Feeding The Ghosts*. She claims that the texts 'produc[e] art which devises subtle strategies of resistance and survival – and celebration'.[79] Given D'Aguiar's apparent pessimism regarding the continuation of damaging legacies of slavery, I would question the extent to which his texts can be seen as a celebratory. Towards the end of *Feeding the Ghosts*, he provides the reader with a glimpse into the kind of happy ending he *could* have written, as Mintah describes the effects of Simon's embrace:

> I am unburdened … The lives of the men, women and children in the hold must benefit from this lightness, this bodiless in my body. Their chains must fall from them and they too must float like me … With such lightness I can take the wheel of the *Zong* and swing it until the *Zong* turns around. (*FG*, 202)

This passage indicates her belief in the beneficial potential of her relationship with Simon – she imagines it possible to turn the slave ship around, and thus halt slavery. Yet this moment quickly passes and the novel's close rejects a reunion between Mintah and Simon: 'She awoke from dozing by her front door. Shade had succeeded sun. Simon had not come' (*FG*, 222). The *Zong* has not, D'Aguiar suggests, been anchored once and for all by the transformative relations between black and white people. In each of the texts I have examined in this chapter, relationships between mixed-race couples have ended in the death of one of the lovers. Borrowing Walcott's trope of the rower, however, Burnett suggests in her essay that D'Aguiar, along with Dabydeen, V. S. Naipaul, Wilson Harris, Derek Walcott and Pauline Melville, shares 'an awareness that while history still hurts, the timeless zone of myth, if imaginatively read, can provide landmarks to progress, so that the mytheopoeic artist may row the people's boat steadily towards a more benign future'.[80] To continue the watery trope, in my reading the *Zong* does not progress to a benign future, but drifts on the high seas in a perpetual mode of postmemorial anguish. This is a state reinforced by *The Longest Memory* and *Bloodlines*; the narrator of the latter text finally realises the impossibility of healing through love the rift between races generated by slavery, and wonders whether he is prepared 'to die and leave Slavery and feel no regret | that white remains white and black is black' (*B*, 159). *The Longest Memory*, *Feeding the Ghosts* and *Bloodlines* may all present the possibility, however fleeting, of a 'benign future' enabled by a transforming relationship between black and white men and women, but ultimately reject the utopian potential of such meetings.

D'Aguiar, perhaps even more pessimistically, indicates in *Bloodlines* that the trauma of slavery can never be entirely 'worked through'. Slavery, he repeatedly tells us, persists in the racism of today. Even twenty-first-century generations of black and white people cannot alter the conditions of how they first met historically, in the violent period of slavery. There is no way of forgetting or assuaging the fact of slavery. As with Christy's unconvincing metamorphosis from rapist to knight, later actions (abolition, twentieth-century migration, anti-discriminatory laws and so on) cannot neatly appease the past.

In this respect, *Bloodlines* challenges the notion proposed by some critics that a text about slavery should be one that offers hope of a positive message of overcoming oppression, or that a traumatic past can be interpreted into a hopeful fictional text. This notion of transformation arguably runs contrary to the work of D'Aguiar, who finds the notion that the past of slavery can be translated in such a way difficult or even impossible to achieve. Instead, *Bloodlines* arguably offers a form of postmemorial mourning described by Hirsch, who writes that

> postmemory seeks connection. It creates where it cannot recover. It imagines where it cannot recall. It mourns a loss that cannot be repaired. And, because even the act of mourning is secondary, the lost object can never be incorporated and mourning can never be overcome.[81]

D'Aguiar's works also suggest that in the absence of living witnesses or accounts from slaves, and where history fails him in returning to the past of slavery, he is compelled creatively to imagine this past. But he, too, cannot overcome mourning; just as his narrator's head 'hum[s] full of Slavery's towering dead', D'Aguiar reveals in his texts that slavery cannot be forgotten or easily dismissed. *Bloodlines*, like *The Longest Memory* and *Feeding the Ghosts*, is not a hopeful text. It can perhaps be read as a 'postmemorial' to slavery, though it does not mark the demise of the trade, but rather mourns the continuation of aspects of this past in the racism of the twenty-first century.

Critical overview and conclusion

The first part of this chapter offers an overview of some of the most significant trends in the critical approaches to the work of Caryl Phillips, David Dabydeen and Fred D'Aguiar. No author has as yet written a book-length study on all three writers, but Lars Eckstein's *Re-Membering the Black Atlantic* (2006) examines Phillips's *Cambridge* and Dabydeen's *A Harlot's Progress* alongside African American author Toni Morrison's novel *Beloved*. Eckstein's work seeks to demonstrate how each text performs a distinct form of remembrance, 'both in the sense of their poetic association with older manifestations of memory in text, image or sound, and in their political positioning against social discourses of memory and their ideologies'.[1] In his reading of *Cambridge*, Eckstein traces Phillips's conspicuous use of historical sources; in so doing, he builds upon earlier work undertaken by such scholars as Evelyn O'Callaghan. In her important essay, 'Historical Fiction and Fictional History: Caryl Phillips's *Cambridge*' (1993), O'Callaghan reads the novel as being inherently self-conscious: 'to a great extent, it is a pastiche of other narratives and … calls attention to its intertextuality'.[2] In exploring the novel's status as a pastiche, O'Callaghan examines relevant passages from *Cambridge* alongside their original sources, such as *The Interesting Narrative of the Life of Olaudah Equiano, or Gustavus Vassa the African* (1789) and Mrs Carmichael's *Domestic Manners and Social Condition of the White, Coloured, and Negro Population of the West Indies* (1833). For O'Callaghan, this intertextuality encourages the reader to recognise, 'with Foucault, that there are no "true" discourses only more or less powerful ones'.[3] Eckstein adopts a similarly detailed approach to *Cambridge* – also examining extracts from the novel alongside passages from these, and other, original sources – and contends that 'the montage of bits of earlier texts ... constitutes the backbone of the novel'.[4] In his concluding remarks about the novel, Eckstein writes that Phillips 'manages to stage not only the confrontation between two fictional characters, but also that between two entire literary and ideological discourses'.[5] Here, Eckstein seems to mean the juxtaposition of an account based on slave testimonies and an account based on colonial travel writing, but I would suggest that he over-exaggerates the oppositional nature of the two discourses. As I have argued in preceding chapters, slave narratives are not straightforward documents and cannot be so easily opposed to the writing produced by white eighteenth- or nineteenth-century authors. We might think, perhaps, of Ignatius Sancho's long and creative friendship with Laurence Sterne, or the considerable role played by white editors in shaping slave testimonies.[6] These narratives were much more closely involved in the literary and ideological discourses of eighteenth-century Britain than Eckstein suggests.

Critical studies published on Phillips's work include Bénédicte Ledent's *Caryl Phillips* (2002), which provides an excellent introduction to his earlier works, focusing particularly on *Higher Ground*, *Cambridge*, *Crossing the River* and *The Nature of Blood*. Ledent's book is less thematically based than the present study, as her main interest lies in recognising the diversity of Phillips's works and inspirations, though she observes that 'displacement plays an all-pervasive role in his writing'.[7] Helen Thomas's *Caryl Phillips* (2006) is a slim volume also interested in displacement, specifically examining the representation of diaspora in selected works. Thomas takes an unusual approach, utilising the astronomical concept of 'black holes' to visualise 'black diasporan historiography, corresponding not only to the ways in which time and space are transformed into a form of "memory" across the diaspora, but representing the erasure of the black psyche from dominant modes of Western discourse, and corresponding models of progression and development'.[8]

While there have been a number of critical essays published on Phillips's works in recent years, many critics seek to locate his texts either within a rhetoric of blame – by which I mean the demand for retribution from white people for their part in the slave trade – or as being concerned solely with 'black history'. In his review of Phillips's novel *A Distant Shore*, for example, Jonathan Heawood suggests that Phillips's work has 'never achieved the popular recognition it deserves', asking, 'Is this because he writes, unremittingly, about being black?'[9] However, rather than writing solely about 'being black', as Heawood asserts, I have demonstrated that Phillips – through his use of contrapuntal voices and 'creolised' narratives – invariably writes about slavery as a past shared by both black *and* white people. In *The Atlantic Sound*, for example, he discusses the racism he endured as a black child growing up in the north of England, but also explores the feeling of unbelonging experienced by a white judge in the United States, ostracised by his own community for his support of black voting rights. Phillips, similarly, has condemned those critics who implied Barry Unsworth's novel about the slave trade, *Sacred Hunger* (1992), was an inappropriate book for a white author to write: 'Those morons ... who suggest he "culturally appropriated" material should ask themselves serious questions about who was involved in slavery. It wasn't just black people, it was white people too. It was *their* history'.[10] In illustrating that slavery has connected people of differing races, Phillips's works signal his political dissent from racially exclusionary and forgetful works of British history that ignore the centrality of slavery. His is not an unguarded optimism for the future, but a tentative hope for a meeting point between people of different races, based on the understanding of a differing, though shared, past.

There have been two collections of essays on David Dabydeen, that appeared a decade apart: Kevin Grant's edited collection *The Art of David Dabydeen* (1997), which also includes some important early interviews with the author, and Lynne Macedo and Kampta Karran's essay collection *No Land, No Mother* (2007). Grant points out in his introduction that 'Dabydeen is unique in being the only poet to employ Guyanese rural English in his work', and the ensuing essays in this collection, with few exceptions, engage with Dabydeen's use of creole in his poetry and novels – most frequently under scrutiny are *Slave Song* and *Coolie Odyssey*.[11] In particular, essays by Mark McWatt, Sarah Lawson Welsh and Benita Parry are all deeply interested in the way in which Dabydeen uses creole language, tracing its potential for decolonisation or subversion.

The focus for Macedo and Karran's book is on the multiple 'points of connection' in Dabydeen's work, specifically exploring how he – and by extension his writing – may be thought of as being located between multiple identifications.[12] Essays range from an examination of masculinity and creole in *Slave Song* to his intertextual relationship with V. S. Naipaul, and three are concerned with his long poem 'Turner'. Aleid Fokkema reads the poem in relation to the Caribbean epic genre, while Tobias Döring investigates terror and the sublime, and Heike H. Härting explores, among other topics, how 'Turner' 'invites us to examine the ways in which the conceptual links between metaphor and transfiguration constitute practices of representation embedded in imperialism'.[13] The many different approaches to Dabydeen's work suggest its richness and complexity, and also illustrate what Bruce King has called in a review of *A Harlot's Progress* 'Dabydeen's puckish sense of humour'.[14] Dabydeen's works are undeniably playful and shifting, suggesting a reluctance to create straightforward, or 'easy', narratives about slavery or Indian indenture. Borrowing from the historical archive, yet mistrustful of this past, his characters are creatively reinvented and irreverently distorted – illustrative of his refusal to both trust, and invest further credibility in, this archive. For Dabydeen, of greater importance than received history are the fragments of the past about which no accounts have been written. These remnants are deemed of little worth – yet, by inclusion in his works, each neglected fragment potentially becomes, in Mungo's words, 'a splendidly adorned memorial and grave'.[15] In the absence of either suitable memorials to, or – often – gravestones for, the Indian indentured labourer and African slave, Dabydeen's works may be seen as providing a point from which to commence remembering this past.

Elizabeth Kowaleski Wallace is attentive to this resistance towards simple narration in her essay 'Telling Untold Stories: Philippa Gregory's *A Respectable Trade* and David Dabydeen's *A Harlot's Progress*' (2000). Referring to the brand of 'TT' on Mungo, which means contradictory things in Dabydeen's text, Kowaleski Wallace writes: 'What is marked *on* Mungo in a confusing and contradictory way is also what is written about Mungo *for* the reader. Dabydeen takes us full circle back to the theme of writing the unwritten, telling the untold: never simply the opposite of the "untold," the told always consists of multiple possibilities or interpretations.'[16] Just as the reader of *A Harlot's Progress* is privy to Mungo's narrative 'inventiveness', readers of Dabydeen's novel *Disappearance* ultimately are invited to 'Pick whatever version of whatever story you prefer'.[17] In his position as both writer and critic,[18] Dabydeen is acutely aware of his readers, and of the varying interpretations of his work. This level of self-consciousness has led McWatt to argue, with particular attention to *The Intended* and *Disappearance*, that 'Prominently identifiable among the fictional techniques of this author are some of the classical counter-discursive strategies associated with post-colonial theory.'[19] For McWatt, one of the most important counter-discursive strategies is Dabydeen's 'writing back' to Empire, via his works' intertextuality. To this end, McWatt carefully traces the relationship between *The Intended* and Joseph Conrad's *Heart of Darkness* and, more complicatedly, between *Disappearance*, Conrad's novella, and Wilson Harris's *The Secret Ladder*. As McWatt puts it, the richness of literary allusions and metafictionality of Dabydeen's novels amounts to 'marvellous literary gamesmanship'.[20]

To date, there has been no book-length study on D'Aguiar, but his novels especially have generated some interesting scholarship. Gail Low's essay 'The Memory of Slavery in Fred D'Aguiar's *Feeding the Ghosts*' (1999) explores not only D'Aguiar's representation of the memory of slavery, but also his decision to gender as female the escaped slave who climbs back aboard the slave ship *Zong*. As Low observes:

> The choice of Mintah is ... bold in so far as it allows
> D'Aguiar to use the issue of Mintah's reproductive ability
> – her body – to explore slavery's severance of kinship
> and familial affiliations. The maternal is privileged in the
> choice of Mintah as the novel's central protagonist; the
> responsibility for the safety of her fellow slaves in the hold
> is marked as a nurturing burden. This makes her failure all
> the more poignant.[21]

Yet, as Low explains, despite his use of the maternal metaphor,
D'Aguiar 'avoids the temptation to reify motherhood and child-
bearing into some kind of mystical feminine status' by ensuring
other metaphors are also used to suggest 'familial belonging and
affiliations'.[22] Low carefully situates this novel within a wider
body of literature on slavery in 'black British' and Caribbean
writing. She argues that the British late twentieth-century
literary interest in slavery means not only that 'a more integra-
tive approach to history' is necessary, but also that these works
reflect 'the wider black diasporic concerns and the formative role
of African-American intellectual and cultural life in the production of a black aesthetics'.[23]

Transatlantic connections are also important in Dave
Gunning's essay 'Reading the "Uncle Tom" Character in Fred
D'Aguiar's *The Longest Memory*' (2005). Gunning persuasively
argues that in this novel D'Aguiar commences the deconstruc-
tion of fixed representations of anti-racist positions: 'Through an
understanding of the mechanics of a society reliant on slavery,
D'Aguiar can outline responses to a discourse around race that
do not rely on the reproduction of stereotypes that work to stifle
the reality of human variety'.[24] In this essay, which explores *The
Longest Memory* alongside Richard Wright's *Native Son*, and
within the context of the legacies of Harriet Beecher Stowe's
Uncle Tom's Cabin, Gunning argues that D'Aguiar rejects not
only the binary opposition, or 'complete discrepancy between
the utterances of master and slave', but also 'the thinking
that reduces the subject positions available to black people to
that of the compliant Uncle Tom or nihilist Bigger Thomas.'[25]

In response to those readers tempted to view Whitechapel uncritically as a kind of 'Uncle Tom' character, and borrowing Homi Bhabha's notion of 'sly civility', Gunning proposes that D'Aguiar 'does not create an Uncle Tom figure entirely without autonomy but rather one whose negotiation of the terms of his oppression takes place through the initial adoption of an accommodating pose.'[26]

Both Low and Gunning avoid making dubious claims about the possibility of drawing a redemptive conclusion from D'Aguiar's works. In my approach to his novels and poetry, I have also aimed to challenge readings that propose a redemptive or celebratory style in his writing about slavery. This is the kind of reading that sees *Bloodlines*, in David Vincent's words, 'strid[ing] through predicament and woe to place love as the only motivational energy for salvation'.[27] The vocabulary chosen by Vincent is telling, indicating his belief that slavery can be 'saved' by romantic relationships between black and white people – a notion ultimately revealed as flawed by the text. Andrew Biswell has similarly suggested that *Bloodlines*, 'displaying a flash of optimism, is prepared to imagine a distant future in which different races will live peacefully together'.[28] D'Aguiar's works, however, seem to propose a much gloomier outlook on the transformative potential of writing about slavery. He offers a sombre view of this past and its continuing legacies and arguably cannot yet foresee the future possibility of different races living 'peacefully together', as Biswell envisages. Instead, his works suggest a much bleaker picture of British and American societies, as unalterably based on racial distinctions that ensure the perpetuation of 'insider-outsider' positions.[29] Such racial polarisation, he contends, feeds the continuity of what he refers to as '*this past, this present, this future, this slavery*', or slavery's longevity.[30] If not completely paralysed by postmemories of slavery, *The Longest Memory*, *Feeding the Ghosts* and *Bloodlines* occupy certainly limited positions – unable to cease traumatic repetitions, they are caught in an ongoing condition of postmemorial anguish which does not allow D'Aguiar entirely to work through the past of slavery. His belief in the unending existence of this past suggests that, for D'Aguiar, this is not something that *can* be worked through. This tendency towards despair ensures that his outlook on slavery is very different from the positions of Phillips and Dabydeen, as my conclusion shall now consider.

In her recent book *Trauma Fiction* (2004), Anne Whitehead remarks upon the propensity of novels by contemporary authors that figure ghosts:

> In contemporary fiction, there has been an abundance of novels which explore haunted histories. The traces of unresolved past events, or the ghosts of those who died too suddenly and violently to be properly mourned, possess those who are seeking to get on with the task of living.[31]

As we can see, Whitehead suggests such hauntings do not occur indiscriminately, but arise specifically from the failure of past events to be resolved, or the living to adequately mourn 'those who died too suddenly and violently'. Such ghosts 'possess' those that are alive, and prevent them from continuing 'the task of living'. Whitehead's comments about the persistence of unresolved pasts to trouble the living may be seen to be particularly resonant with regard to the works of Phillips, Dabydeen and D'Aguiar that I have explored in this book.

Although each author has different motivations for, and concerns with, returning to the past of slavery, the trope of ghostly visitations runs through their works. Such hauntings assume different forms, including manifestations of survivor guilt for those who lived through the middle passage, the guilt of parents that have betrayed their children, and the faint presence of slaves in historical records. As these examples testify, ghosts are figured in different ways, but for Phillips, Dabydeen and D'Aguiar, such spectres collectively signify their shared conviction that legacies of slavery extend into the twenty-first century, as well as indicating that this past continues to haunt their imaginations.

I began this study by noting that slavery has been overlooked in received historical narratives of Britain. The texts I have explored by the above writers attempt to redress this silence surrounding slavery and illustrate why it is important that this past is not forgotten. I have shown that each author has had a particular struggle with creating literature about slavery. We saw that Phillips's works are involved with exploring the pasts absent from received British history; the exclusion of certain groups from this narrative, he proposes, is an instrumental factor in twentieth- and twenty-first-century problems with British national identity. Overlooking the slave past arguably enables the persistent coalition of race and nationality which leaves some Britons feeling excluded or marginalised. On the other hand, Dabydeen appears troubled by the act of representing slavery or Indian indenture without exploiting this past or inadvertently contributing to the ongoing 'pornography of Empire'.[32] While deeply concerned with matters of audience and the reception of works on slavery, he paradoxically produces poems and novels complicit in the very process of representation that he problematises. In contrast, the works of D'Aguiar may be thought of as being held in a static position of postmemorial repetition: there is a need to remember the slave trade, but D'Aguiar wrestles with the means of doing so without re-traumatising or adding to the wealth of received remembrance. Remembering the past of slavery is essential, D'Aguiar suggests, but equally crucial is the *means* of remembrance.

The varying problems and difficulties experienced by all three writers imply that there can be no straightforward representation or remembrance of slavery. Each insists, however, that awareness of this past is vital; D'Aguiar perhaps takes this notion farthest, in suggesting how the legacy of slavery is perpetuated in the present. Such a belief makes trauma impossible to work through, hence perhaps his greater pessimism than the others. Phillips is arguably most optimistic; his works cautiously motioning the possibility of a future meeting, and understanding, between black and white people, though any utopianism is tempered by realism: this meeting is yet to be staged. Dabydeen seems poised in a contradictory position somewhere between the two states outlined above: sceptical about the consumption of works on slavery, his frustration at being unable to control how such texts are received may be seen as leading to a deliberately belligerent approach to issues of audience.

I have suggested that one of the problems often cited by writers like Marcus Wood and James Walvin in thinking about the past of slavery is its lack of appropriate monuments. Alan Rice has also argued that, 'Without memorial sites, memorialization is problematic, especially in such a contested terrain as Britain's slave past'.[33] Perhaps like ghosts, monuments signify something that no longer exists; located in the present, they nevertheless face backwards to the past. Caught between past and present, therefore, they are arguably equally spectral; as Robert Musil has claimed, 'there is nothing in this world as invisible as a monument'.[34] Memorials cannot provide access to the past but signify the prior existence of something which no longer exists, yet needs to be remembered. In a similar way, without physical monuments to the past of slavery, the works of Phillips, Dabydeen and D'Aguiar indicate a possible means of beginning to remember this past which, its ghosts imply, also clamours to be heard. However, unlike monuments, which are necessarily backwards-looking, their texts, while exploring the past of slavery, simultaneously point towards the future. The problems, though, lie in how to create this future. Phillips's liminal diasporan characters search for, but do not find, a place in which they might be accommodated. Using neglected fragments, Dabydeen, we saw, was attempting to create a future possibility, or space, for imagining the African slave or Indian indentured labourer, but he remains confounded by form. D'Aguiar's postmemorial anguish would seem to undermine the likelihood of ever reaching a benevolent morrow. This is not, then, a simple, utopian shared belief in the prospect of creating through literature a just future.

One of the things this book has tried to achieve is to demonstrate that Phillips, Dabydeen and D'Aguiar adopt very different approaches to imagining the past of slavery. Yet, each is acutely aware of the compelling need to explore this past, frustrated as they are by the enduring racial anxieties that threaten twenty-first-century claims to Britain's multiculturalism. It seems it is necessary to look at slavery in order that they might trace the root of these antagonisms. These authors may initially seem, to borrow Whitehead's terminology, 'possessed' by the ghosts of slavery – returning to this past repeatedly in their works. Yet, all are doing so precisely in order that they might confront the challenge of 'get[ting] on with the task of living'. This may be a difficult process, but for Phillips, Dabydeen and D'Aguiar, it is absolutely necessary. Ultimately, their works suggest that it is only by comprehending, and accepting, the past of slavery that the present might be understood, and the future can begin to be envisaged.

Notes

Chapter 1

1 Fred D'Aguiar, *Bloodlines* (London: Chatto & Windus, 2000), p. 150.

2 Peter Fryer, *Staying Power: The History of Black People in Britain* (London and Sterling, VA: Pluto Press, 1984), p. 372. Although Fryer describes these passengers as 'Jamaicans', James Procter is careful to point out that the *Empire Windrush* carried settlers from a number of Caribbean islands and not just from Jamaica. See the introduction to James Procter (ed.), *Writing Black Britain 1948–1998: An Interdisciplinary Anthology* (Manchester and New York: Manchester University Press, 2000), pp. 1–12 (p. 3). For this reason, I shall refer to them as Caribbean migrants.

3 Procter, *Writing*, p. 3.

4 This Act became effective the following year. I cite the mid-sixteenth century as the beginning of Britain's involvement in the slave trade in accordance with Eric Williams, who writes of the voyage of John Hawkins in 1562 as being the 'first English slave-trading expedition'. See Williams, *Capitalism and Slavery* (London: André Deutsch, 1964), p. 30. See also Hugh Thomas, *The Slave Trade: The History of the Atlantic Slave Trade, 1441–1870* (London, Basingstoke and Oxford: Papermac, 1998), p. 12.

5 James Walvin, *Making the Black Atlantic: Britain and the African Diaspora* (London and New York: Cassell, 2000), pp. x–xi.

6 Salman Rushdie, *The Satanic Verses* (London: Viking, 1988), p. 343.

7 Alex Tyrrell and James Walvin, 'Whose History Is It? Memorialising Britain's Involvement in Slavery', in Paul A. Pickering and Alex Tyrrell (eds), *Contested Sites: Commemoration, Memorial and Postwar Politics in Nineteenth-Century Britain* (Aldershot, Burlington, VT: Ashgate, 2004), pp. 147–69 (p. 151).

8   *Ibid.*, p. 148.

9   Fryer, *Staying Power*, pp. 1, 12. Bernardine Evaristo's novel-in-verse *The Emperor's Babe* (2001) playfully explores the black presence in Roman Britain.

10 Jan Marsh, 'The Black Presence in British Art 1800–1900: Introduction and Overview', in Jan Marsh (ed.), *Black Victorians: Black People in British Art 1800–1900* (Aldershot and Burlington, VT: Lund Humphries, 2005), pp. 12–22 (p. 14).

11 As Fryer writes in *Staying Power*, from the early 1950s there had also been a growing number of immigrants from India and Pakistan; by the end of 1958, these numbered around 55,000 (p. 372).

12 See Bob Carter, Clive Harris and Shirley Joshi, 'The 1951–1955 Conservative Government and the Racialization of Black Immigration', in Kwesi Owusu (ed.), *Black British Culture and Society: A Text Reader* (London and New York: Routledge, 2000), pp. 21–36 (p. 24).

13 Robin Cohen, *Frontiers of Identity: The British and the Others* (London and New York: Longman, 1994), p. 49.

14 Paul Gilroy, *'There Ain't No Black in the Union Jack': The Cultural Politics of Race and Nation* (London and New York: Routledge, 2000), p. 86.

15 J. Enoch Powell, *Freedom and Reality*, ed. by John Wood (Kingswood, Surrey: Eliot Right Way Books, 1969), p. 282.

16 *Ibid.*, p. 17.

17 *Ibid.*, p. 281.

18 In addition to *Making the Black Atlantic*, James Walvin's many books on slavery include *England, Slaves and Freedom, 1776–1838* (Basingstoke and London: Macmillan, 1986) and *Black Ivory: A History of British Slavery* (London: HarperCollins, 1992). See also Ron Ramdin, *Reimaging Britain: Five Hundred Years of Black and Asian History* (London and Sterling, VA: Pluto Press, 1999). Other notable exceptions to this claim appear in the Select bibliography.

19 Sam Durrant, *Postcolonial Narrative and the Work of Mourning: J. M. Coetzee, Wilson Harris, and Toni Morrison* (Albany: State University of New York Press, 2004), p. 1.

20 Preface to Caryl Phillips (ed.), *Extravagant Strangers: A Literature of Belonging* (London: Faber & Faber, 1998 [1997]), pp. xiii–xvi (p. xiii).

21 Trevor Phillips, 'Deal with Difference through integration says Trevor Phillips', The Commission for Racial Equality, 24 September

2004, http://www.cre.gov.uk [accessed 2 June 2006] (para. 15 of 16).
Part of the issue here is that 'multiculturalism' means different
things to different people. See the introduction to Tariq Modood
and Pnina Werbner (eds), *The Politics of Multiculturalism in the
New Europe: Racism, Identity and Community* (London and New
York: Zed Books, 1997), pp. 1–25.

22   Mark Stein, *Black British Literature: Novels of Transformation*
(Columbus, OH: Ohio State University Press, 2004), pp. 9–18.

23   *Ibid.*, p. xv.

24   Paul Gilroy, *Small Acts: Thoughts on the Politics of Black Cultures*
(London and New York: Serpent's Tail, 1993), p. 20.

25   Stuart Hall has also warned against minimising the 'immense
diversity and differentiation of the historical and cultural experience of black subjects'; see Hall, 'New Ethnicities' (1989), in David
Morley and Kuan-Hsing Chen (eds), *Stuart Hall: Critical Dialogues
in Cultural Studies* (London and New York: Routledge, 1996), pp.
441–9 (p. 443). See also Gideon Ben-Tovin, 'Why "Positive Action"
is "Politically Correct"' in Modood and Werbner, *Politics of Multiculturalism*, pp. 209–22 (p. 218).

26   Richard Dyer, *White* (London and New York: Routledge, 1999), p. 1.
See also Alistair Bonnett, 'Constructions of Whiteness in European
and American Anti-Racism', in Pnina Werbner and Tariq Modood
(eds), *Debating Cultural Hybridity: Multi-Cultural Identities and
the Politics of Anti-Racism* (London and Atlantic Highlands, NJ:
Zed Books, 1997), pp. 173–92 and Gary Taylor, *Buying Whiteness:
Race, Culture, and Identity from Columbus to Hip Hop* (New York
and Basingstoke: Palgrave, 2005).

27   Alison Donnell (ed.), *Companion to Contemporary Black British
Culture* (London and New York: Routledge, 2002), p. xiii.

28   *Ibid.*

29   Fred D'Aguiar, 'Against Black British Literature', in Maggie Butcher
(ed.), *Tibisiri: Caribbean Writers and Critics* (Sydney; Mundelstrup, Denmark and Coventry: Dangaroo Press, 1989), pp. 106–14
(p. 106). See also Alison Donnell, 'Nation and Contestation: Black
British Writing', *Wasafiri*, 36 (2002): 11–17. It is worth pointing
out that in the same year as his rejection of the label 'black British',
D'Aguiar was still using it in his discussion of 'black British poetry'
in *The New British Poetry*, ed. by Gillian Allnutt, Fred D'Aguiar,
Ken Edwards and Eric Mottram (London: Paladin, 1988), pp. 3–4.

30   Donnell, *Companion*, p. xiv.

31   Stuart Hall, 'Cultural Identity and Diaspora', in Patrick Williams

and Laura Chrisman (eds), *Colonial Discourse and Post-Colonial Theory: A Reader* (Hemel Hempstead: Harvester Wheatsheaf, 1993), pp. 392–403 (p. 402).

32 John McLeod, 'Some Problems with "British" in a "Black British Canon"', *Wasafiri*, 36 (2002): 56–9 (p. 59).

33 Nevertheless, 'within Britain' still suggests a (temporary) geographical grounding which may be troubled by the current habitation of two of these authors in the United States.

34 Maya Jaggi, 'Crossing the River: Caryl Phillips talks to Maya Jaggi', *Wasafiri*, 20 (1994): 25–9 (p. 29).

35 Edward W. Said, *Culture and Imperialism* (London: Chatto & Windus, 1994), p. 1.

36 *Ibid.*, p. 59.

37 Caryl Phillips, *The European Tribe* (London: Faber & Faber, 1999 [1987]), p. 7.

38 Louise Yelin, 'An Interview with Caryl Phillips', in Renée T. Schatteman (ed.), *Conversations with Caryl Phillips* (Jackson, MS: University Press of Mississippi, 2009), pp. 46–52 (p. 48). First published in *Culturefront*, 7(2) (1998).

39 Caryl Phillips, *A New World Order: Selected Essays* (London: Secker & Warburg, 2001), p. 234. In an interview from 2001, Phillips disclosed that he had bought the rights to *The Lonely Londoners*, which he intended to adapt for the National Theatre. See Lars Eckstein, 'The Insistence of Voices: An Interview with Caryl Phillips', *ARIEL*, 32(2) (2001): 33–43 (pp. 34–5).

40 Carol Margaret Davison, 'Crisscrossing the River: An Interview with Caryl Phillips', *ARIEL*, 25(4) (1994): 91–9 (p. 94).

41 Phillips, *New World Order*, p. 304.

42 Wolfgang Binder, 'Interview with David Dabydeen, 1989', in Kevin Grant (ed.), *The Art of David Dabydeen* (Leeds: Peepal Tree, 1997), pp. 140–55 (p. 143).

43 Kay Saunders writes that it was Chief Justice Beaumont who first publicly referred to the system as 'The New Slavery'. See Kay Saunders (ed.), *Indentured Labour in the British Empire 1834–1920* (London and Canberra: Croom Helm, 1984), pp. 52–3.

44 K. O. Laurence, *Immigration into the West Indies in the 19th Century* (Barbados: Caribbean Universities Press, 1971), p. 26.

45 Hugh Tinker, *A New System of Slavery: The Export of Indian Labour Overseas 1830–1920* (London, New York and Bombay: Oxford University Press, 1974), p. 334.

46   Binder, 'Interview with David Dabydeen', p. 144.

47   Lars Eckstein, 'Getting Back to the Idea of Art as Art: An Interview with David Dabydeen', *World Literature Written in English*, 39(1) (2001): 27–36 (p. 31).

48   David Dabydeen, 'West Indian Writers in Britain', in Ferdinand Dennis and Naseem Khan (eds), *Voices of the Crossing: The Impact of Britain on Writers from Asia, The Caribbean and Africa* (London: Serpent's Tail, 2000), pp. 59–75 (pp. 62–3).

49   Binder, 'Interview with David Dabydeen', p. 172. Again, this claim works on the assumption that to be British is to be white.

50   Maria Frías, 'Building Bridges Back to the Past: An Interview with Fred D'Aguiar', *Callaloo*, 25(2) (2002): 418–25 (pp. 421–2).

51   Frank Birbalsingh, 'An Interview with Fred D'Aguiar', *ARIEL*, 24(1) (1993): 133–45 (pp. 133).

52   *Ibid.*, pp. 134–5, 141.

53   Fred D'Aguiar, *Bethany Bettany* (London: Vintage, 2004 [2003]), p. 261.

54   Fred D'Aguiar, 'Further Adventures in the Skin Trade', in W. N. Herbert and Matthew Hollis (eds), *Strong Words: Modern Poets on Modern Poetry* (Tarset: Bloodaxe, 2000), pp. 270–3 (p. 271).

55   Fred D'Aguiar, 'A Gift of a Rose', B*ritish Subjects* (Newcastle: Bloodaxe Books, 1993), p. 62.

56   D'Aguiar, 'Home', *British Subjects*, pp. 63–4 (p. 63).

57   Fred D'Aguiar, *The Longest Memory* (London: Vintage, 1995 [1994]), p. 135.

Chapter 2

1   John McLeod, 'British Freedoms: Caryl Phillips's Transatlanticism and the staging of *Rough Crossings*', *Atlantic Studies*, 6(2) (2009): 191–206 (p. 194).

2   Peter Fryer, *Staying Power: The History of Black People in Britain* (London and Sterling, VA: Pluto Press, 1984), p. 191.

3   Caryl Phillips, *Rough Crossings by Simon Schama* (London: Oberon Modern Plays, 2007), p. 48.

4   Frances Ann Kemble's *Journal of a Residence on a Georgian Plantation in 1838–1839* has been overlooked in other critical works on *Cambridge*, though Phillips draws upon this source in

creating Emily's narrative. Born in England in 1806, Kemble became an actor and journeyed to the US in 1832. There, she married a wealthy American, Pierce Butler, in 1834. She later discovered that her husband was to inherit two plantations in Georgia; by 1849 they were divorced. Vehemently opposed to slavery, Kemble's journal recording the cruelties of the plantations was published in 1863.

5   Letter from Paul Edwards to Caryl Phillips, 10 August 1990, cited in Lars Eckstein, *Re-Membering the Black Atlantic: On the Poetics and Politics of Literary Memory* (Amsterdam and New York: Rodopi, 2006), p. 71.

6   Gayatri Chakravorty Spivak and Geoffrey Hawthorn, 'The Post-Modern Condition: The End of Politics', in Sarah Harasym (ed.), *The Post-Colonial Critic: Interviews, Strategies, Dialogues* (London and New York: Routledge, 1990), pp. 17–34 (p. 31).

7   Undated draft of a letter from Phillips to Edwards, cited in Eckstein, *Re-Membering*, p. 72.

8   See Mrs Flannigan, *Antigua and the Antiguans: A Full Account of the Colony and its Inhabitants from the Time of the Caribs to the Present Day*, 2 vols (London and Basingstoke: Macmillan, 1991), pp. 89–92.

9   Caryl Phillips, introduction to *The Shelter* (Oxford: Amber Lane Press, 1984), pp. 7–12 (pp. 10–11). See also Vron Ware, *Beyond the Pale: White Women, Racism and History* (New York: Verso, 1993 [1992]), especially p. 29.

10 Bénédicte Ledent, *Caryl Phillips* (Manchester and New York: Manchester University Press, 2002), p. 100.

11 Maya Jaggi, 'Crossing the River: Caryl Phillips talks to Maya Jaggi', *Wasafiri*, 20 (1994): 25–9 (p. 26).

12 Caryl Phillips, *Cambridge* (New York: Vintage, 1993 [1991]), p. 97. All subsequent references will be to this edition.

13 Sara Mills, *Discourses of Difference: An Analysis of Women's Travel Writing and Colonialism* (London and New York: Routledge, 1991), p. 3. Similarly, Lady Maria Nugent's journal is poised between these two realms; she is both, as Claudia Brandenstein puts it, a 'dedicated imperialist', yet restricted by her role as a woman, 'located both within and without projects of empire'. See Brandenstein, '"Making the agreeable to the big wigs": Lady Nugent's Grand Tour of Duty in Jamaica, 1801–1805', in Helen Gilbert and Anna Johnston (eds), *In Transit: Travel, Text, Empire* (New York: Peter Lang, 2002), pp. 47, 49.

14   *Ibid.*

15   Elsewhere, Cambridge refers to the 'jolly Union Jack' as an 'English flag' (p. 150); this kind of interchangeable use of 'England' for 'Britain' is something I wish to avoid. For clarity of argument, I refer to English identity, rather than British, in accordance with the narratives of Emily and Cambridge, but the inclusion of the Scottish doctor on the island, Mr McDonald, suggests that Phillips depicts a British, rather than English, society in the Caribbean.

16   Nira Yuval-Davis, *Gender and Nation* (London, Thousand Oaks, CA and New Delhi: Sage Publications, 2000), pp. 12–13.

17   Robert J. C. Young, *Colonial Desire: Hybridity in Theory, Culture and Race* (London and New York: Routledge, 1995), p. 149.

18   An interesting work on the significance of clothing on Jamaican plantations is Steeve O. Buckridge's *The Language of Dress: Resistance and Accommodation in Jamaica, 1760–1890* (Kingston, Jamaica: University of the West Indies Press, 2004).

19   This quotation illustrates the above-mentioned frequent slippage in *Cambridge* between 'English' and 'British'; Mr McDonald is Scottish, which makes it unlikely that he would refer to England as 'our country'.

20   Eric Williams, *Capitalism and Slavery* (London: André Deutsch, 1964), p. 19.

21   Paul Smethurst, *The Postmodern Chronotope: Reading Space and Time in Contemporary Fiction* (Amsterdam and Atlanta: Rodopi, 2000), p. 249.

22   This moment is paralleled with Cambridge's description in the third part of the novel as an 'insane man' (Phillips, *Cambridge*, p. 171).

23   Stuart Hall, 'Cultural Identity and Diaspora', in Patrick Williams and Laura Chrisman (eds), *Colonial Discourse and Post-Colonial Theory: A Reader* (Hemel Hempstead: Harvester Wheatsheaf, 1993), pp. 392–403 (p. 392).

24   Paul Gilroy, *'There Ain't No Black in the Union Jack': The Cultural Politics of Race and Nation* (London: Routledge, 2000), p. 59.

25   Phillips has written about the difficult position of black people in eighteenth-century Britain in reference to Ignatius Sancho: 'There was among these pioneering black Britons a sense of both belonging and not belonging, a sense of being part of the nation and being outside of it.' See Caryl Phillips, 'Foreword', in Reyahn King et al. (eds), *Ignatius Sancho: An African Man of Letters* (London: National Portrait Gallery, 1997), pp. 9–14 (p. 13).

26   Edward Said, *Culture and Imperialism* (London: Chatto & Windus, 1994), p. 408.

27   Carol Margaret Davison, 'Crisscrossing the River: An Interview with Caryl Phillips', *ARIEL*, 25(4) (1994): 91–9 (p. 93).

28   Caryl Phillips, *Crossing the River* (New York: Vintage, 1995 [1993]), p. 1. All subsequent references will be to this edition.

29   Said, *Culture and Imperialism*, p. 1.

30   Edward Said, *The World, the Text, and the Critic* (London: Vintage, 1991), p. 17.

31   *Ibid.*

32   *Ibid.*, p. 24.

33   Similarly, in his novel *Middle Passage* (1990), Charles Johnson's ex-slave narrator Rutherford Calhoun notes: 'Right then I decided our captain was more than just evil. He was the devil'. See Johnson, *Middle Passage* (Edinburgh: Payback Press, 1990), p. 120.

34   Said, *Culture and Imperialism*, p. 59.

35   Walvin, England, *Slaves and Freedom, 1776–1838* (Basingstoke and London: Macmillan, 1986), p. 13.

36   In her refusal to conform to what she sees as village small-mindedness, Joyce prefigures Phillips's character Dorothy in his novel *A Distant Shore*.

37   Just two examples are Bénédicte Ledent, '"Overlapping Territories, Intertwined Histories": Cross-Culturality in Caryl Phillips's *Crossing the River*', *Journal of Commonwealth Literature*, 30(1) (1995): 55–62 (p. 59) and Gail Low, '"A Chorus of Common Memory": Slavery and Redemption in Caryl Phillips's *Cambridge* and *Crossing the River*', *Research in African Literatures*, 29(4) (1998): 122–40 (p. 138).

38   We might remember the way in which Cambridge's wife bore the brunt of people's hostility for their relationship; to recall Cambridge's words, 'she that was under my protection received considerably worse for being in company with a man of colour' (Phillips, *Cambridge*, p. 145).

39   Wendy Webster, *Imagining Home: Gender, 'Race' and National Identity, 1945–64* (London: UCL Press, 1998), p. 48. Despite her use of the loaded term 'unnatural', Webster makes no mention of interracial homosexual relationships.

40   The fact the Joyce is not allowed to go to America with Nash contrasts with the approval wartime brides met when bride and groom were of the same race; see Margaret Randolph Higgonet

et al. (eds), *Behind the Lines: Gender and the Two World Wars* (New Haven and London: Yale University Press, 1987), especially pp. 11–12.

41   Said, *Culture and Imperialism*, p. 36.

42   Jaggi, 'Crossing the River', p. 76.

43   Phillips has also described his writing in *Crossing the River* as 'connecting across centuries' (Davison, 'Crisscrossing the River', p. 93).

44   Edward Said, 'Media, Margins and Modernity' (1986), in Raymond Williams, *The Politics of Modernism: Against the New Conformists*, ed. by Tony Pinkney (London and New York: Verso, 1989), pp. 177–97 (p. 196).

45   Caryl Phillips, *Extravagant Strangers: A Literature of Belonging* (London: Faber & Faber, 1998 [1997]), p. xiv. All subsequent references will be to this edition.

46   Caryl Phillips, *A New World Order: Selected Essays* (London: Secker & Warburg, 2001), p. 192. All subsequent references will be to this edition.

47   Maya Jaggi, 'Caryl Phillips: Rites of Passage', *Guardian*, 3 November 2001 in *NewsBank* http://infoweb.newsbank.com [accessed 17 February 2004] (para. 1 of 46).

48   Said, *Culture and Imperialism*, p. 407.

49   In *The World, the Text, and the Critic*, Said also writes of the 'nuances, principally of reassurance, fitness, belonging, association, and community, entailed in the phrase *at home* or *in place*' (p. 8).

50   Caryl Phillips, 'A Dream Deferred: Fifty Years of Caribbean Migration to Britain', *Kunapipi*, 21(2) (1999): 106–18 (p. 112).

51   Rosemary Marangoly George, *The Politics of Home: Postcolonial Relocations and Twentieth-century Fiction* (Cambridge, New York and Melbourne: Cambridge University Press, 1996), p. 9.

52   Paul Gilroy, *The Black Atlantic: Modernity and Double Consciousness* (London and New York: Verso, 1999), p. 3. A notion Gilroy, in turn, borrows from Werner Sollors; see Sollors, *Beyond Ethnicity: Consent and Descent in American Culture* (New York and Oxford: Oxford University Press, 1986).

53   *Ibid.*

54   *The Oxford English Reference Dictionary*, ed. by Judy Pearsall and Bill Trumble (Oxford and New York: Oxford University Press, 1996), p. 676.

55   Caryl Phillips, *The Atlantic Sound* (London: Faber & Faber, 2000), pp. 122–3. All subsequent references will be to this edition.

56   Homi K. Bhabha, *The Location of Culture* (London and New York: Routledge, 2000), pp. 145–6.

57   Orwell's essay is entitled 'England Your England', but his focus is on Britain, rather than England; evidence, again, of the kind of slippage between England and Britain that I acknowledged in my reading of *Cambridge*.

58   Ian Baucom, *Out of Place: Englishness, Empire and the Locations of Identity* (Princeton: Princeton University Press, 1999), p. 15. Again, while Baucom refers to England, his comments are fully applicable to Britain.

59   Paul Gilroy, *After Empire: Melancholia or Convivial Culture?* (Abingdon: Routledge, 2004), p. 116.

60   *Ibid.*, p. 121.

61   *Ibid.*

62   Ramsay Muir, *A History of Liverpool* (London: Williams & Norgate, 1907), p. 195.

63   Ferdinand Dennis, *Behind the Frontlines: Journey into Afro-Britain* (London: Victor Gollancz, 1988), p. ix.

64   *Ibid.*, p. 17.

65   James Walvin, *Making the Black Atlantic: Britain and the African Diaspora* (London and New York: Cassell, 2000), p. x.

66   Caryl Phillips, *The European Tribe* (London: Faber & Faber, 1999), p. 128.

67   Siddhartha Deb, 'On Belonging', Review of *A New World Order*, *Financial Times*, 20/21 October 2001, section Weekend, p. 4.

68   The 'Homeward Bound Foundation' is also the name of the Pan-Africanist group behind the middle passage monument, sunk 427 kilometres off New York harbour. See Johanna C. Kardux, 'Monuments of the Black Atlantic: Slavery Memorials in the United States and the Netherlands', in Heike Raphael-Hernandez (ed.), *Blackening Europe: The African American Presence* (New York and London: Routledge, 2004), pp. 87–105 (pp. 89–90).

69   Avtar Brah, *Cartographies of Diaspora: Contesting Identities* (London and New York: Routledge, 2002), p. 192.

70   Gilroy, *Black Atlantic*, p. 189.

71   *Ibid.*

72   George also states that 'Belonging in any one place requires a judicious balancing of remembrance and forgetting' (*Politics*, p. 197).

73   Bhabha, *Location of Culture*, p. 161. Bhabha draws upon Ernest

Renan's essay 'What is a Nation?', reprinted in Homi K. Bhabha (ed.), *Nation and Narration* (London and New York: Routledge, 1990), pp. 8–21.

74   The Africentric movement relies on linearity, which colonialism and slavery interrupts; see Gilroy, *Black Atlantic*, p. 190.

75   Gilroy, *Black Atlantic*, p. 19. In *The European Tribe*, Phillips begins the section on Britain by quoting Simone Weil: 'To be rooted is perhaps the most important and least recognized need of the human soul', arguably suggesting a significant shift since this early text in his conceptualisation of diasporan identity (p. 119).

76   *Ibid.*, p. 16.

77   Caryl Phillips, *Where There is Darkness* (Ambergate: Amber Lane Press, 1982), p. 16.

78   Bénédicte Ledent also suggests that 'sound' could mean to explore, or plumb the depths. See Ledent, 'Ambiguous Visions of Home: The Paradoxes of Diasporic Belonging in Caryl Phillips's *The Atlantic Sound*', *EnterText*, 1 (2000) http://www.brunel.ac.uk/faculty/arts/EnterText/Ledent.pdf [accessed 10 April 2004] (para. 5 of 15).

79   In Phillips's play, *Strange Fruit*, his character Alvin also asks: 'What we supposed to do? Live on a raft in the middle of the Atlantic at a point equidistant between Africa, the Caribbean and Britain?' See Phillips, S*trange Fruit* (Ambergate: Amber Lane Press, 1981), p. 99.

80   George, *Politics*, p. 1.

Chapter 3

1   David Dabydeen, 'West Indian Writers in Britain', in Ferdinand Dennis and Naseem Khan (eds), *Voices of the Crossing: The Impact of Britain on Writers from Asia, The Caribbean and Africa* (London: Serpent's Tail, 2000), pp. 59–75 (p. 61).

2   V. S. Naipaul, *The Middle Passage: Impressions of Five Societies – British, French and Dutch – in the West Indies and South America* (London: André Deutsch, 1978 [1962]), p. 82.

3   Dabydeen, 'West Indian Writers', p. 60. He also admits that Vidia from *The Counting House* is a version both of Naipaul and of himself (p. 61).

4   Frank Birbalsingh (ed.), *Frontiers of Caribbean Literature in English* (London and Basingstoke: Macmillan, 1996), p. 172.

5   David Dabydeen, 'Song of the Creole Gang Women', *Slave Song* (Sydney, Mundelstrup and Coventry: Dangaroo, 1984), pp. 17–18

(p. 17). All subsequent references will be to this edition. Dabydeen's translation is provided as: 'Work, nothing but work/ Morning noon and night nothing but work/ Booker owns my cunt/ Booker owns my children/ Pain, nothing but pain/ One million thousand acres cane' ('[Notes to] "Song of the Creole Gang Women"', *Slave Song*, pp, 43–5 (p. 45).

6   Dabydeen, '[Notes to] "Song of the Creole Gang Women"', p. 43.

7   Dabydeen, 'Introduction', *Slave Song*, pp. 9–15 (p. 10).

8   Birbalsingh, *Frontiers*, p. 170.

9   *Ibid.*

10   *Ibid.*, p. 172.

11   David Dabydeen, 'On Not Being Milton: Nigger Talk in England Today', in Maggie Butcher (ed.), *Tibisiri: Caribbean Writers and Critics* (Sydney, Mundelstrup, Denmark and Coventry: Dangaroo Press, 1989), pp. 121–35 (p. 121).

12   Dabydeen, 'Nightmare', *Slave Song*, p. 34. Dabydeen's translation reads: 'One gang of sweaty, stinking niggers/ Drag her off the bed/ Work upon her/ Crack her head/ Give her jigga [a severe itching and peeling of the flesh as a result of contact with putrid matter]/ Between her thighs' ('[Notes to] "Nightmare", *Slave Song*, pp. 61–2 (p. 61).

13   David Dabydeen, 'Coolie Odyssey', *Coolie Odyssey* (London and Coventry: Hansib and Dangaroo: 1988), pp. 9–13 (p. 9). All subsequent references will be to this edition.

14   Graham Huggan, 'Preface', *The Postcolonial Exotic: Marketing the Margins* (Abingdon: Routledge, 2001), pp. vii–xvi (p. viii). However, Huggan later makes the important point that postcolonial literatures in English 'are read by many different people in many different places; it would be misleading, not to mention arrogant, to gauge their value only to Western metropolitan response' (p. 30).

15   David Dabydeen, *A Harlot's Progress* (London: Vintage, 2000 [1999]), p. 5. All subsequent references will be to this edition.

16   In this reading of *The Counting House*, 'subaltern' refers to both Indian indentured labourer and ex-slave.

17   Gayatri Chakravorty Spivak, 'Subaltern Studies: Deconstructing Historiography' (1985), in Spivak, *In Other Worlds: Essays in Cultural Politics* (London and New York: Methuen, 1987), pp. 197–221 (p. 209).

18   David Dabydeen, *The Counting House* (London: Vintage, 1997 [1996]), p. 179. All subsequent references will be to this edition.

19 David Dabydeen and Brinsley Samaroo (eds), *India in the Carib-bean* (London and Basingstoke: Macmillan, 1987), p. 10.

20 Happily, in the years following the publication of *India in the Carib-bean*, we have seen an increase in the number of books published on Indian-Caribbean culture, history and literature, such as Ron Ramdin's *Arising from Bondage: A History of the Indo-Caribbean People* (London: I. B. Tauris, 2000) and Marina Carter and Khal Torabully's *Coolitude: An Anthology of the Indian Labour Dias-pora* (London: Anthem Press, 2002), as well as studies focusing specifically on Indian-Caribbean women's experiences, including Rosanne Kanhai's edited essay collection *Matikor: The Politics of Identity for Indo-Caribbean Women* (St Augustine, Trinidad and Tobago: University of the West Indies Press, 1999) and Brinda J. Mehta's *Diasporic (Dis)locations: Indo-Caribbean Women Writers Negotiate the Kala Pani* (Kingston, Jamaica: University of the West Indies Press, 2004).

21 Madhavi Kale, *Fragments of Empire: Capital, Slavery, and Indian Indentured Labor Migration in the British Caribbean* (Philadel-phia: University of Pennsylvania Press, 1998), p. 14.

22 Walton Look Lai, *Indentured Labor, Caribbean Sugar: Chinese and Indian Migrants to the British West Indies, 1838–1918* (Baltimore and London: Johns Hopkins University Press, 1993), pp. 53–4. The role played by Chinese indentured labourers is arguably an even more neglected area of the history of British imperialism.

23 Kale, *Fragments*, p. 32.

24 A relationship traced by Edward Said in *Culture and Imperialism* (London: Chatto & Windus, 1993).

25 Gayatri Chakravorty Spivak, 'A Literary Representation of the Subaltern', in Spivak, *In Other Worlds*, pp. 241–68 (p. 244).

26 'Sunt lachrimae rerum' is an abbreviation of a phrase by Virgil: 'sunt lachrimae rerum et mentem mortalia tanguant', which can be translated as: 'there are tears for things and mortal things touch the heart'. However, in *The Counting House*, the inscription resides on the gravestone of a plantation owner, and I would suggest that it is also significant that 'rerum' can mean wealth or possessions. Further, Miriam's inability to see that the inscription refers to tears may indeed be linked to her inability to cry. In his novel *The Intended*, Dabydeen's narrator imagines using this phrase to impress his girlfriend: 'I would quote to her the Latin phrase our teacher used in summarising the tragedy of [*Troilus and Criseyde*], "sunt lachrimae rerum" – "there are tears in things". I imagined our conversation would pause at this dual moment of poignancy

and erudition, that she would be moved by both' (London: Secker & Warburg, 1991, p. 121).

27   Gayatri Chakravorty Spivak, *A Critique of Postcolonial Reason: Towards a History of the Vanishing Present* (Cambridge, MA and London: Harvard University Press, 1999), p. 304.

28   Susan M. Pearce, 'Objects as Meaning; or Narrating the Past', in Pearce (ed.), *Interpreting Objects and Collections* (London and New York: Routledge, 1994), pp. 19–29 (p. 23).

29   Marcus Wood, *Blind Memory: Visual Representations of Slavery in England and America 1780–1865* (Manchester and New York: Manchester University Press, 2000), p. 46.

30   See Paul Gilroy, *The Black Atlantic: Modernity and Double Consciousness* (London and New York: Verso, 1999).

31   Ladislas Bugner, *The Image of the Black in Western Art*, 4 vols (Cambridge, MA and London: Harvard University Press, 1989), IV, 1: *From the American Revolution to World War 1: Slaves and Liberators*, ed. by Hugh Honour (1989), p. 20.

32   John Ruskin, *Modern Painters*, 5 vols (Orpington and London: George Allen, 1843–1897), I: *Of General Principles, and of Truth* (1843), pp. 405–6.

33   James Hamilton, *Turner: A Life* (London: Hodder & Stoughton, 1997), p. 285.

34   Ruskin, *General Principles*, p. 405.

35   *Ibid.*, p. 406.

36   Graham Reynolds, *Turner* (London: Thames & Hudson, 1969), p. 179.

37   Wood, *Blind Memory*, p. 17.

38   James Hamilton, *Turner: The Late Seascapes* (New Haven and London: Yale University Press and Williamstown, MA: Sterling and Francine Clark Institute, 2003), p. 47. Hamilton also notes that a biography of William Wilberforce was published that year.

39   Ronald Segal, *The Black Diaspora* (London: Faber Faber, 1995), p. 35. Some critics, however, dispute the claims that Turner's painting was based upon the *Zong*. See, for example, Barry Venning, *Turner* (London and New York: Phaidon, 2003), p. 246. Martin Butlin and Evelyn Joll have suggested that Turner's choice of subject matter was an attempt at securing royal patronage. Butlin and Joll, *The Paintings of J. M. W. Turner* (New Haven and London: Yale University Press, 1984), p. 237.

40   Thomas Clarkson, *The History of the Rise, Progress, and Accomplishment of the Abolition of the African Slave-Trade by the*

British Parliament, 2 vols (London: Longman, Hurst, Rees and Orme, 1808), I (1808), pp. 96–7.

41 *Ibid.*, pp. 14, 15.

42 Exceptions to this rule are, of course, Marcus Wood and James Walvin.

43 S. E. Anderson, *The Black Holocaust for Beginners* (New York: Writers and Readers Publishing, 1995).

44 Ziva Amishai-Maisels, *Depiction and Interpretation: The Influence of the Holocaust on the Visual Arts* (Oxford, New York, Seoul and Tokyo: Pergamon Press, 1993), p. xxxi.

45 David Dabydeen, 'Preface', *Turner: New and Selected Poems* (London: Jonathan Cape, 1994), pp. ix–x (p. x). All subsequent references will be to this edition. In his interview with Lars Eckstein he has been even more candid about the matter: 'I just stated that Turner was getting a great deal of pleasure – pornographic pleasure almost – from the contemplation of that kind of suffering'. See Lars Eckstein, 'Getting Back to the Idea of Art as Art – An Interview with David Dabydeen', *World Literature Written in English*, 39(1) (2001): 27–36 (p. 32).

46 Alex Tyrrell and James Walvin, 'Whose History Is It? Memorialising Britain's Involvement in Slavery', in Paul A. Pickering and Alex Tyrrell (eds), *Contested Sites: Commemoration, Memorial and Postwar Politics in Nineteenth-Century Britain* (Aldershot and Burlington, VT: Ashgate, 2004), pp. 147–69 (p. 148).

47 Wood, *Blind Memory*, p. 93.

48 Introduction to James Procter (ed.), *Writing Black Britain 1948–1998: An Interdisciplinary Anthology* (Manchester and New York: Manchester University Press, 2000), pp. 1–12 (pp. 1–2).

49 Paul Gilroy, *The Black Atlantic: Modernity and Double Consciousness* (London and New York: Verso, 1999), p. 189.

50 Peter Fryer estimates that in 1792 at least 10,000 black people lived in London. See Fryer, *Staying Power: The History of Black People in Britain* (London and Sterling, VA: Pluto Press, 1984), p. 203.

51 Ron Ramdin, *Reimaging Britain: Five Hundred Years of Black and Asian History* (London and Sterling, VA: Pluto Press, 1999), p. 30. Furthermore, Norma Myers claims that this 'decrease' in the nineteenth century is, in fact, a statistical mistake; see Myers, *Reconstructing the Black Past: Blacks in Britain 1780–1830* (London and Portland, OR: Frank Cass, 1996), p. 30.

52 Homi K. Bhabha, *The Location of Culture* (London and New York: Routledge, 2000), p. 161.

53   John Berger, *Ways of Seeing* (London: Penguin, 1972), p. 83.

54   Ruskin indicated to his father that he wished to own the painting, and it was duly bought him as a New Year's present in 1844 (Ruskin, *General Principles*, p. 257). In her novel *Free Enterprise* (2004), Michelle Cliff's character Mary Ellen Pleasant is present at the unveiling of Turner's *Slavers* at the home of its fictional new owner, Alice Hooper. See Cliff, *Free Enterprise* (New York: Plume, 1995), p. 73.

55   Andrew Wilton, *Turner and the Sublime* (London: British Museum Publications, 1980), p. 8.

56   Ruskin, *General Principles*, p. 406.

57   Wood, *Blind Memory*, p. 45.

58   Karen McIntyre, 'Necrophilia or Stillbirth? David Dabydeen's *Turner* as the Embodiment of Postcolonial Creative Decolonisation', in Kevin Grant (ed.), *The Art of David Dabydeen* (Leeds: Peepal Tree Press, 1997), pp. 141–58 (p. 141).

59   Dabydeen's narrator is androgynous: at times both male and female but, according to critical convention, I shall refer to the narrator as 'he'.

60   Dabydeen, 'Turner', *Turner*, pp. 1–40 (p. 15). All subsequent references will be to this edition.

61   James E. Young, *The Texture of Memory: Holocaust Memorials and Meaning* (New Haven and London: Yale University Press, 1993), p. 12.

62   We might also recall that part of Dabydeen's motivation for writing *The Counting House* came from his contention that, in the received history of slavery, 'the Indo-Caribbean is relegated to a footnote' (Dabydeen and Samaroo, p. 10).

63   Jean-François Lyotard, 'The Sublime and the Avante-Garde', in Andrew Benjamin (ed.), *The Lyotard Reader* (Oxford and Cambridge, MA: Blackwell, 1993), pp. 196–211 (p. 196). First published in *Art Forum*, 22(8) (1984).

64   Lyotard, 'The Sublime', p. 203.

65   See Butlin and Joll. Ruskin aside, critics have varied in their appraisal of his painting; Mark Twain summarised the painting as 'a tortoise-shell cat having a fit in a platter of tomatoes'; cited in Jerrold Ziff, 'Turner's "Slave Ship": "What a Red Rag is to a Bull"', *Turner Studies*, 3(2) (1984): 28.

66   Maya Jaggi, 'Out of the torrid waters of colonial culture', interview with David Dabydeen, *Guardian*, 23 April 1994 (28).

67 Laura Mulvey explores in detail Sigmund Freud's concept of scopophilia in 'Visual Pleasure and Narrative Cinema', *Screen*, 16(3) (1975): 6–18.

68 Edward Kamau Brathwaite, *Folk Culture of the Slaves in Jamaica* (London: New Beacon Books, 1981), p. 13.

69 Jacques Derrida, *Memoirs of the Blind: The Self-Portrait and Other Ruins*, trans. by Pascale-Anne Brault and Michael Naas (Chicago and London: University of Chicago Press, 1993), p. 126. First published in French as *Mémoires d'aveugle: L'auto-portrait et autres ruines* (Paris: Réunion des Musées Nationaux, 1990).

70 Frederick Antal, *Hogarth and His Place in European Art* (London: Routledge & Kegan Paul, 1962), p. 12. Also, as M. Dorothy George states, they were highly realistic depictions; see George, *London Life in the XVIIIth Century* (London: Kegan Paul, Trench, Trubner & Co., 1925), p. 113.

71 David Dabydeen, *Hogarth, Walpole and Commercial Britain* (London: Hansib, 1987), p. 12.

72 David Dabydeen, 'Hogarth – The Savage and the Civilised', *History Today*, 31 (1981): 48–51 (pp. 48, 51). Myers similarly concurs that Hogarth seemed to be 'expressing sympathy for the black lower classes or utilizing them in order to make criticisms of white society'. She notes, however, that 'Following Hogarth, caricaturists of blacks tended towards a more overt form of racism, especially as the abolitionist campaign gained momentum' (p. 48).

73 Introduction to Paul Edwards and David Dabydeen (eds), *Black Writers in Britain 1760–1890* (Edinburgh: Edinburgh University Press, 1991), pp. ix–xv (p. xi).

74 Thomas Pringle (1789–1834) edited the memoirs of Mary Prince; Dabydeen's characters are inspired by the historical archive, but creatively transformed.

75 Quobna Ottobah Cugoano, *Thoughts and Sentiments on the Evil of Slavery: And Other Writings*, ed. by Vincent Carretta (New York, London, Victoria, Toronto and New Delhi: Penguin, 1999), p. 110.

76 James Walvin, *An African's Life: The Life and Times of Olaudah Equiano, 1745–1797* (London and New York: Continuum, 2000), p. 194.

77 The irony here is that this image is no longer thought to be a portrait of Equiano; see for example Reyahn King, 'Ignatius Sancho and portraits of the Black Élite', in Reyahn King *et al.* (eds), *Ignatius Sancho: An African Man of Letters* (London, National Portrait Gallery, 1997), pp. 35–6.

78 See Mark Stein, 'David Dabydeen Talks to Mark Stein', *Wasa-firi*, 29 (1999): 29. There are elements of other slave authors in Dabydeen's creation of Mungo; Ignatius Sancho, for example, was a butler to the duke and duchess of Montagu; see Bugner, IV, 2: *American Revolution to World War I*, p. 30.

79 Jack Gratus, *The Great White Lie: Slavery, Emancipation and Changing Racial Attitudes* (London: Hutchinson, 1973), p. 178. Caryl Phillips's Cambridge also used the term in a derogatory way, referring to himself as having been 'dressed in the spiritual and physical guise of *Mungo*'. See Phillips, *Cambridge* (New York: Vintage, 1993 [1991]), p. 136.

80 A twentieth-century version of this notion of assimilation can be found in the Conservative Party election poster of 1983 examined by Paul Gilroy in *'There Ain't No Black in the Union Jack': The Cultural Politics of Race and Nation*, and mentioned in Chapter 2 (London: Routledge, 2000), p. 59.

81 David Dabydeen, 'Dependence, or the Ballad of the Little Black Boy (On Francis Wheatley's *Family Group and Negro Boy* painted in the 1770s)', *Coolie Odyssey*, pp. 48–9 (p. 49).

82 See Bugner, IV, 2, p. 148. A particularly famous example of this use of black subjects for contrast can be found in Eduoard Manet's painting *Olympia* (1865); see Bugner, IV, 2, p. 159. In *Hogarth's Blacks*, Dabydeen also writes of these marginalised figures: 'What emerges from such paintings is a sense of the loneliness and humiliation of blacks in white aristocratic company. The black existed merely to reflect upon the superiority of the white' (p. 30).

83 Cugoano, *Thoughts and Sentiments*, p. 149. Jonathan Jones traces the fallen reputation of Reynolds and suggests that he 'portrays a British history we are less eager to own up to. [Reynolds] portrays the rulers of an empire'. See Jones, 'How the Mighty Fall', *Guardian*, 21 May 2005, section Weekend, pp. 28–37 (p. 32).

84 Introduction to Paul Edwards (ed.), *Equiano's Travels: The Interesting Narrative of the Life of Olaudah Equiano or Gustavus Vassa the African* (Oxford: Heinemann, 1996), pp. xv–xxvii (p. xv).

85 Walvin, *An African's Life*, p. 194. Paul Edwards and James Walvin suggest that the reviser of Cugoano's book may well have been Olaudah Equiano. See Edwards and Walvin (eds), *Black Personalities in the Era of the Slave Trade* (London and Basingstoke: Macmillan, 1983), p. 57.

86 Spivak, 'Subaltern Studies', p. 209.

87 Walvin, *An African's Life*, p. 160.

88 Ignatius Sancho, *Letters of the Late Ignatius Sancho: An African*, ed. by Paul Edwards (London: Dawsons of Pall Mall, 1968), p. 30. Cugoano also tends to refer to black people in a distanced manner; for example: 'Those who have endeavoured to restore to their fellow-creatures the common rights of nature, of which especially the unfortunate Black People have been so unjustly deprived, cannot fail in meeting with the applause of all good men.' See Cugoano, *Thoughts and Sentiments*, p. 9.

89 Peter J. Kitson and Debbie Lee (eds), *Slavery, Abolition and Emancipation: Writings in the British Romantic Period*, 8 vols (London: Pickering & Chatto, 1999), vol 1: *Black Writers*, ed. by Sukhdev Sandhu and David Dabydeen, p. li. Sandhu and Dabydeen also write of Sancho's 'lazily anti-Jewish comments, his would-be flirtatious badinage with young noblewomen ... and his suffocatingly tedious excurses on morality' (p. li).

90 It is also a story with a strongly cyclical element. Mr Gideon, for example, decides to become a slave ship captain only after Mungo has joined him in treating the prostitutes, yet he is also the doctor aboard the slave ship which carried Mungo to Britain. This once again indicates Mungo's resistance to narrating – this time to the linearity of the slave narrative.

91 Cathy Caruth (ed.), *Trauma: Explorations in Memory* (Baltimore and London: Johns Hopkins University Press, 1995), pp. vii–ix (p. vii).

92 In 'Coolie Odyssey', Dabydeen similarly writes of the indulgence of memories: 'In a winter of England's scorn | We huddle together memories, hoard them from | The opulence of our masters' (p. 9).

93 Another example of a literary representation of eighteenth-century London through the eyes of a black man is S. I. Martin's *Incomparable World* (London: Quartet Books, 1996). In this novel, the protagonist Buckram expresses his concern at the anglicised nature of the wealthier black people he encounters: '*Who were these people?* It was as if the memory of slavery had passed them by. As if they'd never known bondage' (p. 111).

94 Douglas Hall, *In Miserable Slavery: Thomas Thistlewood in Jamaica, 1750–86* (London and Basingstoke: Macmillan, 1992), pp. 82, 150.

95 Elizabeth Kowaleski Wallace, 'Telling Untold Stories: Philippa Gregory's *A Respectable Trade* and David Dabydeen's *A Harlot's Progress*', *Novel*, 33(2) (2000): 235–52 (p. 245).

96 As 'Britain' was a relatively new concept created by the Act of Union of 1707, the land Thistlewood yearns for is a nostalgic older England.

97 Cited in Antal, *Hogarth and His Place*, p. 10.

98　Kobena Mercer, *Welcome to the Jungle: New Positions in Black Cultural Studies* (New York and London: Routledge, 1994), p. 173. Mercer's particular focus here is on the work of Robert Mapplethorpe – most notably, *Black Males*. As Mercer notes, 'It is as if, according to Mapplethorpe's line of sight: Black + Male = Erotic/Aesthetic Object ... The "essence" of black male identity lies in the domain of sexuality' (p. 173).

99　*Ibid*. p. 235.

100　Martin Carter, 'After One Year', in *Selected Poems*, ed. by David Dabydeen (Leeds: Peepal Tree Press, 1999), p. 108.

101　Gemma Robinson, 'Introduction to Selected Poems of Martin Carter', Carter, *Selected Poems*, p. 17.

102　Another connection was, of course, Britain's establishment of the colony of 'British Guiana' in 1831.

103　Stein, 'David Dabydeen', p. 29.

104　Sancho, *Letters*, p. 218.

105　Kitson and Lee, *Slavery*, p. li.

Chapter 4

1　Fred D'Aguiar, *Feeding the Ghosts* (London: Vintage, 1998 [1997]), pp. 229–30. All subsequent references will be to this edition.

2　Fred D'Aguiar, 'Further Adventures in the Skin Trade', in W. N. Herbert and Matthew Hollis (eds), *Strong Words: Modern Poets on Modern Poetry* (Tarset: Bloodaxe, 2000), pp. 270–3 (pp. 271–2).

3　Jacques Derrida, 'Plato's Pharmacy', *Dissemination*, trans. by Barbara Johnson (London and New York: Continuum, 2004 [1981]), pp. 69–186 (p. 111). First published in French in *Tel Quel*, 32/33 (1968).

4　*Ibid.*, p. 75.

5　See for example Marianne Hirsch, 'Projected Memory: Holocaust Photographs in Personal and Public Fantasy', in Mieke Bal, Jonathan Crewe and Leo Spitzer (eds), *Acts of Memory: Cultural Recall in the Present* (Hanover, NH and London: University Press of New England, 1999), pp. 2–23 (p. 8).

6　*Ibid.*, p. 8.

7　Fred D'Aguiar, 'The Last Essay About Slavery', in Sarah Dunant and Roy Porter (eds), *The Age of Anxiety* (London: Virago, 1996), pp. 125–47 (p. 131).

8   Derrida, 'Plato's Pharmacy', p. 111. The translation of hypomnēsis is provided elsewhere in 'Plato's Pharmacy' as 're-memoration, recollection, consignation'; for clarity of argument, I shall refer to it as remembering or remembrance (*ibid.*, p. 95).

9   *Ibid.*, p. 130.

10   *Ibid.*, p. 102.

11   *Ibid.*, p. 109.

12   George Lipsitz, *Time Passages: Collective Memory and American Popular Culture* (Minneapolis and London: University of Minnesota Press, 1990), p. 213.

13   Fred D'Aguiar, *The Longest Memory* (London: Vintage, 1995 [1994]), p. 106. All subsequent references will be to this edition.

14   D'Aguiar's novel – whether consciously or not – also reflects an earlier and important text which recounts slavery in America, namely *Long Memory: The Black Experience in America* by Mary Frances Berry and John W. Blassingame. In this, they explain that their choice of title was selected to symbolise their 'rejection of the view of Afro-Americans as an atomized, rootless people who begin each generation without any sense of what preceded them'. Like D'Aguiar's novel, therefore, their text suggests that collective and 'long' memories of slavery may be thought of as synonymous. See Berry and Blassingame, *Long Memory: The Black Experience in America* (New York and Oxford: Oxford University Press, 1982), p. x.

15   D'Aguiar, 'Last Essay', p. 132.

16   D'Aguiar has admitted he had current concerns in mind when writing *The Longest Memory*, stating in an interview that the book was inspired by both a photograph of a former slave, taken in 1963, and his arrival in the United States in 1992 in the aftermath of the riots in Los Angeles: 'America was licking its wounds, trying to come to terms with what had happened. It occurred to me that the book might be a way of talking about contemporary issues in terms of a past event.' See Christina Koning, 'The Past, Another Country', *Independent*, 23 July 1995, Reviews section, p. 32. Returning to the past through the frame of the present can be helpful when examining the legacies of slavery; 'memory' is, of course, like the racism which sparked the riots of 1992, another legacy of this past.

17   The namelessness of Cook is indicative of the scarcity of evidence or historical documentation concerning black female slaves in the United States in the nineteenth century. As Martha Hodes has noted, 'black women's voices are the faintest in the antebellum

historical record'. See Hodes, *White Women, Black Men: Illicit Sex in the Nineteenth-Century South* (New Haven and London: Yale University Press, 1997), pp. 7–8.

18 Andreas Huyssen, 'Monument and Memory in a Postmodern Age', in James E. Young (ed.), *The Art of Memory: Holocaust Memorials in History* (New York and Munich: Prestel-Verlag, 1994), pp. 9–17 (p. 9).

19 Derrida, 'Plato's Pharmacy', p. 75.

20 *Ibid.*, p. 76.

21 *Ibid.*, p. 75.

22 *Ibid.*, p. 142.

23 *Ibid.*, p. 108.

24 D'Aguiar, 'Further Adventures', p. 271.

25 Michel Foucault, 'Nietzsche, Genealogy, History', in Donald F. Bouchard (ed.), *Language, Counter-memory, Practice: Selected Essays and Interviews*, trans. by Donald F. Bouchard and Sherry Simon (Ithaca, NY: Cornell University Press, 1980 [1977]), pp. 139–64 (p. 145, 148). This essay first appeared in French in Suzanne Bachelard et al. (eds), *Hommage à Jean Hyppolite* (Paris: Presses Universaires de France, 1971).

26 Foucault, 'Nietzsche', p. 148.

27 Derrida, 'Plato's Pharmacy', p. 108.

28 D'Aguiar, 'Last Essay', p. 131.

29 In fact, it was a male slave who managed to climb back into the ship. Gail Low explores the implications of D'Aguiar's gendering of the slave as female in her essay 'The Memory of Slavery in Fred D'Aguiar's *Feeding the Ghosts*', in Deborah L. Madsen (ed.), *Post-Colonial Literatures: Expanding the Canon* (London and Sterling, VA: Pluto Press, 1999), pp. 104–19 (pp. 108–9).

30 Derek Walcott, 'The Sea Is History', *The Star-Apple Kingdom* (London: Jonathan Cape, 1980), pp. 25–8 (p. 25). See also Walcott's essay 'The Muse of History', in Orde Coombs (ed.), *Is Massa Day Dead?: Black Moods in the Caribbean* (Garden City, NY: Anchor Books and Doubleday, 1974), pp. 1–28.

31 *Ibid.*

32 Edward Brathwaite, 'Calypso', *The Arrivants: A New World Trilogy* (London, New York and Toronto: Oxford University Press, 1973), pp. 48–50 (p. 48).

33 One of the most successful of these projects is Gail Low's previously

mentioned essay, in which she carefully unravels the novel's relationship not only to 'The Sea is History', but also the poems 'Names' and 'The Schooner *Flight*'; see Low, 'The Memory'.

34 Brathwaite, 'Calypso', p. 48.

35 *Ibid.*

36 *Ibid.*

37 One could see this as illustrative of Brathwaite's desire to avoid cataloguing slaves as 'stock', commonly listed alongside inanimate objects aboard the ships. John Newton, for example, records in his journal entry of 9th March 1751: 'The boat returned, brought 6 casks of water and 6 slaves from Mr Tucker's, 2 men, 1 woman, 1 boy, 2 undersized girls.' See Newton, *The Journal of a Slave Trader*, ed. by Bernard Martin and Mark Spurrell (London: Epworth Press, 1962), p. 39.

38 Marcus Wood, *Blind Memory: Visual Representations of Slavery in England and America 1780–1865* (Manchester and New York: Manchester University Press, 2000), p. 14.

39 The *Zong* has, however, as we have seen, provoked some visual and poetic depictions. Robert Wedderburn recounts the jettison of 'cargo' in his poem 'The Desponding Negro' (1824); see Wedderburn, *The Horrors of Slavery: And Other Writings*, ed. by Iain McCalman (Edinburgh: Edinburgh University Press, 1991), p. 91.

40 Michelle Cliff has also returned to the past of the *Zong* in her novel *Abeng* (1984).

41 Ian Baucom, 'Specters of the Atlantic', *South Atlantic Quarterly*, 100(1) (2001): 61–82 (p. 64).

42 Hugh Thomas, *The Slave Trade: The History of the Atlantic Slave Trade, 1440–1870* (London, Basingstoke and Oxford: Papermac, 1998 [1997]), p. 489.

43 Except for the assertion, already indicated, that the slave that managed to climb back on board was male.

44 Fred D'Aguiar, 'At The Grave of the Unknown African', *An English Sampler: New and Selected Poems* (London: Chatto & Windus, 2001), pp. 65–7 (p. 66). First published in *Callaloo*, 15(4) (1992).

45 D'Aguiar, 'Feeding the Ghosts', *An English Sampler*, p. 22.

46 Theodor W. Adorno, 'Meditations on Metaphysics: After Auschwitz', in *The Adorno Reader*, ed. by Brian O' Connor (Oxford and Malden, MA: Blackwell, 2000), pp. 85–8 (p. 87). First published in German in *Negative Dialektik* (Frankfurt am Main: Suhrkamp Verlag, 1966).

47 *Ibid.*, pp. 86–7.

48 *Ibid.*, pp. 87–8.

49 D'Aguiar, 'Last Essay', p. 131.

50 Dori Laub, 'Bearing Witness or the Vicissitudes of Listening', in Shoshana Felman and Dori Laub, *Testimony: Crises of Witnessing in Literature, Psychoanalysis, and History* (New York and London: Routledge, 1992), pp. 57–74 (p. 67).

51 Ulrich Baer, *Remnants of Song: Trauma and the Experience of Modernity on Charles Baudelaire and Paul Celan* (Stanford, CA: Stanford University Press, 2000), pp. 5–6.

52 D'Aguiar, 'Last Essay', p. 125.

53 The narrator is named Christy, after his father, but in order to avoid confusion, I shall continue to refer to him as 'the narrator'.

54 The ottava rima was introduced by Wyatt, and was popular with Romantic poets like Byron, who used it in such works as *Beppo* (1818) and *Don Juan* (1819–24), and Keats, in 'Isabella' (1820).

55 Fred D'Aguiar, *Bloodlines* (London: Chatto & Windus, 2000), p. 6. All subsequent references will be to this edition.

56 Carole Vance writes that 'Women are encouraged to assent that all male sexuality done to them is pleasurable and liberatory: women really enjoy being raped but can't admit it'. See Vance, 'Pleasure and Danger: Exploring Female Sexuality' (1984) in Sandra Kemp and Judith Squires (eds), *Feminisms* (Oxford and New York: Oxford University Press, 1997), pp. 327–35 (p. 329). For more on the way in which raped women have been blamed for the assault, see Andrea Dworkin, *Pornography: Men Possessing Women* (London: Women's Press, 1981).

57 Berry and Blassingame, *Long Memory*, p. 115. They add that 'Given the belief in the ungovernable passion of blacks, the rape of a black woman by a white man was a legal *non sequitur*. She stood defenseless before the bar of justice because it was always assumed that she had been the seducer' (p. 115).

58 bell hooks, *Ain't I a Woman: Black Women and Feminism* (London: Pluto Press, 1982), p. 52.

59 Bruce King, 'Bloodlines', *World Literature Today*, 75:1 (2001) in *Literature Online* http://lion.chadwyck.co.uk [accessed 22 February 2005] (para. 4 of 5).

60 David Dabydeen, 'On Not Being Milton: Nigger Talk in England Today', in Maggie Butcher (ed.), *Tibisiri: Caribbean Writers and Critics* (Sydney, Mundelstrup, Denmark and Coventry: Dangaroo Press, 1989), pp. 121–35 (p. 121).

61   hooks, *Ain't I a Woman*, p. 53.

62   *Ibid.*, p. 52.

63   D'Aguiar, 'Last Essay', p. 131.

64   *Ibid.*, p. 126.

65   Writing about rape also distances *Bloodlines* from simulating slave narratives, as Cynthia S. Hamilton notes, rape was 'the often alluded to, but unspeakable subject' of nineteenth-century American slave narratives. See Hamilton, 'Revisions, Rememories and Exorcisms: Toni Morrison and the Slave Narrative', *Journal of American Studies*, 30 (1996): 429–45 (p. 435).

66   David Dabydeen, 'Coolie Odyssey', *Coolie Odyssey* (London and Coventry: Hansib and Dangaroo: 1988), pp. 9–13 (p. 9).

67   Derrida, 'Plato's Pharmacy', p. 142.

68   Hirsch introduced the term in her essay 'Past Lives: Postmemories in Exile', *Poetics Today*, 17(4) (1996): 659–86, reprinted in Susan Rubin Suleiman (ed.), *Exile and Creativity: Signposts, Travelers, Outsiders, Backward Glances* (Durham, NC and London: Duke University Press, 1998), pp. 418–46.

69   Hirsch, 'Projected Memory', p. 8.

70   *Ibid.*, p. 8.

71   Marianne Hirsch, 'Surviving Images: Holocaust Photographs and the Work of Postmemory', *Yale Journal of Criticism*, 14(1) (2001): 5–37 (p. 11).

72   Hirsch, 'Projected Memory', p. 9.

73   Hirsch, 'Past Lives', p. 420.

74   D'Aguiar, 'Home', *British Subjects* (Newcastle: Bloodaxe Books, pp. 63–4 (p. 63).

75   Hirsch, 'Past Lives', p. 421.

76   Hirsch, 'Projected Memory', p. 10.

77   Lars Eckstein, 'Getting Back to the Idea of Art as Art – An Interview with David Dabydeen', *World Literature Written in English*, 39(1) (2001): 27–36 (p. 30).

78   Hirsch, 'Projected Memory', p. 16.

79   Paula Burnett, '"Where Else to Row, but Backward?" Addressing Caribbean Futures through Re-visions of the Past', *ARIEL*, 30(1) (1999): 11–37 (p. 34). The other texts under discussion in her essay are David Dabydeen's 'Turner', V. S. Naipaul's *A Way in the World*, Pauline Melville's *The Ventriloquist's Tale*, Wilson Harris's *Palace of the Peacock* and Derek Walcott's *The Bounty*.

80 Burnett, '"Where Else to Row"', p. 35.

81 Hirsch, 'Past Lives', p. 422.

Chapter 5

1   Lars Eckstein, *Re-Membering the Black Atlantic: On the Poetics and Politics of Literary Memory* (Amsterdam and New York: Rodopi, 2006), p. xi.

2   Evelyn O'Callaghan, 'Historical Fiction and Fictional History: Caryl Phillips's *Cambridge*', *Journal of Commonwealth Literature*, 29:2 (1993), 34–47 (34).

3   *Ibid.*, 46.

4   Eckstein, *Re-Membering*, p. 74.

5   *Ibid.*, p. 111.

6   See for example Sukhdev Sandhu, 'Ignatius Sancho and Laurence Sterne', *Research in African Literatures*, 29(4) (1998): 88–105 and Peter Fryer, *Staying Power: The History of Black People in Britain* (London: Pluto, 1984), pp. 94–5.

7   Bénédicte Ledent, *Caryl Phillips* (Manchester: Manchester University Press, 2002), p. 1.

8   Helen Thomas, *Caryl Phillips* (Tavistock: Northcote House, 2006), p. 8. Houston A. Baker Jr adopted the same approach to Richard Wright's work in 'Reassessing (W)right: A Meditation on the Black (W)hole', in Harold Bloom (ed.), *Richard Wright* (New York and Philadelphia: Chelsea House, 1987), pp. 127–61.

9   Jonathan Heawood, 'Distance Learning', *Observer*, 23 March 2003, Reviews section, p. 17. Heawood's claim comes despite Phillips's comment in the same article that, 'As soon as you put a black character into a book in any Western society … the novel will be perceived through a prism of race'.

10 Maya Jaggi, 'Interview with Caryl Phillips', *Brick*, 49 (1994): 73–7 (p. 74).

11 Kevin Grant (ed.), *The Art of David Dabydeen* (Leeds: Peepal Tree Press, 1997), p. 10.

12 Lynne Macedo and Kampta Karran, 'Introduction', in Macedo and Karran (eds), *No Land, No Mother: Essays on David Dabydeen* (Leeds: Peepal Tree Press, 2007), pp. 9–16 (p. 16).

13 Heike H. Härting, 'Painting, Perversion, and the Politics of Cultural Transfiguration in David Dabydeen's *Turner*', in Macedo

and Karran, pp. 48–85 (p. 49). See also Aleid Fokkema, 'Caribbean Sublime: Transporting the Slave, Transporting the Spirit', *ibid.*, pp. 17–31 and Tobias Döring 'Turning the Colonial Gaze: Re-Visions of Terror in Dabydeen's *Turner*', *ibid.*, pp. 32–47.

14   Bruce King, Review of *A Harlot's Progress, Wasafiri*, 30 (1999): 64–6 (p. 64).

15   David Dabydeen, *A Harlot's Progress* (London: Vintage, 2000 [1999]), p. 34.

16   Elizabeth Kowaleski Wallace, 'Telling Untold Stories: Philippa Gregory's *A Respectable Trade* and David Dabydeen's *A Harlot's Progress*', *Novel*, 33(2) (2000): 235–52 (p. 249).

17   David Dabydeen, *Disappearance* (London: Vintage, 1999 [1993]), p. 168.

18   Frank Birbalsingh (ed.), *Frontiers of Caribbean Literature in English* (London and Basingstoke: Macmillan, 1996), p. 170.

19   Mark McWatt, '"Self-consciously Post-colonial": The Fiction of David Dabydeen', in Grant, *Art of David Dabydeen*, pp. 97–107 (p. 97).

20   *Ibid.*, p. 106.

21   Gail Low, 'The Memory of Slavery in Fred D'Aguiar's *Feeding the Ghosts*', in Deborah L. Madsen (ed.), *Post-Colonial Literatures: Expanding the Canon* (London: Pluto Press, 1999), pp. 104–19 (p. 108).

22   *Ibid.*, p. 109.

23   *Ibid.*, p. 118.

24   Dave Gunning, 'Reading the "Uncle Tom" Character in Fred D'Aguiar's *The Longest Memory*' in Judith Misrahi-Barak (ed.), *Revisiting Slave Narratives* (Montpellier: Les Carnets de Cerpac, 2005), pp. 295–310 (p. 296).

25   *Ibid.*, p. 308.

26   *Ibid.*, p. 306.

27   David Vincent, 'Paperbacks', *Observer*, 21 October 2001 in *News-Bank* http://0infoweb.newsbank.com [accessed 29 August 2005] (para. 5 of 13).

28   Andrew Biswell, 'Don Juan in a Lost America', *Daily Telegraph*, 16 December 2000 in *Lexis-Nexis* http://web.lexis-nexis.com/professional [accessed 29 August 2005] (para. 3 of 5).

29   Fred D'Aguiar, 'Further Adventures in the Skin Trade', in W. N. Herbert and Matthew Hollis (eds), *Strong Words: Modern Poets on Modern Poetry* (Tarset: Bloodaxe, 2000), pp. 270–3 (p. 271).

30 Fred D'Aguiar, 'The Last Essay About Slavery', in Sarah Dunant and Roy Porter (eds), *The Age of Anxiety* (London: Virago, 1996), pp. 125–47 (p. 131).

31 Anne Whitehead, *Trauma Fiction* (Edinburgh: Edinburgh University Press, 2004), p. 6.

32 David Dabydeen, 'On Not Being Milton: Nigger Talk in England Today', in Maggie Butcher (ed.), *Tibisiri: Caribbean Writers and Critics* (Sydney, Mundelstrup, Denmark and Coventry: Dangaroo Press, 1989), pp. 121–35 (p. 121).

33 Alan Rice, *Radical Narratives of the Black Atlantic* (London and New York: Continuum, 2003), p. 216.

34 Robert Musil, *Posthumous Papers of a Living Author* (Hygiene, CO: Eridanos Press, 1987), p. 64.

Select bibliography

Books by Phillips

Drama

Strange Fruit (Ambergate: Amber Lane Press, 1981).
Where There is Darkness (Ambergate: Amber Lane Press, 1982).
The Shelter (Oxford: Amber Lane Press, 1984).
The Wasted Years (London: Methuen, 1985).
Playing Away (London: Faber & Faber, 1997).
Rough Crossings (London: Oberon Books, 2007).

Fiction

The Final Passage (London: Faber & Faber, 1985).
A State of Independence (London: Faber & Faber, 1986).
Higher Ground (London: Viking, 1989).
Cambridge (London: Bloomsbury, 1991).
Crossing the River (London: Bloomsbury: 1993).
The Nature of Blood (London: Faber & Faber, 1997).
A Distant Shore (London: Secker & Warburg, 2003).
Dancing in the Dark (London: Secker & Warburg, 2005).
In the Falling Snow (London: Harvill Secker, 2009).

Non-fiction

The European Tribe (London: Faber & Faber, 1987).
Extravagant Strangers: A Literature of Belonging, ed. (London: Faber & Faber, 1997).
The Right Set: An Anthology of Writing on Tennis, ed. (London: Faber & Faber, 1999).
The Atlantic Sound (London: Faber & Faber, 2000).
A New World Order (London: Secker & Warburg, 2001).
Foreigners (London: Harvill Secker, 2007).

Books by Dabydeen

Fiction

The Intended (London: Secker & Warburg, 1991).
Disappearance (London: Secker & Warburg, 1993).
The Counting House (London: Jonathan Cape, 1996).
A Harlot's Progress (London: Jonathan Cape, 1999).
Our Lady of Demerara (Chichester: Dido Press, 2004).
Molly and the Muslim Stick (Oxford: Macmillan Caribbean, 2008).

Non-fiction

Hogarth's Blacks: Images of Blacks in Eighteenth Century English Art (Mundelstrup, Denmark and Kingston-Upon-Thames: Dangaroo Press, 1985).
The Black Presence in English Literature, ed. (Manchester: Manchester University Press, 1985).
Caribbean Literature: A Teacher's Handbook (London: Heinemann Educational, 1985).
Hogarth, Walpole and Commercial Britain (London: Hansib, 1987).
India in the Caribbean, ed. with Brinsley Samaroo (London: Hansib, 1987).
A Reader's Guide to West Indian and Black British Literature, with Nana Wilson-Tagoe (London/Warwick: Hansib/University of Warwick Centre for Caribbean Studies, 1987).
Handbook for Teaching Caribbean Literature (London: Heinemann Educational, 1988).
Black Writers in Britain 1760–1890, ed. with Paul Edwards (Edinburgh: Edinburgh University Press, 1991).
Across the Dark Waters, ed. with Brinsley Samaroo (London and Basingstoke: Macmillan, 1996).
The Oxford Companion to Black British History, ed. with John Gilmore and Cecily Jones (Oxford: Oxford University Press, 2007).

Poetry

Slave Song (Coventry: Dangaroo, 1984).
Coolie Odyssey (London: Hansib, 1988).
Turner: New and Selected Poems (London: Jonathan Cape, 1994).

Books by D'Aguiar

Drama

A Jamaican Airman Foresees His Death (London: Methuen, 1995).

Fiction

The Longest Memory (London: Chatto & Windus, 1994).
Dear Future (London: Chatto & Windus, 1996).
Feeding the Ghosts (London: Chatto & Windus, 1997).
Bethany Bettany (London: Chatto & Windus, 2003).

Poetry

Mama Dot (London: Chatto & Windus, 1985).
Airy Hall (London: Chatto & Windus, 1989).
British Subjects (Newcastle: Bloodaxe Books, 1993).
Bill of Rights (London: Chatto & Windus, 1998).
Bloodlines (London: Chatto & Windus, 2000).
An English Sampler: New and Selected Poems (London: Chatto & Windus, 2001).
Continental Shelf (Manchester: Carcanet, 2009).

Articles, interviews, essays

Birbalsingh, Frank, 'An Interview with Fred D'Aguiar', *ARIEL*, 24(1) (1993): 133–45.

Dabydeen, David, 'Hogarth: The Savage and the Civilised', *History Today*, 31 (1981): 48–51.

Davison, Carol Margaret, 'Crisscrossing the River: An Interview with Caryl Phillips', *ARIEL*, 25(4) (1994): 91–9.

Eckstein, Lars, 'Getting Back to the Idea of Art as Art: An Interview with David Dabydeen', *World Literature Written in English*, 39(1) (2001): 27–36.

——, 'The Insistence of Voices: An Interview with Caryl Phillips', *ARIEL*, 32(2) (2001): 33–43.

Frias, Maria, '"Building Bridges Back to the Past": An Interview with Fred D'Aguiar', *Callaloo*, 25(2) (2002): 418–25.

Goldman, Paula, 'Home, Blood, and Belonging: A Conversation with Caryl Phillips', *Moving Worlds*, 2(2) (2002): 115–22.

Heawood, Jonathan, 'Distance Learning', Interview with Caryl Phillips, *Observer*, 23 March 2003, Reviews section, p. 17.

Jaggi, Maya, 'Crossing the River: Caryl Phillips talks to Maya Jaggi', *Wasafiri*, 20 (1994): 25–9.

Jenkins, Lee M., 'On Not Being Tony Harrison: Tradition and the Individual Talent of David Dabydeen', *ARIEL*, 32(2) (2001): 69–88.

Leusmann, Harald, 'Fred D'Aguiar Talks to Harald Leusmann', *Wasafiri*, 28 (1998): 17–21.

McLeod, John, '*Dancing in the Dark*: Caryl Phillips in Conversation with John McLeod', *Moving Worlds*, 7(1) (2007): 103–14.

Phillips, Caryl, 'A Dream Deferred: Fifty Years of Caribbean Migration to Britain', *Kunapipi*, 21(2) (1999): 106–18.

——, 'Following On: The Legacy of Lamming and Selvon', *Wasafiri*, 29 (1999): 34–6.

Saunders, Kay, 'Caryl Phillips: Interview', *Kunapipi*, 9(1) (1987): 44–52.

Schatteman, Renée T. (ed.), *Conversations with Caryl Phillips* (Jackson, MS: University Press of Mississippi, 2009).

Stein, Mark, 'David Dabydeen Talks to Mark Stein', *Wasafiri*, 29 (1999): 27–9.

Swift, Graham, 'Caryl Phillips Interviewed', *Kunapipi*, 13(3) (1991): 96–103.

Selected criticism

Burnett, Paula, '"Where Else to Row, but Backward?" Addressing Caribbean Futures Through Re-visions of the Past', *ARIEL*, 30(1) (1999): 11–37.

Dawes, Kwame, 'Negotiating the Ship on the Head: Black British Fiction', *Wasafiri*, 29 (1999): 18–24.

Eckstein, Lars, *Re-Membering the Black Atlantic: On the Poetics and Politics of Literary Memory* (Amsterdam and New York: Rodopi, 2006).

Fee, Margery, 'Resistance and Complicity in David Dabydeen's *The Intended*', *ARIEL*, 24(1) (1993): 107–26.

Grant, Kevin (ed.), *The Art of David Dabydeen* (Leeds: Peepal Tree Press, 1997).

Gunning, Dave, 'Reading the "Uncle Tom" Character in Fred D'Aguiar's *The Longest Memory*', in Judith Misrahi-Barak (ed.), *Revisiting Slave Narratives* (Montpellier: Les Carnets de Cerpac, 2005), pp. 295–310.

——, 'Caryl Phillips's *Cambridge* and the (Re)Construction of Racial Identity', *Kunapipi*, 28(1) (2007): 70–81.

Kowaleski Wallace, Elizabeth, 'Telling Untold Stories: Philippa Gregory's *A Respectable Trade* and David Dabydeen's *A Harlot's Progress*', *Novel*, 33(2) (2000): 235–52.

Ledent, Bénédicte, *Caryl Phillips* (Manchester and New York: Manchester University Press, 2002).

——, '"Of, and Not Of", This Place: Attachment and Detachment in Caryl Phillips' *A Distant Shore*', *Kunapipi*, 26(1) (2004): 152–60.

Low, Gail '"A Chorus of Common Memory": Slavery and Redemption in Caryl Phillips's *Cambridge* and *Crossing the River*', *Research in African Literatures*, 29(4) (1998): 122–40.

——, 'The Memory of Slavery in Fred D'Aguiar's *Feeding the Ghosts*', in Deborah L. Madsen (ed.), *Post-Colonial Literatures: Expanding the Canon* (London and Sterling, VA: Pluto Press, 1999), pp. 104–19.

Macedo, Lynne and Kampta Karran (eds), *No Land, No Mother: Essays on David Dabydeen* (Leeds: Peepal Tree Press, 2007).

McLeod, John, '"Between two waves": Caryl Phillips and black Britain', *Moving Worlds*, 7(1) (2007): 9–19.

——, 'British Freedoms: Caryl Phillips's Transatlanticism and the Staging of *Rough Crossings*', *Atlantic Studies*, 6(2) (2009): 191–206.

O'Callaghan, Evelyn, 'Historical Fiction and Fictional History: Caryl Phillips's *Cambridge*', *Journal of Commonwealth Literature*, 29(2) (1993): 34–47.

Parry, Benita, 'David Dabydeen's *The Intended*', *Kunapipi*, 13(3) (1991): 85–90.

Smethurst, Paul, 'Postmodern Blackness and Unbelonging in the Works of Caryl Phillips', *Journal of Commonwealth Literature*, 37(2) (2002): 5–20.

Ward, Abigail, '"Words are All I Have Left of My Eyes": Blinded by the Past in J. M. W. Turner's *Slavers Throwing Overboard the Dead and Dying* and David Dabydeen's "Turner"', *Journal of Commonwealth Literature*, 42(1) (2007): 47–58.

——, 'David Dabydeen's *A Harlot's Progress*: Re-presenting the Slave Narrative Genre', *Journal of Postcolonial Writing*, 43(1) (2007): 32–44.

——, 'An Outstretched Hand: Connection and Affiliation in *Crossing the River*', *Moving Worlds*, 7(1) (2007): 20–32.

General works

Baucom, Ian, *Out of Place: Englishness, Empire, and the Locations of Identity* (Princeton: Princeton University Press, 1999).

——, *Specters of the Atlantic: Finance Capital, Slavery, and the Philosophy of History* (Durham, NC and London: Duke University Press, 2005).

Brah, Avtar, *Cartographies of Diaspora: Contesting Identities* (London and New York: Routledge, 2002).

Caruth, Cathy (ed.), *Trauma: Explorations in Memory* (Baltimore and London: Johns Hopkins University Press, 1995).

——, *Unclaimed Experience: Trauma, Narrative and History* (Baltimore and London: Johns Hopkins University Press, 1996).

Chrisman, Laura and Patrick Williams (eds), *Colonial Discourse and Post-colonial Theory: A Reader* (Harlow: Pearson Education, 1994).

Cohen, Robin, *Frontiers of Identity: The British and the Others* (London and New York: Longman, 1994).

Dennis, Ferdinand and Naseem Khan (eds), *Voices of the Crossing: The Impact of Britain on Writers from Asia, The Caribbean and Africa* (London: Serpent's Tail, 2000).

Felman, Shoshana and Dori Laub, *Testimony: Crises of Witnessing in Literature, Psychoanalysis, and History* (New York and London: Routledge, 1992).

Fryer, Peter, *Staying Power: The History of Black People in Britain* (London and Sterling, VA: Pluto Press, 1984).

George, Rosemary Marangoly, *The Politics of Home: Postcolonial Relocations and Twentieth-century Fiction* (Cambridge, New York and Melbourne: Cambridge University Press, 1996).

Gerzina, Gretchen, *Black England: Life Before Emancipation* (London: John Murray, 1995).

Gikandi, Simon, *Maps of Englishness: Writing Identity in the Culture of Colonialism* (New York: Columbia University Press, 1996).

Gilroy, Paul, *Small Acts: Thoughts on the Politics of Black Cultures* (London and New York: Serpent's Tail, 1993).

——, *The Black Atlantic: Modernity and Double Consciousness* (London and New York: Verso, 1999).

——, *'There Ain't No Black in the Union Jack': The Cultural Politics of Race and Nation* (London: Routledge, 2000).

——, *After Empire: Melancholia or Convivial Culture?* (Abingdon: Routledge, 2004).

Hodgkin, Katharine and Susannah Radstone (eds), *Contested Pasts: The Politics of Memory* (London and New York: Routledge, 2003).

Huggan, Graham, *The Postcolonial Exotic: Marketing the Margins* (Abingdon: Routledge, 2001).

Innes, C. L., *A History of Black and Asian Writing in Britain, 1700–2000* (Cambridge: Cambridge University Press, 2002).

Kale, Madhavi, *Fragments of Empire: Capital, Slavery, and Indian Indentured Labor Migration in the British Caribbean* (Philadelphia: University of Pennsylvania Press, 1998).

King, Nicola, *Memory, Narrative, Identity: Remembering the Self* (Edinburgh: Edinburgh University Press, 2000).

Kundnani, Arun, *The End of Tolerance: Racism in 21st-Century Britain* (London: Pluto Press, 2007).

LaCapra, Dominick, *History and Memory After Auschwitz* (Ithaca, NY and London: Cornell University Press, 1998).

Low, Gail and Marion Wynne-Davies (eds), *A Black British Canon?* (Basingstoke: Palgrave Macmillan, 2006).

Mercer, Kobena, *Welcome to the Jungle: New Positions in Black Cultural Studies* (New York and London: Routledge, 1994).

McClintock, Anne, *Imperial Leather: Race, Gender and Sexuality in the Colonial Contest* (New York and London: Routledge, 1995).

McLeod, John, *Beginning Postcolonialism* (Manchester and New York: Manchester University Press, 2000).

Modood, Tariq and Pnina Werbner (eds), *The Politics of Multiculturalism in the New Europe: Racism, Identity and Community* (London and New York: Zed Books, 1997).

Mongia, Padmini (ed.), *Contemporary Postcolonial Theory: A Reader* (London: Arnold, 1997).

Moore-Gilbert, Bart, *Postcolonial Theory: Contexts, Practices, Politics* (London and New York: Verso, 1997).

Owusu, Kwesi (ed.), *Black British Culture and Society: A Text Reader* (London and New York: Routledge, 2000).

Paul, Kathleen, *Whitewashing Britain: Race and Citizenship in the Postwar Era* (Ithaca, NY and London: Cornell University Press, 1997).

Perryman, Mark (ed.), *Imagined Nation: England After Britain* (London: Lawrence & Wishart, 2008).

Pettinger, Alasdair (ed.), *Always Elsewhere: Travels of the Black Atlantic* (London and New York: Cassell, 1998).

Phillips, Mike and Trevor Phillips, *Windrush: The Irresistible Rise of Multi-Racial Britain* (London: HarperCollins, 1999).

Plasa, Carl, *Textual Politics From Slavery to Postcolonialism: Race and Identification* (Basingstoke and London: Macmillan Press, 2000).

Procter, James (ed.), *Writing Black Britain 1948–1998: An Interdisciplinary Anthology* (Manchester and New York: Manchester University Press, 2000).

——, *Dwelling Places: Postwar Black British Writing* (Manchester and New York: Manchester University Press, 2003).

Ramdin, Ron, *Reimaging Britain: Five Hundred Years of Black and Asian History* (London and Sterling, VA: Pluto Press, 1999).

——, *Arising from Bondage: A History of the Indo-Caribbean People* (London: I. B. Tauris, 2000).

Rice, Alan, *Radical Narratives of the Black Atlantic* (London and New York: Continuum, 2003).

Rogers, David and John McLeod (eds), *The Revision of Englishness* (Manchester: Manchester University Press, 2004).

Rushdy, Ashraf H. A., *Neo-slave Narratives: Studies in the Social Logic of a Literary Form* (New York and Oxford: Oxford University Press, 1999).

Segal, Ronald, *The Black Diaspora* (London: Faber & Faber, 1995).

Stein, Mark, *Black British Literature: Novels of Transformation* (Columbus, OH: Ohio State University Press, 2004).

Thomas, Hugh, *The Slave Trade: The History of the Atlantic Slave Trade, 1440–1870* (London, Basingstoke and Oxford: Papermac, 1998).

Tinker, Hugh, *A New System of Slavery: The Export of Indian Labour Overseas 1830–1920* (London, New York and Bombay: Oxford University Press, 1974).

Walvin, James, *England, Slaves and Freedom, 1776–1838* (Basingstoke and London: Macmillan, 1986).

——, *Black Ivory: A History of British Slavery* (London: HarperCollins, 1992).

——, *An African's Life: The Life and Times of Olaudah Equiano, 1745–1797* (London and New York: Continuum, 2000).

——, *Making the Black Atlantic: Britain and the African Diaspora* (London and New York: Cassell, 2000).

Wambu, Onyekachi (ed.), *Empire Windrush: Fifty Years of Writing About Black Britain* (London: Victor Gollancz, 1998).

Ware, Vron, *Beyond the Pale: White Women, Racism and History* (London and New York: Verso, 1992).

—— *Who Cares About Britishness? A Global View of the National Identity Debate* (London Arcadia Books, 2007).

Webster, Wendy, *Imagining Home: Gender, 'Race' and National Identity, 1945–64* (London: UCL Press, 1998).

Werbner, Pnina and Tariq Modood (eds), *Debating Cultural Hybridity: Multi-Cultural Identities and the Politics of Anti-Racism* (London and Atlantic Highlands, NJ: Zed Books, 1997).

Williams, Eric, *Capitalism and Slavery* (London: André Deutsch, 1964).

Wood, Marcus, *Blind Memory: Visual Representations of Slavery in England and America 1780–1865* (Manchester and New York: Manchester University Press, 2000).

Young, Robert J. C., *Postcolonialism: An Historical Introduction* (Oxford and Malden, MA: Blackwell, 2001).

Yuval-Davis, Nira, *Gender and Nation* (London, Thousand Oaks, CA and New Delhi: Sage, 2000).

Index

Note: 'n.' after a page reference indicates the number of a note on that page.